Work–Life Balance in Times of Recession, Austerity and Beyond

This book reflects the enormous interest in work–life balance and current pressing concerns about the impacts of austerity more broadly. It draws on contemporary research and practitioner experiences to explore how work–life balance and related workplace and social policy fare in turbulent economic times and the implications for employees, employers and wider societies. Authors consider workplace trends, practices and employment relations and the impacts on work, care and well-being of diverse workers. A guiding theme throughout the book is a dual agenda of supporting employee work–life balance, workplace effectiveness and social justice. The final chapters present case studies of innovative processes and organizational practices for addressing the triple agenda, note the important role of social policy context and discuss the challenge of extending debates on work-life balance to include a social justice dimension.

This book will be of interest to academics and postgraduate students of organisational psychology, sociology, human resource management, management and business studies, law and social policy, as well as employers, managers, HR managers, trade unions and policy makers.

Suzan Lewis is Professor of Organizational Psychology at Middlesex University, London, UK.

Deirdre Anderson is a Senior Lecturer in Organizational Behaviour at Cranfield University School of Management, UK.

Clare Lyonette is a Principal Research Fellow at the Warwick Institute for Employment Research (IER), UK.

Nicola Payne is a Health Psychologist and Associate Professor in Psychology at Middlesex University, UK.

Stephen Wood is Professor of Management, School of Business, University of Leicester, UK.

T0295975

Routledge Research in Employment Relations

Series Editors:
Rick Delbridge and Edmund Heery
Cardiff Business School, UK

For a full list of titles in this series, please visit www.routledge.com

Aspects of the employment relationship are central to numerous courses at both undergraduate and postgraduate level.

Drawing from insights from industrial relations, human resource management and industrial sociology, this series provides an alternative source of research-based materials and texts, reviewing key developments in employment research.

Books published in this series are works of high academic merit, drawn from a wide range of academic studies in the social sciences.

33 **Voice and Involvement at Work**
Experience with non-union representation
*Edited by Paul J. Gollan, Bruce E. Kaufman,
Daphne Taras and Adrian Wilkinson*

34 **Corporate Social Responsibility and Trade Unions**
Perspectives from Europe
Edited by Lutz Preuss, Michael Gold and Chris Rees

35 **Gender Equality and Work-Life Balance: Glass Handcuffs
and Working Men in the U.S.**
Sarah Blithe

36 **Board-Level Employee Representation in Europe**
Power and Articulation
Jeremy Waddington and Aline Conchon

37 **Employment Relations under Coalition Government**
The UK Experience, 2010–2015
Edited by Steve Williams and Peter Scott

38 **Work-Life Balance in Times of Recession, Austerity and Beyond**
*Edited by Suzan Lewis, Deirdre Anderson, Clare Lyonette, Nicola
Payne and Stephen Wood*

Work–Life Balance in Times of Recession, Austerity and Beyond

Edited by Suzan Lewis,
Deirdre Anderson, Clare Lyonette,
Nicola Payne and Stephen Wood

Routledge
Taylor & Francis Group

NEW YORK AND LONDON

First published 2017
by Routledge
711 Third Avenue, New York, NY 10017

and by Routledge
2 Park Square, Milton Park, Abingdon, Oxon OX14 4RN

First issued in paperback 2018

*Routledge is an imprint of the Taylor & Francis Group,
an informa business*

Library of Congress Cataloging-in-Publication Data
CIP data has been applied for

ISBN 13: 978-1-138-34096-1 (pbk)
ISBN 13: 978-1-138-92644-8 (hbk)

Typeset in Sabon
by Apex CoVantage, LLC

Contents

List of Figures   vii
List of Tables   viii
List of Contributors   ix
Introduction   xv

1 Working Time Trends and Work–Life Balance in
   Europe since the Onset of the Great Recession   1
   COLETTE FAGAN AND GREET VERMEYLEN

2 Work–Life Balance, Health and Well-Being in
   Times of Austerity   23
   GAIL KINMAN AND ALMUTH MCDOWALL

3 Employer Support for Work–Life Balance in Recession:
   Findings for Britain from the Workplace Employment
   Relations Survey   45
   LUCY STOKES AND STEPHEN WOOD

4 Work–Life Balance and Austerity: Implications of New
   Ways of Working in British Public Sector Organisations   63
   CLARE LYONETTE, DEIRDRE ANDERSON, SUZAN LEWIS,
   NICOLA PAYNE AND STEPHEN WOOD

5 Regulating Work and Care Relationships in a Time of
   Austerity: A Legal Perspective   78
   NICOLE BUSBY AND GRACE JAMES

6 Trade Unions and Work–Life Balance: The Impact of
   the Great Recession in France and the UK   93
   SUSAN MILNER

 7 Work–Life Balance and Class: In Search of Working-Class
    Work-Lives   112
    TRACEY WARREN

 8 Self-Employment in Times of Economic Crisis:
    Work–Life Challenges   131
    LAURA DEN DULK, ANNE ANNINK AND BRAM PEPER

 9 The Physical Workplace and Work–Life Balance:
    Perspectives from Practice   149
    ZIONA STRELITZ

10 Revisiting the Dual Agenda: Why Companies Miss the
    Point if They Retract Flexible Work Arrangements during
    Bad Times   165
    HYOSUN KIM, LOTTE BAILYN AND DEBORAH M. KOLB

11 Towards a Triple Agenda for Work–Life Balance beyond
    Recession and Austerity   180
    DEIRDRE ANDERSON, JONATHAN SWAN AND SUZAN LEWIS

    Index   191

Figures

1.1 Trends in work schedules for the employed in the European
Union, 2000–2010: (a) Proportion who work at weekends
at least once a month, (b) Proportion who work during the
evenings and at night at least once a month, (c) Proportion who
work shifts and who work fixed hours, days and start and finish
times   6

3.1 Employees perceiving managers to be supportive of their
work–life balance needs   56

3.2 Work–life conflict, according to number of changes employee
experienced in recession   59

7.1 Hours of weekly labour market work. Employees aged
18–64. 2012–13   118

7.2 Employees (aged 18–64) reporting 'financial difficulties/
just about getting by', by occupation   123

7.3 Proportion of dual-employed working age mixed-sex
couples who both report being in financial difficulties   125

7.4 Proportion of working age mixed-sex couples who both
report being in financial difficulties   126

8.1 Trends in self-employment across EU countries, 2005–2014   133

Tables

1.1   Employment and unemployment trends for the EU-27
across the Great Recession   3

3.1   Availability of flexible working arrangements, 2004 and
2011   51

3.2   Family-friendly provision, 2004 and 2011   53

3.3   Employees perceiving managers to be supportive of their
work–life balance needs, 2004 and 2011   55

3.4   Use of flexible working arrangements, according to
employees' experiences of recession   57

Contributors

Deirdre Anderson is a Senior Lecturer in Organizational Behaviour at Cranfield University School of Management. Research interests include flexibility, work and family, inclusion and diversity, gendered careers, and women's management pipeline. Prior to her academic career, she spent over 15 years as an independent business psychology consultant with an emphasis on assessment and individual and group development. Deirdre has written several book chapters and published in academic journals including the *British Journal of Management, International Journal of Human Resource Management* and *Human Relations.* She is a member of the British Psychological Society and an Academic Fellow of the CIPD.

Anne Annink (MSc) is a PhD candidate at Erasmus University Rotterdam, faculty of social sciences, department of public administration, in the Netherlands. Her PhD research is about the work–life balance of self-employed workers across Europe. This thesis aims to explain differences in work–life balance and well-being among the self-employed by comparing types of self-employment across different national contexts. The research is based on policy analysis, large comparative surveys and cross-national interview data.

Lotte Bailyn is the T Wilson (1953) Professor of Management emerita at MIT's Sloan School of Management. She is an authority on the relation of workplace practices to employees' personal lives, with a particular emphasis on gender equity in business organisations and academia. She is the author of *Breaking the Mold: Redesigning Work for Productive and Satisfying Lives* (Cornell University Press) and co-author of *Beyond Work-Family Balance: Advancing Gender Equity and Workplace Performance* (Wiley).

Nicole Busby is a Professor of Labour Law at Strathclyde Law School. Her research explores the relationship between paid work and unpaid care, the constitutionalisation of labour rights and claimants' experiences of the UK's Employment Tribunal system. She has published widely in these areas. She is co-director (with Grace James) of the AHRC-funded Families and Work Network.

Laura Den Dulk is Associate Professor at Erasmus University Rotterdam, Department of Public Administration and Sociology, the Netherlands. Her main area of expertise is cross-national research on work–life policies in organisations. Current research interests include the integration of work and personal life at the individual level (how people manage their work and personal/family life), the organisational level (the role of managers, workplace flexibility) and the country level (cross-national comparisons). In 2014, she received the Rosabeth Moss Kanter Award for Excellence in Work-Family Research for a paper in the *European Management Journal*. She is co-editor of *Community, Work and Family*.

Colette Fagan is a Professor of Sociology at the University of Manchester. Her research focuses on employment and public policy with particular interests in gender inequalities and gender mainstreaming; working conditions and job quality; working-time (and time-use more broadly); and international comparative analysis. She is the UK national academic expert in the European Commission's Expert Network on Employment and Gender Equality and a member of the Eurofound Advisory Committee on Working Conditions. Her international research collaborations include the EC FP6 Network of Excellence 'Reconciling Work and Welfare in Europe' (RECWOWE, 2007–11) and the International Panel on Social Progress (2015–17). Her other engagements as an academic consultant to the policy community include research reports for the European Commission, Eurofound, the European Parliament, the European Trade Union Institute, the International Labour Office and the OECD.

Grace James is a Professor of Law at the University of Reading, where she teaches Employment and Discrimination Law. The main focus of her research has been pregnancy–related discrimination and carer rights at work—and she has published widely in this field. She is co-director (with Nicole Busby) of the AHRC-funded Families and Work Network.

Hyosun Kim is an Associate Professor of Management at College of Business, Chung-Ang University, in Korea and the co-founder of Future Workplace Institute. She is interested in workplace innovation that would allow employees to balance work and life, as well as to contribute meaningfully to their organisation. She participated in several government-led initiatives on improving work–family balance at the workplace, including government accreditation programme on family-friendly workplaces. Her research results and reports were utilized as a basis for establishing work–family legislation and other government-led workplace innovation initiatives in Korea. Currently, her research focuses on how IT infrastructure helps organisations to embrace flexible work arrangements in public and private domain. She also serves as a member of International Committee at Work Family Research Network (WFRN).

Gail Kinman is Professor of Occupational Health Psychology in the Department of Psychology at the University of Bedfordshire. She is a Chartered Psychologist and an Associate Fellow of the British Psychological Society and is co-founder and co-chair of the British Psychological Society Working Group for Work–life Balance. Gail's main area of expertise is work-related stress, recovery and work–life balance in emotionally demanding professions such as health and social care, education and within the emergency and security services. She has a particular interest in developing interventions to support the well-being of workers in such jobs and has published widely on these topics. A more recent area of interest is the ways in which people can manage information communication technologies for work purposes in a healthy and sustainable way.

Deborah Kolb is Deloitte Ellen Gabriel Professor for Women and Leadership (Emerita) and the co-founder of Center for Gender in Organizations at the Simmons College School of Management. From 1991–94, she was Executive Director of the Program on Negotiation at Harvard Law School. She is a Senior Fellow at the Program where she co-directs The Negotiations in the Workplace Project. Deborah is an authority on gender issues in negotiation and leadership. Her most recent, *Negotiating at Work: Turn Small Wins into Big Gains* (Jossey-Bass/John Wiley, 2015), was named by Time.com as one of the best negotiation books of 2015.

Suzan Lewis is Professor of Organizational Psychology at Middlesex University, London. Her research focuses on work–personal life issues and workplace practice, culture and change in diverse national contexts. She has published numerous books and articles on these topics as well as policy-related reports, for example, for the European Commission and International Labour Organization. Suzan has led many national and international research projects and has worked with employers and policy makers on work–life issues and workplace change in Europe, Asia and North America. She was a founding editor of the international journal Community, Work and Family and Vice President of the Work-Family Researchers Network from 2015–17.

Clare Lyonette is a Principal Research Fellow at the Warwick Institute for Employment Research (IER). She has worked at IER since February 2009 and has been involved in a number of research projects focusing on workforce issues and work–family balance and conflict, careers, inequalities, gender roles, atypical working and flexible working/part-time work. Before joining IER, she also worked on several ESRC-funded projects on employment and the family while at City University. She has extensive knowledge of conducting both quantitative and qualitative research and data analysis and has published widely in her fields of expertise.

Almuth McDowall is a Chartered and Registered Practitioner psychologist. She is Senior Lecturer in Organizational Psychology at Birkbeck University of London and Programme Director for the MSc in Human Resource Development. Her interests are work–life balance, individual performance, and ethical behaviours in the workplace. Her research focuses on tangible practical outcomes; she is co-founder of the Division of Occupational Psychology (British Psychological Society) Working Group on Work–life Balance, and committed to bringing academic research into organisational practice. Almuth acts as a professional adviser to a number of organisations in her academic capacity and is a regular presence in the media.

Susan Milner is Associate Professor in European politics at the University of Bath and the author of *Comparative Employment Relations* (Palgrave Macmillan, 2015). She has researched the role of trade unions in the development of work–life balance policies in France and the UK, and more recently in Sweden and Denmark. She is a member of a team (led by Sophie Pochic, ENS, Paris) investigating gender equality agreements in France (2016–17).

Nicola Payne is a Health Psychologist and Associate Professor in Psychology at Middlesex University. She has run the MSc Health Psychology at Middlesex for more than ten years and her primary research interests are within the field of occupational health psychology. These include work–life balance, occupational stress, the impact of work on health behaviours and behaviour change interventions and issues related to combining work and fertility treatment.

Bram Peper is Lecturer at the Tilburg University, Department of Sociology, and Assistant Professor at the Erasmus Law School (criminology). His main research is cross-national research regarding work–family arrangements in organisations in different welfare state regimes. He co-edited *Flexible Working, Organizational Change and the Integration of Work and Personal life* (Edward Elgar, 2005) and *Diversity, Standardization and Social Transformation. Gender, Ethnicity and Equality in Europe* (Ashgate, 2011). His current research focuses on the well-being of employees, work–life balance and the role of managers, and boundary management in relation to work–life issues.

Lucy Stokes is a Senior Research Fellow at the National Institute of Economic and Social Research. Her principal research interests cover issues relating to employment, education and public sector performance. Lucy was part of the research team for the 2011 Workplace Employment Relations Survey (WERS) and is one of the co-authors of the primary analysis of the

2011 WERS, reported in the book *Employment Relations in the Shadow of Recession* (Palgrave Macmillan). She has also previously provided advice to users of the WERS data as part of the former WERS 2004 Information and Advice Service.

Ziona Strelitz is a Social Anthropologist, Town Planner and Interior Designer specialising in research and strategy to shape responsive, sustainable settings that serve their protagonists' and users' needs. As Founder Director of ZZA Responsive User Environments, her work links social, cultural, design and management perspectives. Her repertoire of study and practice at the intersections of physical and virtual activity, space and place, spans multiple spatial scales, locations, building types and business sectors, including government, technology, media, professional services, property, police and academia. Ziona is highly experienced as a judge of workplace awards, member of expert panels, author, lecturer and international presenter.

Jonathan Swan is the Policy and Research Officer at Working Families, the UK's leading work–life organsiation. Jonathan has researched and written on a wide range of work–life integration issues, including: fathers and work, flexible working in senior roles, productivity and performance, organisational culture and active ageing. He is responsible for the annual Top Employers for Working Families benchmark for organisations and the Time, Health and Family series of reports.

Greet Vermeylen is Research Manager in the Working Conditions and Industrial Relations Unit in the European Foundation for the Improvement of Living and Working Conditions (Eurofound). She is involved in designing and running the European Working Conditions Survey and the European Company Survey (both of which are regular European-wide surveys) and research projects concerned with working time, work–life balance and work organisation, and the Eurofound's network of European observatories (European Working Conditions Observatory). She previously worked in the European Commission (DG Employment and Social Affairs) and a Belgian Presidency Taskforce for the Presidency of the European Union dealing with social protection issues.

Tracey Warren is a Professor of Sociology at the University of Nottingham. Her research interests lie in the sociologies of work and employment, and of social divisions. More specifically, these include work time, inequalities of gender, class and ethnicity, work–life balance, time poverty, job quality, financial hardship and the transmission of economic dis/advantage. She has published her work in such journals as *the British Journal of Sociology*; *Work, Employment and Society*; *Sociology*; *Gender, Work and Organization*; and *Feminist Economics* and she co-authored the book *Work and Society: Sociological Approaches, Theories and Methods* (Routledge).

Stephen Wood is Professor of Management, University of Leicester and an Academician of the British Academy of Social Science and Academic Fellow of the Chartered Institute of Personnel and Development. He has a broad range of expertise in employment relations, human resource management and work–family relations. He is on the editorial board of *Journal of Management, International Journal of Human Resource Management, Administrative Sciences, Industrial Relations*, and was a *Chief Editor of the British Journal of Industrial Relations* (1998–2003) and is on its International Advisory Board. He was a Co-Director of the Economic and Social Research Council Centre for Organisation and Innovation (2001–6) and Deputy Director of the Institute of Work Psychology (2001–10) at the University of Sheffield.

Introduction

This book reflects enormous ongoing interest in work–life balance (WLB), as well as pressing concerns about the impacts of the post-2008 recession on individuals, workplaces and societies. Traditional gendered workplace cultures, and expectations about ideal workers and the separation of work and nonwork lives, have been exacerbated by global competitive capitalism and technological connectedness, making it even more difficult for many people to manage their work and personal lives. Nevertheless, prior to the financial crisis and subsequent turbulent economic times, workplace policies and practices to support time flexibility and combining working and caring were growing in many contexts. This book explores the challenges for WLB and related workplace practices and social policy when governments are following austerity policies, and considers the implications for the achievement of the triple agenda of meeting the needs of employees, employers and social justice. Below, we discuss three key terms and themes used throughout the book: austerity, work–life balance and the triple agenda, before introducing the aims and chapters of the book.

There is no simple agreed definition of financial austerity but this usually refers to government spending cuts to reduce budget deficits, following a period of recession or poor economic performance. Many politicians and economists view austerity as the only way that national economies can recover from the ongoing impact of the 2008 financial crash, whereas others view it as a value-laden political strategy that disproportionately impacts on women and vulnerable sectors of society (Guerrina, 2015; Walby, 2015). The chapters in this book explore the implications of national and/or workplace responses to difficult economic contexts for aspects of WLB, including employer policies and practices, experiences of working and caring, employment relations, health and well-being, workplace innovation, fairness and social justice.

WLB is usually defined in terms of having the time (and energy) for both work and personal life activities, that is, without work dominating people's lives. However, although the WLB discourse is widely used by scholars, policy makers, employers, the media and the general public, its meaning is contested (Fleetwood, 2007; Lewis et al., 2007). A very basic criticism is that work (paid and unpaid) is part of life and not something separate to be balanced with life (Gambles et al., 2006). Suggestions for alternative terminologies, which attempt to counter this false dichotomy, include the integration or harmonisation of paid work and personal life (Gambles et al., 2006). However, these terms do not trip off the tongue in the same way as WLB. Moreover, the language of WLB, however problematic, has focused awareness on issues raised by current trends, including the intensification of work and blurring of work–nonwork boundaries by technology. Given its persistence in popular discourse, we use the term WLB in this book, applying a critical lens where appropriate. In fact, there is no single understanding or use of the term WLB. Rather, multiple and overlapping WLB discourses are dynamic, shifting over time and place (Lewis et al., 2007; Lewis et al., 2016). WLB can be used as a noun to refer to an outcome or aspiration to be achieved by individuals, or as an adjective to describe practices or other means of contributing to such outcomes. The former usage typically implies that WLB is an important but often elusive aspect of well-being which is a major focus of this book. The latter is commonly used in relation to workplace initiatives, such as flexible working arrangements, for managing time and work–nonwork boundaries. These are often referred to as WLB policies, provisions or practices, which are also discussed in a number of chapters.

There is also a growing critical literature which argues that the use of the term workplace WLB policies or practices implies an employee-led focus or "favours" which can mask the employer benefits of some so-called WLB policies and practices (Smithson and Stokoe, 2005; Fleetwood, 2007; Lewis et al., 2007; Gatrell and Cooper, 2008; Özbilgin et al., 2011; Lewis et al., 2016), as well as masking the effects of wider global competitive capitalism and spread of neo-liberal values (Fleetwood, 2007). This raises issues of fairness and social justice. The WLB discourse has also been criticised for implying gender neutrality (Smithson and Stokoe, 2005; Lewis et al., 2007). However, austerity is deepening gender inequalities (Walby, 2015), and gender inequity is a key aspect of social justice, considered in this book.

The impact on WLB of financial turbulence and austerity is examined through a triple agenda lens throughout the book. That is, authors consider, in various ways, the impact of the economic context on three important outcomes: individuals' WLB and well-being, workplace effectiveness and social justice. The notion of a dual agenda of both workplace effectiveness and WLB (and especially gender equity) is not new (Rapoport et al., 2002; Bailyn and Harrington, 2004) and is similar in some respects to the business-case agenda for WLB support, insofar as it emphasises that both the business and WLB agendas are equally important. The triple agenda, which has the potential to extend debates about WLB by foregrounding aspects of fairness and social justice, is more challenging.

This book is based on an Economic and Social Science Research Council research seminar series, 'Work–Life Balance in the Recession and Beyond,' which took place in the UK in 2014–15. The main aims of this

interdisciplinary seminar series were, first, to understand the WLB challenges for employees, employers and policy-makers posed by the recession
and subsequent economic challenges and, secondly, to provide a forum for
academic researchers and a range of research users, including employers,
policy-makers, unions, charities and non-governmental organisations, to
debate how to address these challenges post-recession. These aims are mir-
rored in the aims of the book, which includes research on how WLB and
WLB policies and practices have been affected by the 2008 recession and
associated austerity programmes. We have also endeavoured to incorporate
some of the ideas emerging from the practitioner–academic discussions. Like
the seminar series, the book aims to move beyond documenting problems
in supporting WLB and concludes by focusing on ideas for strategies for
sustaining a triple agenda to support WLB.

Overview of the Book

The main aim of the book is to assess the impact of recession and austerity policies on WLB and supports for it, and particularly how they affect
our ability to achieve the triple agenda of individuals' WLB and well-being,
workplace effectiveness and social justice, drawing on state-of-the-art
research in the UK and elsewhere. In Chapter 1, Colette Fagan and Greet
Vermeylen provide a European-wide overview of inequalities in employment and WLB since the onset of the 2008 recession, while also highlighting
relevant country-level policy changes in the context of austerity. Using the
European-wide European Working Conditions Survey, they outline differences by country, as well as by gender, age and occupational groupings. In
Chapter 2, Gail Kinman and Almuth McDowall consider how features of
the economic downturn, such as the intensification of work, increased job
insecurity, financial hardship and non-standard or precarious work arrangements, coupled with longer-term trends in flexible working practices and
technological change, may have detrimental effects for WLB, health and
well-being. They argue that such negative effects are likely to be accentuated by the persistence of traditional gendered assumptions which associate
long hours with career success and devalue certain types of flexible working. Chapter 3, by Lucy Stokes and Stephen Wood, focuses on the provision
of WLB practices and management's attitudes towards WLB before and
after the recession. Using data from Britain's Workplace Employment Relations Survey (WERS) series, they show that the main changes took place
within the public sector, as managers became less supportive of employees' WLB needs and employees, who experienced recessionary action, were
less likely than others to make use of some WLB practices. All employees
who experienced such action had greater levels of work-nonwork conflict.
Clare Lyonette, Deirdre Anderson, Suzan Lewis, Nicola Payne and Stephen
Wood in Chapter 4 highlight the strategic use of what they call evolved flexible working arrangements, including enforced remote working, in order to

manage austerity-related financial cuts in the British public sector. Drawing on qualitative data from interviews with HR directors in local councils, they highlight that this strategy has been aided by the longer-term trend in IT developments, and they also discuss the implications for employees, line managers and service delivery. In Chapter 5, Nicole Busby and Grace James examine how changes in employment law, welfare provisions and public sector cuts impact particularly on women's capacity to work and care, and also exacerbate gender inequality. They challenge current conceptualisations of austerity and offer an alternative feminist response capable of guarding against the reversal of gains made in gender equality on the grounds of political ideology. Susan Milner in Chapter 6 discusses the impact of the economic crisis on trade unions' policies towards WLB. Comparing France and the UK, she shows that the ability of trade unions to develop and pursue WLB policies has been adversely affected by the recession. The legal protection for collective bargaining in France has meant that the effect has been lower in large companies; the general trend applies to both countries, however, and so the provision of WLB practices at the workplace remains concentrated in large organisations.

Tracey Warren in Chapter 6 focuses on the financial insecurity engendered by the recession. She argues that financial security is a vital and potentially neglected contributor to WLB, a neglect that reflects an overemphasis on middle-class lifestyles in discussions (and research) on WLB and the time pressures associated with them. Laura Den Dulk, Anne Annink and Bram Peper extend this discussion in Chapter 7, which concentrates on the neglected category of self-employed workers. Using a comparative case study of independent professionals in Spain and the Netherlands, they highlight the financial and personal insecurities generated by the fluctuations in work and the difficulties of finding clients, and show that the role of the family in providing support is much stronger in Spain than in the Netherlands. In Chapter 9, Ziona Strelitz examines the physical workplace, focusing on two trends that affect WLB in opposing ways: the consolidation of large organisations' workspace in single locations, which imposes strains on employees through longer journeys to work that on-site lifestyle amenities fail to offset, and the increasing use of third places to support working close to, but away from, the home. Both trends commenced before the recession, but it has promoted them. If centralizing organizations adopt flexible work strategies, as some do, the impact of the first trend can be partially mitigated. Hyosun Kim, Lotte Bailyn and Deborah Kolb, in Chapter 10, note that employers often reverse their use of remote working in difficult economic times and argue that this reflects their emphasis on the control of labour, which is counterproductive. The authors present an alternative collaborative approach that aims to challenge traditional assumptions about working practices in order to reconcile the triple agenda of employee and employer needs and the gender equity aspect of social justice. This is illustrated with collaborative interactive action research cases in the USA and South Korea.

Finally, Deirdre Anderson, Jonathan Swan and Suzan Lewis in Chapter 11 draw on the findings from earlier chapters, as well as case studies of organisations from the public, private and small business sectors to consider whether social justice, insofar as it was ever implied in the WLB agenda, gets lost in turbulent economic times or whether the three prongs of the triple agenda can be reconciled. They note that although employers appear to find it difficult to articulate the third (social justice) aspect of the triple agenda, there have been some attempts to extend a fairness dimension, even in post-recessional times, leading to some promising changes in workplace practices. However, in most cases these initiatives fall short of fundamental organisational change and tend to apply to relatively privileged workers, while the struggles of the most vulnerable, including those in low-paid and/ or precarious work remain less visible. National social policy and regulation are important bases for social justice in this respect. The chapter concludes by discussing ways of addressing the triple agenda and the challenge of extending debates on WLB by rethinking and redesigning work to achieve its three objectives.

References

Bailyn, L., & Harrington, M. (2004). Redesigning work for work–family integration. *Community, Work & Family*, 7(2): 197–208.

Fleetwood, S. (2007). Why work–life balance now? *The International Journal of Human Resource Management*, 18(3): 387–400.

Gambles, R., Lewis, S., & Rapoport, R. (2006). *The Myth of Work-Life Balance: The Challenge of Our Time for Men, Women and Societies*. Chichester: John Wiley & Sons.

Gatrell, C.J., & Cooper, C.L. (2008). Work-life balance: Working for whom? *European Journal of International Management*, 2(1): 71–86.

Guerrina, R. (2015). Socio-economic challenges to work-life balance at times of crisis. *Journal of Social Welfare and Family Law*, 37(3): 368–377.

Lewis, S., Anderson, D., Lyonette, C., Payne, N., & Wood, S. (2016). Public sector austerity cuts in Britain and the changing discourse of work–life balance. *Work, Employment and Society*. Online first: 1–16.

Lewis, S., Gambles, R., & Rapoport, R. (2007). The constraints of a 'work–life balance' approach: An international perspective. *The International Journal of Human Resource Management*, 18(3): 360–373.

Ozbilgin, M.F., Beauregard, T.A., Tatli, A., & Bell, M.P. (2011). Work-life, diversity and intersectionality: A critical review and research agenda. *International Journal of Management Reviews*, 13(2): 177–198.

Rapoport, R., Bailyn, L., Fletcher, J.K., & Pruitt, B.H. (2002). *Beyond Work-Family Balance: Advancing Gender Equaity and Workplace Performance*. San Francisco, CA: Jossey-Bass.

Smithson, J., & Stokoe, E.H. (2005). Discourses of work–life balance: Negotiating 'genderblind' terms in organizations. *Gender, Work & Organization*, 12(2): 147–168.

Walby, S. (2015). *Crisis*. Cambridge: Policy Press.

1 Working Time Trends and Work–Life Balance in Europe since the Onset of the Great Recession

Colette Fagan and Greet Vermeylen

This chapter examines how working time trends have been shaped by the disruption of the 2008 Great Recession and its aftermath. Following the financial crisis in 2008, austerity measures were introduced across Europe, which were geared towards government budget deficit reduction through public expenditure cuts and increased taxation (Anderson and Minneman, 2014). These expenditure cuts fell primarily on the public sector and its welfare services. They impacted particularly harshly on the living standards of low-income households and women through budget cuts for welfare and public services which triggered job loss, pay cuts and increased job insecurity for the public sector workforce, at least 70% of which are women. These measures have also affected the delivery of services which are intended to improve quality of life and work–life balance (WLB), such as the infrastructure of childcare, schools, health and eldercare services. It has meant that households—normally women—have taken on more unpaid work to substitute for services which the state no longer provides or which they can no longer afford to purchase (Bettio, 2012, European Parliament, 2013).

The recession occurred in the context of long-term trends in working time that can be traced back to the late 1970s when changes began to be made to laws and regulations to permit more diverse working-time arrangements (Messenger, 2004). This restructuring of working time was driven largely by employers' operational requirements for more flexible working practices and extended operating hours, but has also been shaped by personnel strategies to accommodate workers' preferences for some forms of flexibility, such as flexitime, some types of part-time work and some full-time schedules (e.g. nine-day fortnights). Furthermore, the Internet and related technological developments have eroded the boundaries of the working day through remote working, instantaneous communication and handover across different time zones and so forth. The combined effect of these economic and political forces, and technological developments, means that there has been an increase in part-time employment, in schedules which include evening, night or weekend work and working-time arrangements which are more variable and less predictable.

We start this chapter with an overview of the widening of employment inequalities which occurred during the recession, followed by a discussion of the impact of the recession on working time in section two. Section three reviews the working-time inequalities that have persisted through the recession, and section four considers how reforms to reconciliation measures made during the recession have either enhanced or reduced workers' capabilities to obtain working-time arrangements which improve their WLB (Lee and McCann, 2006; Hobson, 2014). The closing section presents our conclusions.

The Rise in Unemployment and Widening Employment Inequalities during the Great Recession

The core years of the Great Recession (2008–10) and its aftermath produced wider labour market inequalities and more polarised employment conditions in most European countries (Eurofound, 2013a). By 2014 there were six million fewer Europeans in employment than in mid-2008 (Eurofound, 2015a). The magnitude of the recession varied between countries, but a broadly similar pattern of employment polarisation occurred in each one, in contrast to different national patterns of employment restructuring prior to the onset of the financial crisis in 2008 (Eurofound, 2013b:1).

The first wave of job losses in 2008 hit the middle of the pay distribution hardest, with a concentration on male-dominated jobs in construction and manufacturing. Subsequent job losses fell largely on women employed in the public sector and private sector services at low-middle pay levels (Fagan and Norman, 2011; Bettio et al., 2013; Karamessini and Rubery, 2013. Higher-paid occupations were less exposed to job loss and, in some activities, employment continued to expand despite the recession, mostly in knowledge-intensive services in the public (health, education) and private sectors.

The unemployment rate rose after 2008, reversing the modest decline over the previous eight years, and, by 2014, reached 10% of the labour force aged 15–64 years in the EU-27 (Table 1.1). The rise in unemployment was particularly acute in Greece and Spain, where the unemployment rate reached 25–27% by 2014, followed by another 11 Member States where the unemployment rate was 11–16% (Bulgaria, Cyprus, Ireland, Italy, Latvia, Lithuania, Portugal and Slovakia). In every country, the rise in unemployment fell particularly hard on young people, who entered the recession with the highest unemployment rate and continued to be more at risk of unemployment than other workers.

The more rapid rise in the male unemployment rate eroded the pre-recession gender gaps in unemployment and employment rates. As shown in Table 1.1, by 2014, the unemployment rate was similar for men and women at the EU-27 level, and the gender gap in the employment rate narrowed. This was because the male employment rate fell after 2008 and has not recovered, while the female employment rate resumed the pre-recession upward trajectory after 2011. This long-term rise in the female employment

Table 1.1 Employment and unemployment trends for the EU-27 across the Great Recession

Unemployment rate

EU-27	2005	2008	2011	2014
Men (aged 15–64)	8.4	6.6	9.7	10.3
Women (aged 15–64)	9.7	7.5	9.8	10.4
Older workers (aged 50–64)	6.7	5.1	6.8	7.4
Younger workers (aged 15–24)	18.6	15.6	21.6	22.0
All (aged 15–64)	**9.0**	**7.0**	**9.7**	**10.3**

Employment rate

EU-27	2005	2008	2011	2014
Men (aged 15–64)	70.8	72.7	70.0	70.2
Women (aged 15–64)	56.2	58.9	58.5	59.6
Older workers (aged 50–64)	53.2	56.4	57.4	60.7
Younger workers (aged 15–24)	36.0	37.3	33.4	32.5
All (aged 15–64)	**63.5**	**65.8**	**64.2**	**64.9**

rate has been supported by improvements in childcare services and other work–family reconciliation measures that began prior to the recession, galvanised by the European Union's Employment Strategy, which introduced a target for a higher female employment rate at the 2000 Lisbon Summit and a target for improving the supply of pre-school childcare places at the 2002 Barcelona Summit (Fagan et al., 2005; European Commission, 2007; Plantenga and Remery, 2009). Nonetheless, the gender gap in employment rate exceeds 6% in every EU Member state except the three Nordic countries and three low-income post-communist countries (Bulgaria, Latvia and Lithuania).

The employment rate for older workers has also risen during the recession years, as governments extend working lives within the framework of the Europe 2020 employment strategy by enacting reforms to pension and retirement systems, combined with equal treatment legislation to counter age discrimination. As shown in Table 1.1, by 2014, the employment rate for older men aged 50–64 years had reached 60.7%, just ahead of the rate for women.

Economic inequalities have widened. Pay freezes or cuts have been widespread, and wage negotiations have frequently focussed on trading wage concessions for saving jobs, except in some managerial and professional jobs where earnings have continued to rise (Eurofound, 2013b: 12). The proportion of residents in the European Union who reported that their households had 'some or great difficulties' in making ends meet rose from 38% in 2007 to 45% in 2011–2012, according to the most recent European Quality of Life Survey; almost one in three people reported that their situation had deteriorated over a 12-month period, and 35% expected it to get worse (Eurofound, 2013a: 3–4; Eurofound, 2014). Low-skilled manual workers and migrant workers, already vulnerable to poverty, are the most likely to report lower earnings and increased job insecurity (Eurofound, EIRO, 2013). More EU nationals are migrating in search of better employment prospects within the EU or further afield, although the scale of this migration is dwarfed by the number of refugees entering the EU from non-EU countries.

Such issues of poverty and lower earnings during the recession are linked to the intensification of the pre-existing expansion of precarious forms of employment and job insecurity, facilitated by legal reforms in a small number of countries. Fixed-term contracts, agency work and fragile types of self-employment have increased, along with newer fragmented forms of precarious employment such as zero-hours contracts and digital crowdsource employment platforms, and undeclared casual work has expanded in poorly regulated sectors (Smith, 2009; Bettio et al., 2013; Eurofound, 2013c; Karamessini and Rubery, 2013; Howcroft and Bergvall-Kåreborn, 2014; Rubery et al., 2014). Among those employed, women are more likely than men to have an insecure or low-paid job (European Parliament—Committee on Women's Rights and Gender Equality, 2014: 26). There are also national differences; the example of Spain illustrates that in a given labour market, one form of precarious employment may contract while another expands. In Spain, the proportion of employees with a fixed-term contract declined from 32% in 2007 to 24% in 2014, according to the European Labour Force Survey, since these workers were the first to lose their jobs, but other forms of precarious employment have expanded, including self-employment start-up.

The increase in unemployment and precarious forms of employment, deteriorating wage conditions and the widespread organisational restructuring triggered by the recession has created an environment in which an increased proportion of the employed consider that they have an insecure job, poor WLB or high levels of job-related stress (as discussed by Kinman and McDowall, Chapter 2), all of which reduce well-being (Eurofound, 2013c). In the next section, we focus on trends in working time during the recession and how this impacts on WLB.

Developments in Working-Time Arrangements and the Impact on WLB

The volume of hours worked, when they are scheduled and workers' control over their working-time arrangements can impact negatively on WLB. The volume of hours worked is a key working-time dimension which reduces or improves WLB. For example, long working hours have a pronounced negative impact on men's and women's self-assessment of the quality of their working time and their WLB, as well as on health outcomes (Fagan et al., 2012, 2014; Tucker and Folkard, 2012). Long working hours are also associated with above average levels of work intensity (Eurofound,

2012a). Work intensity, due to heavy workloads, tight deadlines and pressurised work environments, can create a strain between the demands of employment and personal life, compounding the fatigue caused by long working hours.

The schedule and control over when hours are worked also impact on WLB. Regular schedules during daytime weekday hours generally make it easier for workers to plan and coordinate their employment and private lives, as do work practices which give workers some autonomy, by which we mean discretion and control, to decide when and where they do their work. Employed men and women are more likely to report a poor WLB if they work non-standard work schedules (working in the evening, at night, early morning or at weekends) or if their employer changes their schedule at short notice, than those who work daytime, weekday and predictable schedules (Fagnani and Letablier, 2004; Eurofound, 2012a; Fagan et al., 2012; Ingre et al., 2012). When workers have working-time autonomy to fix or vary their start and finish hours, or their place of work, or take time off at short notice, this reduces the negative effects of long and unsocial hours but does not eradicate them (Fagan and Burchell, 2002; Burchell et al., 2007).

Hours Worked

A comparison of working-time trends since 2005 reveals more continuity than disruption across the core years of the recession (2008–2010). The most notable change was in part-time employment. Prior to the recession, the rate of part-time employment was on a long-term upward trend but once the recession started, the increase became more pronounced, particularly for employed men. By 2014, 9% of employed men and 32% of employed women in the EU-27 were employed part-time. However, much of this increase was due to a rise among both men and women in involuntary part-time working, i.e. working reduced hours because they had been unable to find full-time employment. By 2014, 40% of male part-time employment and 26% of female part-time employment was involuntary.

Short-time working, with incentives to undertake training, and partial retirement schemes, were introduced in countries such as Germany, Austria and France for certain manufacturing sectors, construction and banking. These schemes reduced full-time working hours as a tool to job share and mitigate job loss (Eurofound, 2009, 2010). On the other hand, the average hours for the full-time employed remained fairly stable between 2005 and 2014, at just over 42 hours per week for men and 40 hours per week for women, according to the European Labour Force Survey. While a recession can reduce overtime working for some workers, in other workplaces, job losses can result in an increased workload and longer working hours—paid or unpaid—for the smaller team which remains (see also Lyonette et al., Chapter 4). While the proportion of full-timers who worked long weekly hours declined during the recession, a sizeable proportion remained

(Eurofound, 2012a, 2015a). In the 2010 European Working Conditions Survey, nearly one in three full-time employed men and one in five full-time employed women reported that they worked more than 45 hours per week.

Furthermore, a large proportion of full-time and part-time employed workers report a mismatch between their actual and preferred working hours, and this continued during the recession. More than half of those working more than 40 hours a week would prefer shorter hours. Over one third of part-timers, rising to 45% of part-timers in short hour jobs, would like to increase their working time, compared to just 10% of those working more than 34 hours a week. While part-timers are more likely than full-timers to report that they have a good WLB, they are less likely to consider they have good career prospects (Eurofound, 2012a).

Work Schedules

The expansion of non-standard work schedules during the 1990s slowed and stabilised during the following decade (Evans et al., 2001; Eurofound, 2007, 2012a). The European Working Conditions Survey shows little, if any, increase in the proportion of the workforce who work in the evening, at night or at weekends in the period 2000–2010, and a focus on the situation in 2005 and 2010 indicates that the onset of the recession in 2008 did not trigger an increase in non-standard work schedules (Figure 1.1).

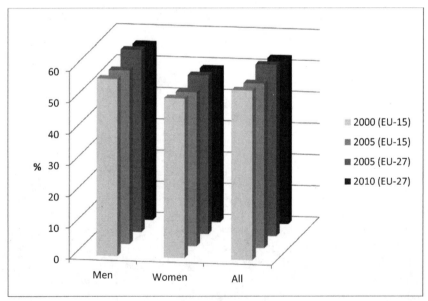

Figure 1.1 Trends in work schedules for the employed in the European Union, 2000–2010

(a) Proportion who work at weekends at least once a month

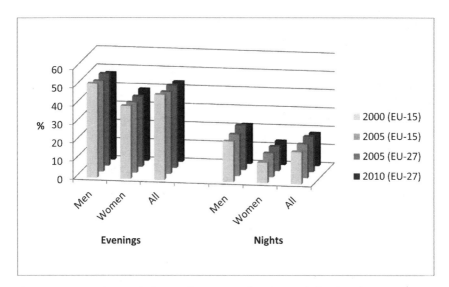

(b) Proportion who work during the evenings[1] and at night[2] at least once a month

1 for at least two hours between 6pm and 10pm
2 for at least two hours between 10pm and 5am

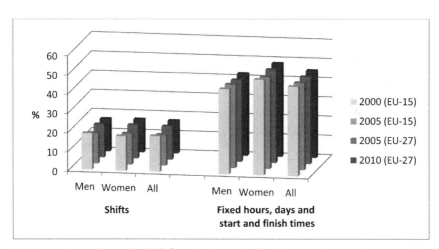

(c) Proportion who work shifts[1] and who work fixed hours, days and start and finish times[2]

1 Shifts include daily split shifts (with a break of at least four hours in between), permanent shifts (morning, afternoon or night) and alternating or rotating shifts.
2 This category captures those who work the same number of days each week, the same number of hours each day and has fixed start and finish times each day worked (and hence the same number of hours per day).

Note: data is not provided for the EU-27 in 2000 because the survey covered only the EU-15.

Source: Eurofound, the European Working Conditions Survey 2000, 2005, 2010

The preliminary results available for 2015 suggest little subsequent change (Eurofound, 2016a).

Nonetheless, the data show that some types of non-standard work schedules are common. This applies more for employed men than women, although the gender gap is narrowing for some features of work schedules. In 2010, more than half of the employed worked at least one day at the weekend over a four-week period, with Saturday work more common than Sunday work. Evening work was undertaken by four in ten employed men and women, with a modest decline for men and a slight increase for employed women between 2005 and 2010. Night work remained stable across the period, and in 2010 nearly one in five employed men and one in ten employed women did some night work over a four-week period, with 10% of the workforce working at least five nights in that period. The proportion of employed men and women who work shifts declined between 2000 and 2005 and then stabilised, with the rate similar for men and women (although the type of shift pattern may still differ). In 2010, 17% of the employed worked shifts and just over one-fifth were on call (Eurofound, 2012a). By 2015 the incidence of shiftwork had risen and a modest increase in nightwork had occurred (Eurofound, 2016a).

Fixed schedules (the same daily start and finish times and the same number of days per week) became slightly more common after 2005 and applied to 43% of employed men and 49% of employed women. For the employed with more variable schedules, some of the variation will come from using working-time options which provide workers with some discretion and flexibility in their schedule, such as flexible working and working time accounts, as well as teleworking options. Likewise, some will have sought a part-time schedule in order to better combine employment with their private life (Fagan, 2004; Anxo et al., 2007; Fagan et al., 2012, 2014). Yet for others, the schedule variation is driven by the employers' operational needs for flexibility, for example in annualised hours agreements or a requirement to be available for schedule changes at short notice, such as the recent rapid growth in zero-hours contracts in the UK. In the EU-27 in 2010, more than one in three of the employed had unpredictable schedules (37% of employed men and 35% of employed women), including 19% of employed men and 13% of employed women whose schedules changed regularly with no more than 24 hours' notice (Eurofound, 2012a). Such unpredictability and short notice changes in work schedule requirements is unconducive to WLB.

ICT and Teleworking

The increased porosity of the work day and spillover from employment into personal time has been facilitated by the increased use of the Internet, making it more difficult to measure actual working time. The proportion of the employed that use the Internet and email in their jobs rose from

14% in 1991 to 40% in 2010, including 30% who use it for most or all of their work (Eurofound, 2012a). Eurofound (2012a) estimates that a quarter of European workers are 'e-nomads' who use ICT for their work and who do part of their work at sites other than their employers or their own work premises. Opportunities for telework and mobile work patterns can provide workers with flexibility options to enhance their WLB (although Kinman and McDowall, Chapter 2, discuss how ICT use must be carefully managed to avoid potential detriments to WLB). Telework also provides an opportunity for employers to save costs by reducing office space, which may impact negatively on the workforce's working conditions (see Lyonette et al., Chapter 4).

Inequalities in Working Time and WLB

There are pronounced national and occupational differences in working-time arrangements: in the incidence of long full-time hours, the amount and quality of part-time employment, the schedules worked and the amount of discretion and flexibility which workers have over their working time (Fagan and Burchell, 2002; Messenger, 2004; Riedmann et al., 2006, 2010; Burchell et al., 2007; Chung et al., 2007; Hegewisch, 2009). The national differences across Europe arise from a combination of economic, political and historical conditions. These include the industrial structure of the economy; state policies and collective bargaining concerning working time; and the size and composition of the labour supply. The latter is shaped by welfare programmes for the unemployed, the adequacy of the grants and allowances made to young people in training and post-compulsory education, welfare arrangements for the unemployed, retirement systems and pensions for older workers, and the quality of the reconciliation measures to enable family care responsibilities to be combined with employment.

These national institutional factors shape the working-time culture and practices at the workplace and the extent to which workers have opportunities to obtain flexibility through arrangements such as flexitime, working-time accounts, individual rights to request reduced or flexible hours, working from home, flexible retirement schemes and so forth. Furthermore, men's and women's working-time expectations and capabilities to secure their desired working-time arrangements are shaped by the extent to which gender-egalitarian employment and family roles are promoted by the gender regime that is constructed by government policies, institutional arrangements and cultural values (Lee and McCann, 2006; Fagan and Walthery, 2011; Hobson, 2014).

The recession has had no discernible impact on gender differences in the household division of employment, housework and care responsibilities. We saw in the previous section that during the recession, the gender gap in employment rates continued to narrow but women still work shorter hours in employment, particularly in countries where part-time employment is common. Women continue to do almost two-thirds of the unpaid work across the EU (European Commission, 2016). The average employed woman in the EU-27 has a longer total working week (paid and unpaid work combined) than the average employed man. The gender gap is smallest in countries where government policy has established high standards of labour rights and gender equality, exemplified by the Nordic countries, followed by France and Belgium (Eurofound, 2013c; European Commission, 2016).

Occupational differences and inequalities in the quality of working-time arrangements have persisted during the recession, alongside the widening earnings inequalities. A comparison of the working-time arrangements of managers and professionals, on one hand, and manual occupations, on the other, illustrates these inequalities (see Warren, 2003, 2015; and Chapter 7, this volume). Typically, managers and professionals work long hours and have heavy workloads, but they are better paid and usually have more autonomy over their work schedules than do other occupational groups (Fagan, 2001; Fagan et al., 2008). They are more prone to having their work spill into evenings and weekends, particularly if they are e-nomads who do much of their work using laptops and smart phones (Eurofound, 2012a).

In contrast, manual workers are more likely to have work schedules which involve shifts, nights and weekend work, to have their hours changed at short notice by their employer, and to be compelled by low pay and financial pressures to work long hours when opportunities for overtime or multiple job holding arise (Fagan et al., 2008, 2012). They have higher levels of work intensity and less working-time autonomy than managers and professionals (Burchell et al., 2007; Eurofound, 2012a; Fagan et al., 2012).

Part-time work also varies by occupational group. Among managerial and professional occupations, the option to work part-time is more developed in female-dominated professions and in countries where there have been explicit measures introduced to facilitate part-time employment, such as through introducing an individual right to request reduced working hours. Part-time employment is often confined to the lower career rungs and at the cost of reduced prospects for career development and promotion (Fagan et al., 2014). Nonetheless, the earnings and quality of part-time jobs in this part of the occupational hierarchy are vastly superior to manual part-time jobs. The growth in involuntary part-time work during the recession has been concentrated in manual service jobs.

Across Europe, flexible working options for employees (such as flexitime, opportunities to switch to part-time hours, to work from home, etc.) are more developed and used in affluent economies, in the public sector and in large private sector workplaces, where a trade union is recognised or where more than half of the workforce is female (Anxo and Boulin, 2005; Riedmann et al., 2010). The available evidence suggests that this pattern of inequalities has persisted during the recession (Präg and Mills, 2014). There has been no major change in the proportion of workers with flexible work options and in 2011–12 around six out of ten of the employed had no flexibility in their working hours (Eurofound, 2012a).

Developments in Reconciliation Policies to Support WLB during the Recession

Well-designed and coherent reconciliation measures are a social investment which deliver benefits for the triple agenda of employee well-being and quality of life, workplace productivity and social justice. They are also central to the national gender equality action plans which exist in all EU member states (European Commission, 2015a), and to the family policy agenda, advocated by organisations which promote the well-being of children and their families (COFACE, 2015). Reconciliation measures bring economic benefits to firms through improved workforce recruitment and retention, staff morale and loyalty, as well as other productivity gains from reductions in long hours working and innovation in work schedules (Golden, 2012). Reconciliation measures include those which are focused on supporting the employment of people with care responsibilities through investment in an infrastructure of care services and family-related leave (maternity, paternity, parental, leave to care for sick relatives), and options for other working-time adjustments such as the legal 'right to request' reduced or rescheduled hours which may extend beyond those with care responsibilities. Regulatory upper limits on working hours are also an important element of a coherent policy framework.

Across Europe, there are examples of policy reforms and cuts made during the recession which have made it more difficult for workers to improve their WLB. There are also examples of reforms designed to improve reconciliation measures and thus increase workers' concrete opportunities, or capabilities (Lee and McCann, 2006), to secure an improved working-time arrangement and WLB, including some designed to protect and target protection for the lowest income households. Selected examples are given below.

The public expenditure cuts which have fallen on families have mainly concentrated on increased targeting and means testing, and cuts to benefit rates, tax credits and allowances, rather than on direct cuts to care services or family-related leave entitlements (Bettio et al., 2013: 21; European Parliament, 2014: 15; Eurofound, 2015b). This has reduced the living standards of those who are eligible and those who no longer qualify under the targeted eligibility conditions. Furthermore, cuts to earnings, benefits and tax allowances make it more difficult for households to pay for care services. As a result, there is a risk that new categories of economically disadvantaged families are being created because they no longer have access to universal provision (Eurofound, 2015b).

Care Services

The increased financial pressure on low- and middle-income households is compounded by persistent shortfalls in care services. The scale of the deficit is illustrated by the limited progress towards meeting the EU's Barcelona childcare targets set in 2002 (childcare for 33% of children under the age of three and 90% for those between three and the mandatory school age). More than a decade later, and despite the considerable progress made in some countries, only six member states have reached both targets—Denmark, Sweden, Belgium, France, Slovenia and Spain (European Commission, 2013). Sixty per cent of parents in the EU report that they face difficulties in accessing childcare (waiting lists, lack of services) (COFACE, 2015: 59). In addition to childcare, the demand for eldercare continues to grow and to outstrip supply as the elderly population expands. While the European Union has not set targets for eldercare services, such provision is constrained by public expenditure budget cuts, compounded by appropriately skilled labour supply shortages in eldercare services in some countries (Bettio et al., 2013).

Member states had different reconciliation policies in place prior to the recession, and the changes made during the economic crisis have varied due to different national economic, cultural and political conditions. The provision of care services has been less vulnerable to budget cuts in those countries where the policies were the most developed and longstanding prior to the recession, such as the Nordic countries, Belgium, France and the Netherlands (Eurofound, 2015b). In contrast, countries which entered the crisis with relatively limited provision and in a poorer economic situation have experienced some of the most acute pressures to cut care services and related reconciliation measures, such as the Southern Mediterranean countries (Greece, Spain, Italy) and some of the Central–Eastern European countries (Bulgaria, Estonia, Latvia, Croatia) (Eurofound, 2015b).

Some countries have taken action to increase the supply of childcare during the recession (Eurofound, 2015b). For example, Belgium enacted plans to expand childcare services in 2008 and later years, including subsidies for parents using the more expensive private providers due to a shortage of public sector childcare places. The French government similarly approved plans to increase the number of childcare places for under-threes in 2013, including a target for an expansion of places provided by childminders. In Poland, the supply of childcare places was increased by a 2011 amendment to the Nursery Act to permit a wider range of childcare service providers to operate, in conjunction with the 2011 Toddler programme, which provided resources for municipalities to develop and co-finance services for children under three.

There are also examples of countries where childcare services have been cut or charges increased for parents due to the financial pressures on public sector childcare services (Bettio et al., 2013: 21; European Parliament, 2014: 15; Eurofound, 2015b). In Finland, for example, the universal right to full-time public daycare for all children aged under seven was reduced in 2013 to a part-time entitlement if one parent was on family leave or unemployed. Slovenia introduced stricter means testing of childcare allowances in 2012. In Spain, childcare subsidies and services for children under three have been reduced since 2011 due to cuts in pre-primary education budgets, the 2012 cancellation of the programme to build more childcare facilities (The *Educa3* programme) and, in 2013, a new education law meant that services for children under the age of three were no longer recognised as the first stage of early education. Greece, on the other hand, has targeted support at the most disadvantaged families. Since 2008, low-income employed and unemployed women have been entitled to a childcare voucher to help pay for public or private childcare services, and in 2012, subsidised pre-school childcare was introduced for some categories of disadvantaged families (Karamessini, 2014; Eurofound, 2015b). Like Greece, the UK provides another example where the expansion of pre-school childcare has been targeted, with the free, part-time childcare entitlement for three- and four-year-olds extended to two-year-olds in the most economically disadvantaged families in England.

Countries also took divergent pathways in their approach to supporting low-income households with children. In France, the amount of benefit paid to those on the lowest incomes was raised. Finland cut the rate of universal child benefit from 2013 for three years to help curb the public debt, but combined this cut with increased support targeted on low-income families (Eurofound, 2015b). By contrast, in the UK, the universal child benefit has been cut, with plans for further cuts in 2017, so that it is payable only for the first and second child; support for low-income families has been reduced further by cuts to means-tested benefit rates and childcare tax credits.

Leave Entitlements

There have been fewer changes to family-related leave entitlements, and the changes made have been mainly to improve entitlements for fathers and to encourage a more gender equal sharing of leave (Eurofound, 2015b, 2015c, 2015d). In Poland, since 2010, the maternity leave period has been extended progressively in four stages and paternity leave has been introduced and extended. The German parental leave system has also been reformed to facilitate the combination of part-time employment and paid leave, and increased the flexibility of paid leave entitlements to both parents, with a bonus period of an additional four months of leave if both parents work part-time simultaneously for at least four months (*Elterngeld Plus)*. In Sweden, a Gender Equality Bonus was introduced in 2008, providing an economic incentive for mothers and fathers to use parental leave more equally. Parents were granted the option to take a month of leave together in 2012, and in 2014 were permitted to spread the leave over a longer period (Duvander et al., 2015).

More modest improvements were made in some other countries. For example, in the UK the Shared Parental Leave scheme was introduced in 2015, which increases the paid leave entitlement for fathers, providing the mother transfers part of her maternity leave. However, take-up is predicted to be low given the low, flat-rate payment and some administrative complexities in the system (Trades Union Congress, 2013). Modest improvements have also been introduced to paternity leave in Italy in 2013 and to the unpaid parental leave entitlement in Greece, where they also extended maternity leave allowances to self-employed women in 2012 (Eurofound, 2015b). The Netherlands is an example of where parental leave support has been eroded because the tax reduction for all parents taking parental leave was abolished in 2015 as part of government budget cuts (Remery, 2014).

Rights to Flexible Working Arrangements

Some countries have extended employee rights to flexible working, as part of a longer-term policy trajectory of expansion across countries which pre-dates the recession (Fagan et al., 2012). The efficacy of these rights varies according to the detail of the legal provision. The Netherlands provides one of the most effective pieces of legislation with regard to persuading employers to agree to requests, (Fagan et al., 2006). In the Netherlands, new improvements to the Flexible Working Act passed in 2015 to allow employees to request more flexibility in their working hours and place of work (Govaert, 2015). In the UK, the right to request flexible or reduced hours was extended progressively in 2007, 2009 and 2014, so that now all employees, not just those with care responsibilities, have this statutory right, although employers can refuse on business grounds. In Germany, the *Familienpflegezeit* (family caring time), introduced in 2012, allows employees to reduce their working time to a minimum of 15 hours per week for up to two years for care responsibilities and in 2015 a new *Pflegezeit* (caring time) entitlement was introduced to allow employees of care-dependent relatives to take up to 10 days of paid care leave at 90% of their income (Blum and Erler, 2015). In Hungary, mothers have gained the right to return to employment part-time, following maternity leave, until their child is aged three (European Union, 2016). Other entitlements to request part time or flexible work have been developed post-recession, for example in Finland (Eurofound, 2015b) and Italy (Giovannini, 2010).

Legal rights to flexible working options have been curtailed in some countries, however. The Belgian career break scheme is a long-running and high-profile example which is often used as a good practice exemplar in policy debates. It provides opportunities for a period of leave or reduced hours (career break scheme for public sector workers, with a time credit scheme in the private sector) but has been progressively cut back since 2011 as part of the measures introduced to cut public expenditure (Merla and Deven, 2010, 2015). In Spain, flat-rate payments provided by regional governments to support parents reducing their work hours were abolished in 2011, and in Catalonia, the right for public sector employees to reduce hours to part-time at full pay was abolished in 2012 (Escobedo et al., 2015). Furthermore, in the context of widespread job insecurity and heavier workloads, it is likely that employees will feel less able to use their 'right to request' or other flexible working options to adjust or reduce their work hours for their personal needs. If they do seek a change, the employer may be less willing or able to accommodate it (Fagan and Walthery, 2011).

Length of Working Hours

Finally, only a few countries have introduced reforms to facilitate longer working hours (e.g., Hungary, Portugal and Romania) and, overall, there have been no major changes in legislation or collectively agreed weekly work hours since the onset of the recession in 2008 (Eurofound, 2016). National provisions must, as a minimum, respect the provisions of the EU Working Time Directive (WTD), which limit daily and weekly working hours. National differences in working-time regulations and the length of the working week persist within this framework, including two countries (Malta, the UK) which have implemented the opt-out of the 48-hour limit on the working week (Eurofound, 2012a). Collective bargaining continues to play an important role in setting standards for working time, even in countries where union density is low. The Nordic countries, France, Belgium, the Netherlands and Germany have the shortest average collectively agreed-upon working week, circa 35–38 hours, in contrast to much longer full-time hours in many of the Central and Eastern European countries. In 2012, Estonia had the EU's longest annual working hours, where employees worked the equivalent of seven more weeks per year than in France (Eurofound, 2012a).

In summary, despite positive changes in reconciliation measures in some countries, the overall picture of policy development is one of stalled progress at the European level. On 1 July 2015, the Commission withdrew its 2008 proposal to reform the 1992 Maternity Leave Directive because the co-legislators failed to reach an agreement and adopt the proposed legislation (European Commission, 2015b). The Commission hopes to break the deadlock with a 'new start' initiative in its Work Programme for 2016. This will recognise the need to modernise and adapt the current legal and policy framework of the EU so that parents with children, or those with dependent relatives, can better balance their caring responsibilities and professional life. On 18 November 2015, a public consultation was launched in the hope that a wide range of stakeholders, particularly social partners, will contribute their ideas on how to improve WLB and reduce obstacles to female labour market participation (European Union, 2015). Similarly, attempts to revise the Working Time Directive (2003/88/EC), which establishes minimum standards to protect workers from excessive hours and provides entitlements for rest periods and holidays, failed to reach agreement in 2011 and 2012, and talks were suspended after more than a year of negotiations (Eurofound, 2013d; European Commission, undated).

Conclusions

A well-designed set of WLB initiatives can meet a triple agenda of enhancing employee WLB and well-being, workplace effectiveness and investment for wider social benefits and social justice, including progressing gender equality and improving the health and well-being and personal relationships of carers, children and elderly relatives.

Workers are more likely to consider that they have a good WLB, and have fewer health problems, if they work moderate full-time or part-time hours, have regular schedules and can adjust their working time, rather than having hours set by their employer, through personal working-time discretion and entitlements made explicit in policies such as the right to request, flexitime schemes and provision for emergency leave at short notice to take care of family or personal needs. There are also economic benefits for employers, in that effective WLB initiatives increase productivity by reducing recruitment and retention problems, supporting workers' well-being and organisational loyalty and stimulating innovation in work systems. This also links to the policy objective of sustaining and prolonging working lives. People who are able to reconcile work with their care responsibilities for children, grandchildren and other dependants in need of care—such as disabled or elderly parents—are more likely to be able to continue in, or resume, employment. The combination of effective government policies (working time options, leaves and social provisions), company practices (working time arrangements) and an infrastructure of care services will increase men and women's capabilities to combine employment with changing care responsibilities across their working lives (Eurofound 2012c, 2015e).

Socio-economic inequalities in working-time arrangements and the opportunities to obtain a better fit between employment and personal life have persisted during the recession and are likely to have been exacerbated for low- and middle-income households by the employment polarisation that has grown in the recession. Certainly the crisis has negatively affected the living standards of families already in a disadvantaged situation, such as lone parents, families with three or more children and jobless families (Eurofound, 2014).

When governments and employers are dealing with the economic pressures of a recession, there is a risk that WLB measures are seen as a non-essential cost, rather than an investment to support both family well-being during economic hardship and organisational effectiveness with which to build economic recovery and support the vulnerable in society. Our review of national policy development has shown that public expenditure cuts have impacted on the public sector care infrastructure in some countries, whereas in others, this infrastructure has been protected and, in some cases, expanded. Statutory family-related leave entitlements have also been protected or extended.

Nonetheless, the recession has helped distract attention from the triple-agenda imperative to reactivate the stalled process of EU negotiations on improving the directives on maternity leave or working time. Furthermore, the issue of how to build working-time arrangements which enable older workers to care for the growing number of frail, elderly relatives continues to grow in importance, yet, unlike childcare, it still lacks the political focus and momentum which target setting can bring, as in the Barcelona childcare targets. Currently, 13% of Europeans aged 50–64 care for an elderly or disabled family member every day or several times a week. This informal care accounts for 80% of all the care provided (COFACE, 2015: 18). We can expect the proportion of workers with such care commitments to increase, and so there is a pressing need for concerted action now. However, the recession and public expenditure cuts have distracted political and economic will from this part of the reconciliation policy jigsaw.

Finally, the recession may have reduced men's and women's capability to use the working-time options which are—in principle—open to them. The combination of heightened job insecurity, wider earnings inequalities and increased financial pressures on households are likely to have reduced the ability to ask for, and obtain, reduced or flexible working time options at their workplace, or to take their entitlement to parental leave and other family-related leave. This is especially the case if employees fear that this sends a negative message to their employer that they are less committed, less productive or becoming difficult to manage. In order to build WLB into the economic recovery, it is important that policies are designed and implemented in ways which give workers a genuine sense of entitlement and support and reward line managers who create innovative personnel practices and work systems to enhance the quality of WLB for their team.

Acknowledgement

We are grateful to Dr Helen Norman for research assistance in connection with data preparation, including the collation of policy developments.

References

Anderson, B., & Minneman, E. (2014). The abuse and misuse of the term "Austerity": Implications for OECD countries. *OECD Journal on Budgeting*, 14(1): 109–122.

Anxo, D., & Boulin, J.Y. (2005). *Working Time Options Over the Life Course*. Dublin: European Foundation for the Improvement of Living and Working Conditions.

Anxo, D., Fagan, C., Letablier, M.T., Perraudin, C., & Smith, M. (2007). *Part-time Work in European Companies*. European Foundation for the Improvement of Living and Working Conditions, Luxembourg: Office for Official Publications of the European Communities.

Bettio, F., Corsi, M., D'Ippoliti, C., Lyberaki, A., Samek, M.L., & Verashchagina, A. (2013). *The Impact of the Economic Crisis on the Situation of Women and Men and on Gender Equality Policies*. External report commissioned by and presented to the EU Directorate-General for Justice, Unit D1 'Equality between Women and Men', available at http://ec.europa.eu/justice/gender-equality/files/documents/130410_crisis_report_en.pdf

Blum, S., & Erler, D. (2015). 'Germany country note', in: P. Moss (ed.) *International Review of Leave Policies and Research 2015*, available at http://www.leavenetwork.org/lp_and_r_reports/

Burchell, B., Fagan, C., O'Brien, C., & Smith, M. (2007). *Working Conditions in the European Union: The Gender Perspective*. Luxembourg: Office for Official Publications of the European Communities.

Chung, H., Kerkhofs, M., & Ester, P. (2007). *Working Time Flexibility in European Companies*. European Foundation for the Improvement of Living and Working Conditions, Luxembourg: Office for Official Publications of European Communities.

COFACE. (2015). *European Reconciliation Package*. Confederation of Family Organisations in the European Union, available at http://www.coface-eu.org/en/upload/ERP/ERP_COFACE_2015_web.pdf

Duvander, A.-Z., Haas, L., & Hwang, C.P. (2015). 'Sweden country note', in: P. Moss (ed.) *International Review of Leave Policies and Research 2014*: 311–320, available at http://www.leavenetwork.org/lp_and_r_reports/

Escobedo, A., Meil, G., & Lapuerta, I. (2015). 'Spain country note', in: P. Moss (ed.) *International Review of Leave Policies and Research 2015*, available at http://www.leavenetwork.org/lp_and_r_reports

Eurofound. (2007). *Fourth European Working Conditions Survey*. Luxembourg: Publications Office of the European Union.

Eurofound. (2009). *ERM Report 2009: Restructuring in Recession*. Luxembourg: Office for Official Publications of the European Communities of the European Union, Luxembourg.

Eurofound. (2010). *ERM Report 2010: Extending Flexicurity—The Potential of Short-time Working Schemes*. Luxembourg: Office for Official Publications of the European Communities of the European Union, Luxembourg.

Eurofound. (2012a). *Fifth European Working Conditions Survey*. Luxembourg: Publications Office of the European Union.

Eurofound. (2012b). *European Quality of Life Survey*. Publications Office of the European Union, Luxembourg.

Eurofound. 2012c. *Working time and work-life balance in a life course perspective*, Publications Office of the European Union, Luxembourg.Eurofound. (2013a). *Employment Polarisation and Job Quality in the Crisis: European Jobs Monitor 2013*, Eurofound, Dublin.

Eurofound. (2013). *EIRO: Wages and Working Conditions in the Crisis*. Dublin: Eurofound, available at www.eurofound.europe.eu

Eurofound. (2013a). *Employment Polarisation and Job Quality in the Crisis: European Jobs Monitor 2013*. Dublin: Eurofound.

Eurofound. (2013b). *Impact of the Crisis on Working Conditions in Europe.* Eurofound, Dublin.

Eurofound. (2013c). *Women, Men and Working Conditions in Europe.* Luxembourg: Publications Office of the European Union.

Eurofound. (2013d). *Cross-sector Social Partners Fail to Agree on Working Time.* Dublin, 23 January. http://www.eurofound.europa.eu/observatories/eurwork/articles/industrial-relations-working-conditions/cross-sector-social-partners-fail-to-agree-on-working-time

Eurofound. (2014). *Third European Quality of Life Survey—Quality of Life in Europe: Families in the Economic Crisis.* Luxembourg: Publications Office of the European Union.

Eurofound. (2015a). *Eurofound Year Book 2014: Living and Working in Europe.* Luxembourg: Publications Office of the European Union.

Eurofound. (2015b). *Families in the Economic Crisis: Changes in Policy Measures in the EU.* Luxembourg: Publications Office of the European Union.

Eurofound. (2015c). *Maternity leave provisions in the EU member states: duration and allowances,* Publications office of the European Union, Luxembourg.

Eurofound. (2015d). *Promoting uptake of parental and paternity leave among fathers in the European Union,* Publications Office of the European Union, Luxembourg.

Eurofound. (2015e). *Sustainable work throughout the life course: concept paper,* Publications Office of the European Union, Luxembourg.

Eurofound. (2016a). *First findings: Sixth European Working Conditions Survey,* Publications Office of the European Union, Luxembourg.

Eurofound. (2016b). *Working Time Developments in the 21st Century: Work Duration and Its Regulation in the EU.* Luxembourg: Publications Office of the European Union.

European Commission. (2007). *Ten Years of the European Employment Strategy.* Luxembourg: Office for Official Publications of the European Communities.

European Commission. (2013). *Barcelona Objectives the Development of Childcare Facilities for Young Children in Europe with a View to Sustainable and Inclusive Growth.* Report from the Commission to the European Parliament, the Council, the European Economic and Social Committee and the Committee of the Regions, Luxembourg: Publications Office of the European Union.

European Commission. (2015a). *Strategic Engagement for Gender Equality 2016–19.* Staff Working Document SWD(2015) 278 final, Brussels 3.12.2015.

European Commission. (2015b). *Delivering for Parents: Commission Withdraws Stalled Maternity Leave Proposal and Paves the Way for a Fresh Approach,* available at http://europa.eu/rapid/press-release_IP-15–5287_en.htm

European Commission. (2016). *Women and Unpaid Work: Recognise, Reduce, Redistribute!.* Employment Social Affairs and Inclusion, available at http://ec.europa.eu/social/main.jsp?langId=en&catId=89&newsId=2492&furtherNews=yes

European Commission. (undated). *Working Conditions—Working Time Directive,* available at http://ec.europa.eu/social/main.jsp?catId=706&langId=en&intPageId=205

European Parliament—Committee on Women's Rights and Gender Equality. (2013). *Report on the Impact of the Economic Crisis on Gender Equality and Women's Rights (2012/2301(INI)) Committee on Women's Rights and Gender Equality A7–0048/2013 28.2.2013,* available at http://www.europarl.

europa.eu/sides/getDoc.do?pubRef=-//EP//TEXT+REPORT+A7–2013–0048+0+DOC+XML+V0//EN

European Parliament—Committee on Women's Rights and Gender Equality. (2014). *Report on the EU Strategy for Equality between Women and Men Post 2015 (2014/2152(INI)) A8–0163/2015,13.5.2015*, available at http://www.europarl.europa.eu/sides/getDoc.do?type=REPORT&reference=A8–2015–0163&language=GA

European Union. (2015). *European Commission Launches Public Consultation on Work-life Balance and Female Labour Market Participation*, available at http://europa.eu/epic/news/2015/20151203_public-consultation-on-work-life-balance_en.htm

European Union. (2016). *Hungary: Developing Childcare Services to Help Parents Back to Work*, available at http://europa.eu/epic/countries/hungary/index_en.htm

Evans, J., Lippoldt, D., & Marianna, P. (2001). *Trends in Working Hours in OECD Countries*. Labour Market and Social Policy Occasional Papers, No. 45, OECD, available at http://www.oecd-ilibrary.org/social-issues-migration-health/trends-in-working-hours-in-oecd-countries_674061356827

Fagan, C. (2001). The temporal re-organisation of employment and household rhythm of work schedules: The implications for gender and class relations. *The American Behavioural Scientist*, 44(7): 1199–1212.

Fagan, C. (2004). Gender and working-time in industrialized countries: Practices and preferences. In J. Messenger (ed) *Working-time and Workers' Preferences in Industrialized Countries: Finding the Balance*: 108–146. London and New York: The Institute for Labour Studies of the International Labour Organization.

Fagan, C., & Burchell, B. (2002). *Gender, Jobs and Working Conditions in the European Union*. Luxembourg: Eurofound, Publications Office of the European Union.

Fagan, C., Hegewisch, A., & Pillinger, J. (2006). *Out of Time: Why Britain Needs a New Approach to Working-time Flexibility*. London: Trades Union Congress.

Fagan, C., Lyonette, C., Smith, M., & Saldaña-Tejeda, A. (2012). *The Influence of Working Time Arrangements on Work-Life Integration or 'Balance': A Review of the International Evidence*. Conditions of Work and Employment Series No. 34, International Labour Organisation, Geneva, available at http://www.ilo.org/travail/whatwedo/publications/WCMS_187306/lang—en/index.htm

Fagan, C., McDowell, L., Perrons, D., Ray, K., & Ward, K. (2008). Class differences in mothers' work schedules and assessments of their 'work–life balance' in dual-earner couples in Britain. In J. Scott, S. Dex & H. Joshi (eds) *Women and Employment: Changing Lives and New Challenges*: 199–212. Cheltenham: Edward Elgar Publishing.

Fagan, C., & Norman, H. (2011). *Assessing the Impact to Date of the Gender Aspects of the Economic Downturn and Financial Crisis in the UK*. Briefing report submitted to the FGB, Italy for the European Parliament Study 'Gender aspects of the economic downturn and the financial crisis'.

Fagan, C., Norman, H., Smith, M., & González Menéndez, M.C. (2014). *In Search of Good Quality Part-time Employment*. Conditions of Work and Employment Series No. 43, International Labour Organisation, Geneva, available at http://www.ilo.org/travail/whatwedo/publications/WCMS_237781/lang—en/index.htm

Fagan, C., Rubery, J., Grimshaw, D., Smith, M.J., Hebson, G., & Figueiredo, H. (2005). Gender mainstreaming in the enlarged European Union: Recent developments in the European employment strategy and social inclusion process. *Industrial Relations Journal*, 36(6): 568–591.

Fagan, C., & Walthery, P. (2011). Individual working-time adjustments between full-time and part-time working in European firms. *Social Politics*, 18(2): 269–299.

Fagnani, J., & Letablier, T. (2004). Work and family life balance: The impact of the 35-hour laws in France. *Work, Employment and Society*, 18(3): 5551–572.

Giovannini, D. (2010). 'Italy country note', in: P. Moss (ed.) *International Review of Leave Policies and Research 2010*, available at http://www.leavenetwork.org/lp_and_r_reports/

Golden, L. (2012). *Effects of Working Time on Productivity*. Conditions of Work and Employment Series No. 33, International Labour Organisation, Geneva, available at http://www.ilo.org/travail/whatwedo/publications/WCMS_187307/lang—en/index.htm

Govaert, M. (2015). *Dutch Flexible Working Act*. Norton Rose Fulbright, available at http://www.nortonrosefulbright.com/knowledge/publications/127797/dutch-flexible-working-act

Hegewisch, A. (2009). *Flexible Working Policies: A Comparative Review*. Manchester: Equality and Human Rights Commission.

Hobson, B. (ed). (2014). *Worklife Balance: The Agency and Capabilities Gap*. Oxford: Oxford University Press.

Howcroft, D., & Bergvall-Kåreborn, B. (2014). *Crowd Sourcing Employment Platforms: The Case of Amazon Mechnical Task*. FairWRC Research Briefing No. 6, available at www.mbs.ac.uk/fairwrc

Ingre, M., Åkerstedt, T., Ekstedt, M., & Kecklund, G. (2012). Periodic self-rostering in shift work: Correspondence between objective work hours, work hour preferences (personal fit), and work schedule satisfaction. *Scandinavian Journal of Work, Environment and Health*, 38(4): 327–336.

Karamessini, M. (2014). *Country Fiches on Gender Equality and Policy Developments: Greece, Quarter 3, 2014*. Report submitted to the European Commission's European Network of Experts on Gender Equality, available at www.enege.eu

Karamessini, M., & Rubery, J. (eds). (2013). *Women and Austerity: The Economic Crisis and the Future for Gender Equality*. Abingdon and New York: Routledge.

Lee, S., & McCann, D. (2006). Working time capability: Toward realizing individual choice. In J.-Y. Boulin, M. Lallement, J. Messenger & F. Michon (eds) *Decent Working Time—New Trends, New Issues*: 65–91. Geneva: International Labour Office.

Merla, L., & Deven, F. (2010). 'Belgium country note', in: P. Moss (ed.) *International Review of Leave Policies and Research 2010*, available at http://www.leavenetwork.org/lp_and_r_reports

Merla, L., & Deven, F. (2015). 'Belgium country note', in: P. Moss (ed.) *International Review of Leave Policies and Research 2015*, available at http://www.leavenetwork.org/lp_and_r_reports

Messenger, J. (ed). (2004). *Working Time and Workers' Preferences in Industrialized Countries: Finding the Balance*. London and New York: Routledge.

Plantenga, J., & Remery, C. (2009). *The Provision of Childcare Services: A Comparative Review of 30 Countries*. Luxembourg: Office for Official Publications of the European Communities.

Präg, P., & Mills, M. (2014). *Family-related Working Schedule Flexibility Across Europe*. Statistical Report No. 6 RAND report under contract JUST/2011/GEND/

PR/1081/A4, European Union, available at http://www.rand.org/pubs/research_reports/RR365.html

Remery, C. (2014). *Country Fiches on Gender Equality and Policy Developments: The Netherlands, Quarter 3*. Report submitted to the European Commission's European Network of Experts on Gender Equality, available at www.enege.eu

Riedmann, A., Bielenski, H., Szczurowska, T., & Wagner, A. (2006). *Working Time and Work–Life Balance in European Companies*. Luxembourg: Office for Official Publications of the European Communities.

Riedmann, A., van Gyes, G., Roman, A., Kerkhofs, M., & Bechmann, S. (2010). *European Company Survey 2009*. Luxembourg: Office for Official Publications of the European Communities.

Rubery, J., Grimshaw, D. & Hebson, G., (2014). *Zero Hours Contracts in Social Care*. FairWRC Research Briefing No. 3, available at www.mbs.ac.uk/fairwrc

Smith, M. (2009). *Analysis Note: Gender Equality and Recession*. Analysis note financed by and prepared for the use of the European Commission, Directorate-General for Employment, Social Affairs and Equal Opportunities, available at www.ec.europa.eu/social/BlobServlet?docId=2839&langId=en

Trades Union Congress (TUC). (2013). *Just One in 172 Fathers Taking Additional Paternity Leave*, available at http://www.tuc.org.uk/workplace-issues/just-one-172-fathers-taking-additional-paternity-leave

Tucker, P., & Folkard, S. (2012). *Working Time, Health, and Safety: A Research Synthesis Paper*. International Labour Organisation Conditions of Work and Employment Series No. 31, International Labour Organisation, Geneva, available at http://www.ilo.org/travail/whatwedo/publications/WCMS_181673/lang—en/index.htm

Warren, T. (2003). Class- and gender-based working time? Time poverty and the division of domestic labour. *Sociology*, 37(4): 733–752.

Warren, T. (2015). Work-time underemployment and financial hardship: Class inequalities and recession in the UK. *Work, Employment and Society*, 29(2): 191–212.

2 Work–Life Balance, Health and Well-Being in Times of Austerity

Gail Kinman and Almuth McDowall

The notion that the experience of work, or the lack of it, has a profound impact on the well-being of individuals and families is not new (Jahoda, 1982). Nonetheless, features of the most recent economic downturn set it apart from previous recessions, requiring a fresh discussion about austerity, work–life balance (WLB) and well-being. This recession was deeper and longer than any experienced since the Second World War; it saw the Gross Domestic Product (GPD) in the UK fall by over 6% and the economy is still recovering from its effects. A range of stringent austerity measures has been implemented in the UK that, at the time of writing, remain ongoing. While the impact of the economic downturn on factors such as organisational performance and consumer spending has been debated extensively (Gregg and Wadsworth, 2010), little focus has been placed on how it has affected individuals who have been asked to do more with less. The implications of austerity for the working conditions, well-being and WLB of individuals and their families are the focal points of this chapter. It focuses predominantly on the position within the UK, but draws on relevant research from other contexts and makes international comparisons where relevant data are available. The chapter considers how features of the economic downturn, such as the intensification of work, increased job insecurity, financial hardship and non-standard or precarious work arrangements, can threaten the well-being and WLB of employees and their families. The implications of flexible working practices and technological change, which have increased during the financial downturn, for recovery processes, WLB and health in times of austerity are also considered. Finally, the importance of line manager support for WLB is discussed.

Well-Being in Times of Austerity

A number of studies have tracked the work-related well-being of employees in the UK and other countries before, during and after the recession. Some conclude that levels of stressors and strains remained stable during this period, while others report a steep decline. The findings of the UK Labour Force Survey (HSE, 2015) suggested that the overall rate of self-reported work-related stress, depression and anxiety had not increased in the previous ten years, but features of work intensification, such as overload, tight deadlines and feelings of pressure, were the work-related stressors that were most commonly reported. Other studies, however, have linked the economic crisis to an increase in psychosocial risk factors within the workplace, as well as rising rates of ill health and absenteeism (Buss, 2009; Shoss and Penney, 2012). Longitudinal research within the National Health Service (data obtained yearly from 2009 to 2014) has observed a steady increase in working hours over this period and rising pressure to work overtime (Powell et al., 2014).

Both the Workplace Employment Relations Study (WERS; Van Wanrooy et al., 2013; see also Stokes and Wood in Chapter 3) and the European Working Conditions Survey (EWCS, 2015) have observed a rapid growth in work intensification over the last ten years or so. More specifically, the Skills and Employment Survey (Felstead et al., 2013) reported that the proportion of UK employees who strongly agreed that their job required them to work "very hard" had increased substantially between 2004 (32%) and 2012 (45%). Perceptions of rising demand were also highlighted in research conducted by the Chartered Institute for Personnel and Development over the same period, which were generally attributed to rising workloads and escalating pressure to meet targets (CIPD, 2014a). Respondents who were experiencing more pressure at work typically blamed the recession for their deteriorating employment conditions. The study found that satisfaction with sense of achievement and the scope for using initiative had increased over time, but the level of satisfaction with job security had fallen. The implications of job insecurity for WLB and well-being are discussed later in this chapter.

Large-scale longitudinal surveys of occupational groups, such as civil servants and academics, have documented increased demands and reduced control and rising levels of work-related stress since the start of recession (Houdmont et al., 2012; Kinman and Wray, 2016). Data obtained from more than 3,000 UK workers from different sectors provide further support for the negative effects of recession on well-being and the role played by work intensification. Green et al. (2016) found that levels of work-related enthusiasm and contentment remained stable between 2001 and 2006, but declined sharply between 2006 and 2012. Factors related to austerity, such as increased effort, downsizing, job insecurity and accelerated change, made particularly strong contributions to reductions in well-being. Analysis of data obtained from 1,000 Americans each day between January 2008 and December 2010 revealed a steep decline in quality of life and positive affect and a substantial increase in worry and stress during this period (Deaton, 2012). Obtaining data on a daily basis from such a large number of individuals must have been onerous for all concerned, but allowed the researcher to capture unfolding hedonic experiences during recession and track responses to specific factors, such as the strength of the stock market.

The research reviewed above suggests that the well-being of employees has reduced markedly since the recession and highlights the role of increasing workload and time pressure. Nonetheless, there is some evidence that workers may accommodate challenging working conditions over time. Analysis of data from the Behavioural Risk Factor Surveillance System (that draws on responses from over 800,000 workers across the USA aged 25 to 55) between 2005 and 2011 showed that the association between macro-economic conditions (i.e. the percentage of people employed at the state level) and both health risk behaviours and outcomes had weakened through the recession (Tekin et al., 2013). The importance of interrogating econometric data at an individual as well as an aggregate level was highlighted, as some demographic differences were found. For example, some ethnic minorities were at greater risk of health problems and people who were better educated tended to report poorer mental health, presumably due to the greater opportunity cost of job loss. Analysis of panel data from workforce surveys in the UK, such as the WERS, the Labour Force Survey and the Whitehall Study II, has strong potential to reveal patterns of change (both positive and negative) in psychosocial risk factors and health status and identify priority areas for intervention at the sector and individual level.

WLB, Boundary Management and Austerity

Few studies have focused directly on the implications of recession and austerity measures for work-life outcomes. As much of the available research was conducted during times of economic growth, the extent to which the findings are relevant during times of financial constraints is uncertain. There is, however, some evidence that work-life conflict has increased for some employees. For example, a survey of more than 2,500 UK workers found that the proportion of respondents who reported blurred boundaries between their work and personal life had risen from 16 percent to 28 percent in the previous 12-month period (ADP, 2014).

When examining the implications of the financial crisis for WLB, it is important to consider how the relationships between work and personal life have been conceptualised. Although work can undoubtedly enrich one's personal life, most studies have utilised a conflict paradigm where incompatible pressures are seen to arise from roles in the work and family domains (Greenhaus and Beutell, 1985; Carlson et al., 2009). This approach draws upon resource-drain theory, which maintains that personal resources (such as time and energy) are finite, and fulfilling the demands of one role will deplete those available to meet the demands of other roles (Edwards and Rothbard, 2000). In the light of the evidence provided above for the growing intensification of work, a resource-drain perspective seems a particularly appropriate lens through which to explore the implications of austerity for WLB and well-being more generally.

Conflict between roles within work and personal life can manifest itself in several ways, but time-based conflict (where time spent working reduces the time available to recover from work and to fulfil personal responsibilities) and strain-based conflict (where tiredness or negative emotional states engendered by the job role are transferred into the personal domain) are most commonly examined (Greenhaus and Beutell, 1985). Strong associations have been found between both types of conflict and a range of negative outcomes such as ill health, relationships difficulties and reduced life satisfaction (Byron, 2005; Amstad et al., 2011). For several reasons discussed below, there is clear potential for the financial crisis to intensify both time-based and strain-based work-life conflict.

The findings of research conducted with almost 24,000 workers aged between 15 and 60 in 27 European Union countries offers support for the negative impact of work-life conflict on health. It also provides indirect evidence that austerity measures have increased the potential for such conflict (Lunau et al., 2014). In this study, work-life conflict was conceptualised as a lack of 'fit' between working hours and family or social commitments and this variable was correlated with health status. Findings revealed that variations in welfare regimes between countries had strong effects on perceptions of work-life conflict that, in turn, had serious consequences for physical and mental health. Norway and Denmark reported the most favourable balance overall, whereas Spain and Greece (who were hit particularly hard by the financial crisis) had the poorest. The Nordic states are widely recognised for their support for employees with caring roles and their comparatively low levels of work-life conflict (Fernandez-Crehuet et al., 2015). The findings of this study suggest that social democratic regimes may be better equipped to minimise the threat of recession on the personal life of employees, although the extent of the recession is also an important factor.

The notion that work and life are different spheres of operation is common across most theoretical paradigms relevant to work–life balance (see Edwards and Rothbard, 2000) and underpins the conflict and resource-drain approaches. Nonetheless, the extent to which individuals prefer their work and home roles to be segmented or integrated, and the behaviours they use to manage the boundaries between these roles, varies considerably (Kossek and Lautsch, 2007). Regardless of whether people prefer to differentiate between work and personal life in general, and the degree to which they seek satisfaction from either or both, opportunities for respite and recovery from work are crucial for well-being (Sonnentag et al., 2010; Kinnunen et al., 2015). Ruminating about work problems during leisure time is a well-established risk factor for health (Berset et al., 2011; Querstret and Cropley, 2012). Confirming its relevance as an explanation for reduced well-being during times of austerity via strain-based work-life conflict, there is evidence that perseverative cognitions about work tend to be more frequent under conditions of high workload and unjust treatment (Cropley and Zijlstra, 2011). Moreover, although sharing problems can benefit health, co-rumination (or excessive discussion with others about work concerns) has the potential to impair rather than improve well-being by further restricting opportunities for respite and recovery (Boren, 2013; Sensky et al., 2015). Individual and collective rumination about job insecurity and financial pressures may be particularly likely therefore to impact on WLB and health and will be discussed further below.

Evidence has been provided that well-being and WLB have deteriorated since the recession and that intensification of work is likely to have played a key role. The next section considers the implications of other factors, such as reduced job security, economic hardship and an increase of non-standard working arrangements, for the health and personal life of employees and their families. Their potential to increase time-based and strain-based conflict will also be examined.

The Impact of Job Insecurity

Rising unemployment rates, job insecurity and an increase in non-standard or 'precarious' employment are defining features of an economic downturn. The most recent UK Skills and Employment survey found a higher level of insecurity among both public and private sector employees than any time in the previous twenty years (Felstead et al., 2013). As noted above, research conducted by the CIPD also revealed that satisfaction with job security had decreased considerably over a similar time-scale. In order to gain insight into the impact of job insecurity on well-being and its relevance to the financial crisis, it is crucial to explore the ways in which it is conceptualised. 'Objective' insecurity is an inherent feature of temporary work owing to its limited time span (De Witte, 2005), whereas 'subjective' insecurity refers to the perceived threat of job loss and encompasses feelings of powerlessness and a lack of control over the continuity of work (Greenhalgh and Rosenblatt, 1984). Research findings indicate that both objective and subjective job insecurity have risen substantially in line with the economic downturn (Burke, 2013).

Subjective job insecurity is one of the most damaging work stressors (Burchell, 2011). It has been linked with a wide range of negative outcomes such as anxiety, depression, burnout, psychosomatic complaints, as well as decreased job commitment and performance (De Witte, 2005; Burgard et al., 2012; Burke, 2013). Fear of job loss can diminish the quality of personal life in several ways. Employees may engage in extra-role behaviour and work longer and more intensely in an attempt to avoid job loss (Brandes et al., 2008), increasing the potential for time-based work-life conflict and reducing recovery opportunities. Furthermore, ruminating excessively about job insecurity and financial concerns is likely to engender strain-based conflict (Greenglass et al., 2013). Recurring and intrusive negative thoughts about work may also lead to social withdrawal, thus limiting the opportunities to gain support from others—an important buffer of the negative effects of work-related stress on well-being (O'Driscoll et al., 2006).

Clearly, labour market conditions will influence employees' reactions to job insecurity, whereas those who are more 'employable' are likely to experience fewer adverse effects. It has been argued that people tend to overestimate the power of the economic situation in influencing their working conditions (Houdmont et al., 2012), but increasingly robust welfare reforms in the UK and other countries are likely to have compounded any pre-existing fears of unemployment (Graham and McQuaid, 2014; Daly and Kelly, 2015). Indeed, there is evidence that simply hearing about organisations facing financial challenges, or being exposed to media reports of financial crises at the national or global level, can engender job insecurity and anxiety (Rocha et al., 2006; Greenglass et al., 2013).

More research is required from a psychological perspective on the impact of objective and subjective job insecurity during times of austerity. It has been suggested that research incorporating multi-level economic pressures and employees' perceptions of their employability into existing models of work-related stress can provide more insight into the long-term impact of the recession (Giorgi et al., 2015). The job-demands resources model and the conservation of resources model (Hobfoll, 1989; Bakker and Demerouti, 2007) may be particularly appropriate frameworks through which to examine these effects. The extent to which perceptions of job insecurity persevere when employment rates are subsequently rising should be examined, together with the mechanisms underlying these effects. Future studies should also explore the impact of perceptions of economic threat from different sources, such as co-ruminating with colleagues and family and engaging with media reports, on the well-being and personal life of employees and their families.

Economic Hardship

Concerns about future financial deprivation (characterised by feelings of job insecurity) can seriously threaten physical and mental health, but the negative effects of actual, rather than anticipated, economic hardship have also been highlighted (Malach-Pines and Zaidman, 2013). One potential mechanism for these effects is maladaptive health behaviours which have clear implications for long-term health (Macy et al., 2013). In terms of recession, EU studies have found strong links between changes in unemployment levels and health status and mortality rates, including suicide (Stuckler et al., 2011; Evans-Lacko et al., 2013). Although few studies have explored the impact of financial concerns on the work-home interface, there is some evidence that they can engender work-life conflict—especially among men (Schieman and Young, 2011), presumably due to the role expectations and pressures of being a 'good provider'. Financial concerns may also be particularly threatening to the well-being of carers due to feelings of responsibility for the well-being of others. For example, a study of women who worked full-time alongside significant elder care-giving responsibilities found that the association between work interfering with the caring role and distress was strengthened in those who were experiencing more financial strain (Kim and Gordon, 2014).

Economic hardship can not only affect individual employees, but also influence the well-being of their family members. This could be explained by the shared environment but, supporting the negative impact of co-rumination discussed above, a study conducted by Afifi et al. (2015) found that discussing financial concerns increased biological markers of stress across partners. These effects were particularly pronounced in women who, prior to the stressful conversation with their spouse, felt more financially secure. It should be acknowledged, however, that failing to discuss serious issues with partners that would affect the family unit, such as financial problems and feelings of job insecurity, is likely to have an adverse impact on well-being and on the quality of the relationship itself. There is evidence that setting guidelines and boundaries for financial decision making is a key component of a successful relationship (Washburn and Christensen, 2008).

In terms of the impact of financial stress on the family unit, a particularly well-designed study of over 500 Finnish mother-father-child triads found strong associations between economic pressure and mental health and parenting styles (Leinonen et al., 2002). The outcomes were also gender specific: for fathers, financial hardship was associated with anxiety and social dysfunction that, in turn, was linked to hostile marital interactions, low marital support and punitive, non-involved fathering; for mothers, it was related to anxiety leading to more authoritative mothering styles. Instrumental and emotional support from the mother, however, tended to compensate for the negative impact of financial pressure on parenting. Later research with the same triads found that a subsequent reduction in family income further threatened the children's well-being via impairments in parental mental health, marital relationships and parenting styles (Solantaus et al., 2004). Cohort studies have strong potential to identify the negative influence of financial hardship on the next generation on outcomes such as achievement orientations, work values and health status over time, as well as the factors that intensify and minimise the risks (Das-Munshi et al., 2013; Mortimer et al., 2014; Johnson and Mortimer, 2015).

Non-Standard Work Arrangements

Non-standard or precarious work arrangements, such as temporary contracts and casual (or zero-hours) working, increased substantially in the UK and most other EU countries since the recession (Eurofound, 2015). Fixed-term contracts can be beneficial for organisations by helping them adjust employment levels to fluctuations in demand, whereby staff can be hired during periods of economic growth and laid off during stagnation. Nonetheless, there are disadvantages for employees as temporary jobs tend to be of poorer quality than their permanent equivalents in that they are lower paid and less secure and are typically characterised by higher demands, lower control and fewer training opportunities (Benach and Muntaner, 2007; Cutuli and Guetto, 2013). There is also evidence that temporary workers are at greater risk of illness and injury than those in permanent jobs, but are more likely to continue to work while sick (Inoue et al., 2011; Wagenaar et al., 2013). Taking sick leave may be considered a sign of weakness under conditions of job insecurity that make employees more vulnerable to job loss. For this reason, it has been recognised that 'presenteeism' may be partially responsible for the decline in sickness absence figures recently observed in the UK (CIPD, 2014b). Nonetheless, presenteeism can be considerably more costly for organisations than absenteeism, as working while sick can not only delay recovery, but also reduce productivity and increase the risk of sickness absence over the longer term (Kivimaki et al., 2005; Johns, 2011).

While frameworks such as Warr's Vitamin model (1987) highlight the potential benefits of work for mental health, there is evidence that precarious and poor quality work can be more damaging than no work at all. For example, a study of middle-aged workers conducted by Broom et al. (2006) found that unemployed people reported worse health and more general medical practitioner visits than those who were working. Nonetheless, the health status of people in low-quality jobs (characterised by insecurity, job strain and low employability) were typically poorer than those whose jobs involved fewer or no stressors, whereas the health of those in jobs with three or more of these stressors was similar to those who were unemployed. The analysis of seven waves of Australian panel data (>7,000 participants) also found that the health benefits of gaining employment were dependent upon the quality of the job, with the transition from unemployment to poor-quality work being more detrimental to mental health than remaining jobless (Butterworth et al., 2011).

Although the negative effects of temporary and poor-quality work on the well-being of employees have been highlighted, little research has directly explored the implications for WLB. As outlined above, the insecurity and financial worries inherent in non-standard working arrangements have clear potential to increase time-based and strain-based conflict. The uncertainty inherent in such work may be particularly challenging for people with caring responsibilities who lack domestic support (Mauno and Ruokolainen, 2015). Casual workers, in particular, are likely to work highly irregular hours (often across multiple jobs) and are often required to engage in "diverse and complex negotiations and strategies" to balance paid work with their caring responsibilities (Dyer et al., 2011: 685). When considering the impact of temporary work on well-being and WLB, however, it is crucial to acknowledge its heterogeneous nature; salary, holiday entitlement and sick pay, and the extent to which this mode of working is by choice rather than circumstance, will moderate its impact (De Cuyper and de Witte, 2007). The extent to which employees are able to accommodate the demands of their non-working lives when workload and working hours are unpredictable will also be a key factor in determining work-life outcomes.

Flexible working, facilitated by the use of information communication technology (ICT), has increased substantially during the economic downturn. Although having the potential to help employees manage the competing demands of work and personal life more effectively, there is evidence that flexible working practices may not necessarily be beneficial for WLB and well-being. This issue is explored in the next section.

Flexibility and WLB in Times of Recession

Flexible working is defined as "a way of working that suits an employee's needs: e.g. having flexible start and finish times, or working from home" (GOVUK, 2014). Flexible arrangements are typically categorised under four headings: variable hours (such as flexi-time and zero hours contracts); restructured hours (such as job sharing); reduced hours (such as working part-time); and leave options (to fulfil caring responsibilities or take career breaks). While the majority of industrialised countries have legislation to facilitate working time adjustments, many restrict these opportunities to workers with caring responsibilities (Hegewisch, 2009). From 2014, all UK employees who had worked for their employer for at least 26 weeks became eligible to request flexible working. Employers are required to consider such requests, but can refuse them if there are valid business reasons to do so.

The extension of the right to request flexible working arrangements is predicated on the notion that flexibility has wide-ranging benefits for employers and employees, such as more successful adaptation to volatile market conditions and the ability to attract a wider talent pool, together with enhanced productivity, reduced absenteeism and lower turnover of employees (Reilly, 1998; Kalleberg, 2001; Gajendran and Harrison, 2007). Employees' attitudes towards flexible working are also typically positive (ADP, 2014; CIPD, 2014a). Indeed, before the UK Government extended the right to request flexible working from parents of young children to all employees, a survey reported that approximately half of the sample intended to take this up given the opportunity, and around one-third believed that their productivity and WLB would improve if they worked flexibly (CIPD, 2012). Some reviews of the literature highlight some benefits of workplace flexibility on work-life integration (Hill et al., 2010). Nonetheless, despite these positive views, a robust systematic review shows that the benefits of flexibility are modest, and only apparent if employees have control over flexible work options (Joyce et al., 2010). Another systematic review of 148 published studies also found no clear business case for flexibility (De Menezes and Kelliher, 2011). The papers reviewed considered relationships between different flexible arrangements (e.g. schedule, remote working and reduced hours), organisational outcomes (e.g. financial performance, productivity, absence and employee turnover), individual performance outcomes (e.g. productivity and ratings of work quality) and attitudinal, health and well-being outcomes (e.g. stress, role conflict, job satisfaction and commitment). The findings differed according to flexibility type and many contradictions emerged: for example, individual studies found positive, negative and non-significant relationships between flexible working and outcomes such as job satisfaction and commitment to the organisation. Moreover, evidence emerged that employees' perceptions of improved productivity due to flexible working were not necessarily shared by their managers.

The findings of other studies suggest that some types of flexibility have the potential to intensify rather than reduce stress and enhance rather than decrease work-life conflict (Ashford et al., 2000; Kelliher and Anderson, 2008; Glavin and Schieman, 2012). Remote working, for example, may reduce organisational costs and remove the stress of commuting, but can increase the risk of social isolation, role stress and family-to-work conflict (Golden et al., 2006). A study of 24,436 workers in 75 countries conducted by Hill et al. (2010) found evidence that flexible workers may actually work longer hours, highlighting an increased risk of time-based conflict. Moreover, analysis of data from the US-based National Survey of the Changing Workforce indicated that employees with more schedule control tended to bring work home more frequently and perceive more, rather than less, conflict between their work and home roles (Schieman and Glavin, 2008). These findings support those of studies suggesting that a combination of high work demands and schedule flexibility can lead to enabled intensification, where employees use flexibility to work longer and harder rather than to facilitate adequate recovery and improve their WLB (Kelliher and Anderson, 2008).

Due to the extension of the right to request flexible working mentioned above, the relevance of research that has examined the utilisation and impact of flexible working initiatives prior to 2014 is questionable under current conditions. A systematic evaluation of the implications of the extended right to request flexible working for individuals and organisations is therefore urgently required. Managers' attitudes and practices will be crucial in influencing the uptake and effectiveness of flexible options and commitment to ensuring their success is required (Cooper and Baird, 2015). As discussed by Stokes and Wood in Chapter 3, the finding that the proportion of managers who believe that WLB is a 'private' concern has grown significantly since 2004 (Van Wanrooy et al., 2013) is therefore a potential cause for concern. Such views were also expressed in an interview study of HR managers in the UK public sector (Lewis et al., 2016; also see Lyonette et al. in Chapter 4) and may reflect perceptions that their organisation already provides sufficient WLB opportunities. Alternatively, they may highlight a tendency to allow business needs to take precedence over initiatives to improve employees' experiences of work during times of financial constraint. These issues are considered further later in the chapter.

Organisations and individuals appear to have very high expectations of flexibility in improving well-being and ensuring organisational success. Nonetheless, mere access to flexible working arrangements is not in itself a panacea; its effectiveness depends upon the type of flexibility offered and the extent to which uptake is encouraged and supported, as well as other factors such as work and family role centrality and boundary management preferences (Kossek et al., 2005; Schieman and Glavin, 2008). There is evidence that organisations are increasingly 'imposing' remote working, as a way of managing financial pressures rather than as an initiative to improve WLB (Lewis et al., 2016; also see Lyonette et al. in Chapter 4). It should also be recognised that not all employees may wish to work flexibly: indeed, some may prefer the more predictable working patterns that are typically present in blue-collar working environments (Poppleton et al., 2008). Introducing flexible working without providing choice, or without a careful consideration of its appropriateness and potential effectiveness, is likely to be costly, especially during times of financial constraints.

A wide range of WLB initiatives is available but, although the right to request flexible working has been extended, there is evidence that the economic downturn has constrained the development of further initiatives requiring financial investment (Lewis et al., 2016). Nonetheless, barriers to taking up the WLB initiatives that are available have been identified. Employees may be reluctant to request flexible working or to take their full entitlement due to concerns about job insecurity and future advancement in the organisation—worries that may be compounded during times of financial constraints. Research findings demonstrate that flexible working may be equally stigmatised by employers and employees and by younger as well as older workers. A longitudinal study of seven companies conducted by Kelliher and Anderson (2008) found that flexible workers were generally considered less motivated and less worthy of promotion than those who had fixed hours of work.

Despite widespread attempts to highlight its benefits to all workers, flexible working is still typically viewed as the "mommy track" and the essence of responsible fatherhood continues to be full employment (Norman et al., 2014). There is evidence that men who wish to work flexibly are subject to particularly negative perceptions. A scenario-based study conducted by Rudman and Mescher (2013) found that hypothetical male employees who requested family leave were believed to possess more of the weak, "feminine" qualities (such as uncertainty) and fewer agentic "masculine" traits (such as dominance and ambition). Perceptions of weakness in these men were directly related to the extent to which participants considered that they should be rewarded (e.g. recommended for promotion) or penalised (e.g. given a salary reduction, or fewer responsibilities at work). Interestingly, female participants were just as likely as males to stigmatise men who requested family leave, but women tended to express stronger views that such men were poor workers. While participants in this study were young adults who may not have had much work experience, other research findings highlight the potential career penalties for requests for flexible working for caring purposes. For example, Leslie et al. (2012) found that flexible work requests were viewed favourably if they were made for business reasons, but seen as synonymous with poor performance if made for family reasons.

ICT Use and Organisational Support

Two key issues require further consideration in the debate on flexible working during austerity. These are (a) the role of technology and (b) the importance of direct supervisory support. The deployment of information communication technology (ICT) has considerable advantages for business during a financial downturn by offering greater flexibility in the location and modality of work. The potential for ICTs to help employees manage the demands of multiple roles is also recognised (Gozu et al., 2015). Nonetheless, technological acceleration has been a key driver of work intensification (Demerouti et al. 2014), which, as discussed above, can threaten well-being and WLB. ICT use can enhance time-based conflict by enabling employees to work longer hours and increasing employers' expectations of their availability (Major and Germano, 2006; Towers et al., 2006). The 'switching costs' of multi-tasking (Spink et al., 2008) will also extend the time required to complete work tasks with strong potential to extend working hours. Mobile technologies can also increase strain-based conflict by making the work role more psychologically salient outside contracted working hours, allowing emotional reactions to work to spill over to personal life (Park et al., 2011). Habitual use of ICT for work purposes out of formal work hours can engender resentment in family members and feelings of guilt in employees (Middleton, 2008). The increasing evidence that a high level of engagement with ICT can increase the occurrence of cognitive failures (Hadlington, 2015), also raises concerns for job performance.

Research exploring the relationship between technology use and work-life outcomes is still in its infancy. ICTs have strong potential to improve WLB, but it is crucial to provide organisations and individuals with evidence-based guidance on how it can be used in a healthy and sustainable manner. Such information is vital under current working conditions where financial constraints, work intensification and expectations to demonstrate high commitment may encourage employees to increase their availability for work. The finding that employees commonly engage with technology for work purposes autonomously, rather than in response to external demands, poses a further challenge for interventions (Schlachter et al., 2016). There is evidence that the use of different devices can strengthen boundaries between work and personal life, but the implications for well-being are as yet unclear (Fleck et al., 2015). Moreover, the use of ICTs for leisure purposes, such as digital gaming, may help employees detach themselves from work concerns quickly and effectively (Collins and Cox, 2014). It should be emphasised, however, that individual differences, such as preference for separation or integration between work and home roles and segmentation norms within organisations and families, appear to be crucial in determining the impact of ICT use on work-life outcomes (Park et al., 2011). This suggests that interventions to manage ICT use should be sufficiently flexible to accommodate individuals' preferences and practices. Line managers have some responsibility for providing their employees with evidence-based guidance to help them engage with ICT in a healthy and effective way.

Support for WLB during Austerity

The important role played by managers in protecting the well-being and WLB of staff has long been highlighted. Supervisors can be a powerful source of support for people with caring responsibilities: indeed, they are the 'linking pins' between formal WLB policies and how these are enacted. Research conducted by Hammer et al. (2007) identified several supportive line manager behaviours, such as emotional support (learning about personal WLB needs and listening to problems); instrumental support (helping employees avoid work-to-home conflict and vice versa); role modelling (demonstrating effective personal WLB behaviours) and creative WLB management (using innovative options to reduce work-life conflict). Supervisor behaviours that are 'WLB specific' can have wide-ranging benefits for the personal life of employees (Kossek et al., 2011). This is in line with other robust research outlining the crucial role played by line managers in preventing work-related stress (Donaldson-Feilder et al. 2011).

Although their role is crucial, research that explores the nature and impact of supportive supervisor behaviours during austerity is extremely limited. Nonetheless, there is some evidence that support for WLB from line managers may be particularly beneficial when employees are experiencing economic strain (Lauzun et al., 2012). However, as discussed above, there is also evidence that UK managers are increasingly viewing WLB as an individual responsibility. The factors that underpin such attitudes should be explored, together with their implications for the success of WLB initiatives that operate under challenging financial conditions. Whether the negative views of managers compound the existing stigmatisation of the uptake of WLB initiatives should also be considered. Supportive manager behaviours cannot work in isolation, however, and should be firmly embedded within an organisational culture where all employees are helped to achieve an effective WLB and the benefits for all stakeholders are recognised.

While there is little doubt that organisations need to offer adequate support, employees also have responsibility for maintaining a healthy balance between their work and their personal lives. Initiatives that emphasise a dual responsibility for WLB are likely to be more effective than those that place the onus on the individual employee or the organisation (Kossek et al., 2011; see also Kim et al. in Chapter 10). For example, Kim et al. discuss action research which involves collaboration between workers, managers and researchers and can engender interventions that support individual workers as well as workplace effectiveness. Competency frameworks, that identify the behaviours of employees and employers that are helpful in managing WLB in different occupational contexts, can also be particularly helpful in raising awareness and informing interventions (Kinman and Grant, 2014; McDowall and Lindsay, 2014). The emphasis on facilitating behaviours that help employees manage the interface between work and personal life are likely to be more cost effective than those that require structural change or other major investment (see also Donaldson-Feilder et al., 2011).

Conclusions

This chapter has demonstrated that the link between financial constraints, the work-home interface and well-being is complex. Job insecurity may encourage employers and employees to 'trade' WLB for organisational success and continued employment over the short term, without recognising the potentially serious consequences for health, personal relationships and job performance over the longer term. Although there is firm evidence to the contrary, employers and employees still consider long working hours to be a fundamental requirement for career success, but the detrimental effects on WLB are acknowledged (Burke and Cooper, 2008). Nonetheless, it should be recognised that the risks to well-being during austerity are likely to stem as much from work intensification as long working hours—with serious risks for recovery and WLB. The role played by technology in enabling intensification as well as facilitating flexibility is also evident. Evidence has been provided that organisations may see flexible working as a panacea for WLB and well-being but, to be effective, employees need choice and control over their working patterns. How the stigmatisation of alternative ways of working, especially for caring purposes, can impact on the uptake of flexible initiatives and the evident carer risks should be recognised and steps taken to increase their acceptability. Supervisor support is another crucial consideration, as this can buffer detrimental health outcomes, but is more effective when targeted specifically at WLB issues and where employees are encouraged to share this responsibility.

More research is clearly needed to examine the long-term impact of the recession and its legacy on the well-being and WLB of employees. Although some insight has been gained, studies have focused predominantly on the implications of austerity measures on business outcomes rather than on individuals. It seems crucial to identify the features of organisations and employees that help them manage the financial downturn more effectively and those that place them at greater risk. As these factors are likely to be context specific, one-size fits all interventions are unlikely to be effective. There is a need to develop more creative and inclusive initiatives to improve work-life outcomes, bearing in mind the key role of control and choice in determining their effectiveness. Focus should also be placed on how organisations and employees can work together to craft and develop a WLB that suits their own preferences and their family's needs, while at the same time benefiting organisations.

Finally, this chapter draws upon research conducted in different national contexts. The extent to which the findings of research conducted in one country or region can be validly applied to another should be carefully considered, as experiences of recession and its aftermath will differ according to labour market conditions, employment practices and culture. It is clear, however, that macro-economic factors influence health and well-being and WLB. Future organisational practice and policy therefore needs to be guided by more robust, evidence-based national and international policy directives.

References

ADP. (2014). *Getting the Right Work-life Balance: White Paper Workforce View 2014/15*, available at http://www.adp.co.uk/workforce-view-insights/work-life-balance-tw

Afifi, T., Davis, S., Merrill, A.F., Coveleski, S., Denes, A., & Afifi, W. (2015). In the wake of the Great Recession: Economic uncertainty, communication, and biological stress responses in families. *Human Communication Research*, 41(2): 268–302.

Amstad, F.T., Meier, L.L., Fasel, U., Elfering, A., & Semmer, N.K. (2011). A meta-analysis of work–family conflict and various outcomes with a special emphasis on cross-domain versus matching-domain relations. *Journal of Occupational Health Psychology*, 16(2): 151.

Ashford, B.E., Kreiner, G.E., & Fugate, M. (2000). All in a day's work: Boundaries and micro-role transitions. *Academy of Management Review*, 25(3): 472–491.

Bakker, A.B., & Demerouti, E. (2007). The job demands-resources model: State of the art. *Journal of Managerial Psychology*, 22(3): 309–328.

Benach, J., & Muntaner, C. (2007). Precarious employment and health: Developing a research agenda. *Journal of Epidemiology and Community Health*, 61(4): 276–277.

Berset, M., Elfering, A., Lüthy, S., Lüthi, S., & Semmer, N.K. (2011). Work stressors and impaired sleep: Rumination as a mediator. *Stress and Health*, 27(2): e71–e82.

Boren, J.P. (2013). The relationships between co-rumination, social support, stress, and burnout among working adults. *Management Communication Quarterly*, 28(1): 3–25.

Brandes, P., Castro, S.L., James, M.S., Martinez, A.D., Matherly, T.A., Ferris, G.R., & Hochwarter, W.A. (2008). The interactive effects of job insecurity and organizational cynicism on work effort following a layoff. *Journal of Leadership & Organizational Studies*, 14(3): 233–247.

Broom, D.H., D'Souza, R.M., Strazdins, L., Butterworth, P., Parslow, R., & Rodgers, B. (2006). The lesser evil: Bad jobs or unemployment? A survey of mid-aged Australians. *Social Science & Medicine*, 63(3): 575–586.

Burchell, B. (2011). A temporal comparison of the effects of unemployment and job insecurity on wellbeing. *Sociological Research Online*, 16(1): 9, available at http://socresonline.org.uk/16/1/9.html

Burgard, S.A., Kalousova, L., & Seefeldt, K.S. (2012). Perceived job insecurity and health: The Michigan recession and recovery study. *Journal of Occupational and Environmental Medicine*, 54(9): 1101–1106.

Burke, R.J. (2013). Economic recession, job insecurity and employee and organizational health. In A. Alexander-Stamatious & C.L. Cooper (eds) *The Psychology of the Recession on the Workplace*: 143–154. Cheltenham: Edward Elgar Publishing.

Burke, R.J., & Cooper, C.L. (2008). *The Long Work Hours Culture: Causes, Consequences and Choices.* Bingley: Emerald Group Publishing.

Buss, P. (2009). Public health and the world economic crisis. *Journal of Epidemiology and Community Health*, 63(6): 417.

Butterworth, P., Leach, L.S., Strazdins, L., Olesen, S.C., Rodgers, B., & Broom, D.H. (2011). The psychosocial quality of work determines whether employment has benefits for mental health: Results from a longitudinal national household panel survey. *Occupational and Environmental Medicine*, 68(11): 806–812.

Byron, K. (2005). A meta-analytic review of work–family conflict and its antecedents. *Journal of Vocational Behaviour*, 67(2): 169–198.

Carlson, D.S., Grzywacz, J.G., & Zivnuska, S. (2009). Is work-family balance more than conflict and enrichment? *Human Relations*, 62(10): 1459–1486.

Chartered Institute of Personnel and Development. (2012). *Flexible Working Provision and Uptake*, available at http://www.cipd.co.uk/binaries/5790%20Flexible%20Working%20SR%20(WEB2).pdf

Chartered Institute of Personnel and Development. (2014a). *Megatrends: The Trends Shaping Work and Working Lives*, available at http://www.cipd.co.uk/hr-resources/research/megatrends-trends-shaping-work-lives.aspx

Chartered Institute of Personnel and Development. (2014b). *Absence Management 2014*, available at https://www.cipd.co.uk/binaries/absence-management_2014.pdf

Collins, E., & Cox, A.L. (2014). Switch on to games: Can digital games aid post-work recovery? *International Journal of Human-Computer Studies*, 72(8): 654–662.

Cooper, R., & Baird, M. (2015). Bringing the 'right to request' flexible working arrangements to life: From policies to practices. *Employee Relations*, 37(5): 568–581.

Cropley, M., & Zijlstra, F.R.H. (2011). Work and rumination. In J. Langan-Fox & C. Cooper (eds) *Handbook of Stress in the Occupations*: 487–503. Cheltenham: Edward Elgar Publishing.

Cutuli, G., & Guetto, R. (2013). Fixed-term contracts, economic conjuncture, and training opportunities: A comparative analysis across European labour markets. *European Sociological Review*, 29(3): 616–629.

Daly, M., & Kelly, G. (2015). *Families and Poverty: Everyday Life on a Low Income.* Bristol, UK: Policy Press.

Das-Munshi, J., Clark, C., Dewey, M.E., Leavey, G., Stansfeld, S.A., & Prince, M.J. (2013). Does childhood adversity account for poorer mental and physical health in second-generation Irish people living in Britain? Birth cohort study from Britain (NCDS). *BMJ Open*, 3(3), available at http://bmjopen.bmj.com/content/3/3/e001335.full

Deaton, A. (2012). *The Financial Crisis and the Well-being of Americans 2011.* OEP Hicks Lecture. *Oxford Economic Papers*, 64(1): 1–26.

De Cuyper, N., & De Witte, H. (2007). Job insecurity in temporary versus permanent workers: Associations with attitudes, well-being, and behaviour. *Work & Stress*, 21(1): 65–84.

De Menezes, L.M., & Kelliher, C. (2011). Flexible working and performance: A systematic review of the evidence for a business case. *International Journal of Management Reviews*, 13(4): 452–474.

Demerouti, E., Derks, D., Lieke, L., & Bakker, A.B. (2014). New ways of working: Impact on working conditions, work–family balance, and well-being. In C. Korunka & P. Hoonakker (eds) *The Impact of ICT on Quality of Working Life*: 123–141. Dordrecht: Springer.

De Witte, H. (2005). Job insecurity: Review of the international literature on definitions, prevalence, antecedents and consequences. *SA Journal of Industrial Psychology*, 31(4): 1–6.

Donaldson-Feilder, E., Lewis, R., & Yarker, J. (2011). *Preventing Stress in Organizations: How to Develop Positive Managers*. Chichester, UK: John Wiley & Sons.

Dyer, S., McDowell, L., & Batnitzky, A. (2011). Migrant work, precarious work–life balance: What the experiences of migrant workers in the service sector in Greater London tell us about the adult worker model. *Gender, Place & Culture*, 18(5): 685–700.

Edwards, J.R., & Rothbard, N.P. (2000). Mechanisms linking work and family: Clarifying the relationship between work and family constructs. *Academy of Management Review*, 25(1): 178–199.

Eurofound. (2015). *Recent Developments in Temporary Employment*, available at https://www.eurofound.europa.eu/sites/default/files/ef_publication/field_ef_document/ef1557en.pdf

Evans-Lacko, S., Knapp, M., McCrone, P., Thornicroft, G., & Mojtabai, R. (2013). The mental health consequences of the recession: Economic hardship and employment of people with mental health problems in 27 European countries. *PLoS One*, 8(7): e69792.

EWCS. (2015). *Sixth European Working Conditions Survey 2015*, available at http://www.eurofound.europa.eu/surveys/2015/sixth-european-working-conditions-survey-2015

Felstead, A., Gallie, D., Green, F., & Inanc, H. (2013). *Work Intensification in Britain: First Findings from the Skills and Employment Survey 2012*. London: Centre for Learning and Life Chances in Knowledge Economies and Societies, Institute of Education.

Fernandez-Crehuet, J.M., Gimenez-Nadal, J.I., & Recio, L.E.R. (2015). The National Work–Life Balance Index: The European case. *Social Indicators Research*, 1–19. **doi:** 10.1007/s11205-015-1034-2

Fleck, R., Cox, A.L., & Robison, R.A.V. (2015). *Balancing Boundaries: Using Multiple Devices to Manage Work-Life Balance Conference on Human Factors in Computing Systems—Proceedings*, 2015-April, doi:10.1145/2702123.2702386

Gajendran, R.S., & Harrison, D.A. (2007). The good, the bad, and the unknown about telecommuting: Meta-analysis of psychological mediators and individual consequences. *Journal of Applied Psychology*, 92(6): 1524–1541.

Giorgi, G., Shoss, M.K., & Leon-Perez, J.M. (2015). Going beyond workplace stressors: Economic crisis and perceived employability in relation to psychological distress and job dissatisfaction. *International Journal of Stress Management*, 22(2): 137.

Glavin, P., & Schieman, S. (2012). Work–family role blurring and work–family conflict: The moderating influence of job resources and job demands. *Work and Occupations*, 39(1): 71–98.

Golden, T.D., Veiga, J.F., & Simsek, Z. (2006). Telecommuting's differential impact on work-family conflict: Is there no place like home? *Journal of Applied Psychology*, 91(6): 1340–1350.

GOVUK. (2014). *Flexible Working*, available at https://www.gov.uk/flexible-working/overview

Gözü, C., Anandarajan, M., & Simmers, C.A. (2015). Work–family role integration and personal well-being: The moderating effect of attitudes towards personal web usage. *Computers in Human Behavior*, 52(November): 159–167.

Graham, H., & McQuaid, R. (2014). *Exploring the Challenges and Opportunities Facing Lone Parents*. Glasgow Centre for Population Health, available at https://dspace.stir.ac.uk/bitstream/1893/20454/1/GCPH_lone_parents_Literature_Review_FINAL%200514.pdf

Green, F., Felstead, A., Gallie, D., & Inanc, H. (2016). Job-related wellbeing through the Great Recession. *Journal of Happiness Studies*, 17(1): 389–411.

Greenglass, E., Marjanovic, Z., & Fiksenbaum, L. (2013). The impact of the recession and its aftermath on individual health and well-being. In G. Alexander-Stammatios & C. Cooper (eds) *The Psychology of the Recession in the Workplace*: 42–58. Cheltenham: Edward Elgar Publishing.

Greenhalgh, L., & Rosenblatt, Z. (1984). Job insecurity: Toward conceptual clarity. *Academy of Management Review*, 9(3): 438–448.

Greenhaus, J.H., & Beutell, N.J. (1985). Sources of conflict between work and family roles. *Academy of Management Review*, 10(1): 76–88.

Gregg, P., & Wadsworth, J. (2010). Employment in the 2008–2009 recession. *Economic & Labour Market Review*, 4(8): 37–45, Office for National Statistics.

Hadlington, L.J. (2015). Cognitive failures in daily life: Exploring the link with Internet addiction and problematic mobile phone use. *Computers in Human Behavior*, 51(October): 75–81.

Hammer, L.B., Kossek, E.E., Zimmerman, K., & Daniels, R. (2007). Clarifying the construct of family supportive supervisory behaviors (FSSB): A multilevel perspective. In P. Perrewe & D. Ganster (eds) *Research in Occupational Stress and Well-being* 6: 171–211. Amsterdam: Elsevier.

Health and Safety Executive. (2015). *Work-related Stress, Anxiety and Depression Statistics in Great Britain 2015*, available at http://www.hse.gov.uk/statistics/causdis/stress/stress.pdf

Hegewisch, A. (2009). *Flexible Working Policies: A Comparative Review*. Manchester: Equality and Human Rights Commission.

Hill, E.J., Erickson, J.J., Holmes, E.K., & Ferris, M. (2010). Workplace flexibility, work hours, and work-life conflict: Finding an extra day or two. *Journal of Family Psychology*, 24(3): 349–358.

Hobfoll, S.E. (1989). Conservation of resources: A new attempt at conceptualizing stress. *American Psychologist*, 44(3): 513–524.

Houdmont, J., Kerr, R., & Addley, K. (2012). Psychosocial factors and economic recession: The Stormont Study. *Occupational Medicine*, 62(2): 98–104.

Inoue, M., Tsurugano, S., & Yano, E. (2011). Job stress and mental health of permanent and fixed-term workers measured by effort-reward imbalance model, depressive complaints, and clinic utilization. *Journal of Occupational Health*, 53(2): 93–101.

Jahoda, M. (1982). *Employment and Unemployment: A Social-psychological Analysis (Vol. 1)*. CUP Archive.

Johns, G. (2011). Attendance dynamics at work: The antecedents and correlates of presenteeism, absenteeism, and productivity loss. *Journal of Occupational Health Psychology*, 16(4): 483–500.

Johnson, M.K., & Mortimer, J.T. (2015). Reinforcement or compensation? The effects of parents' work and financial conditions on adolescents' work values during the Great Recession. *Journal of Vocational Behavior*, 87(2): 89–100.

Joyce, K., Pabayo, R., Critchley, J.A., & Bambra, C. (2010). Flexible working conditions and their effects on employee health and wellbeing. *Cochrane Database of Systematic Reviews*, Issue 2(Art. No.: CD008009): 1–88. doi:10.1002/14651858. CD008009.pub

Kalleberg, A.L. (2001). Organizing flexibility: The flexible firm in a new century. *British Journal of Industrial Relations*, 39(4): 479–504.

Kelliher, C., & Anderson, D. (2008). For better or for worse? An analysis of how flexible working practices influence employees' perceptions of job quality. *The International Journal of Human Resource Management*, 19(3): 419–431.

Kim, N., & Gordon, J.R. (2014). Addressing the stress of work and elder caregiving of the graying workforce. *Human Resource Management*, 53(5): 723–747.

Kinman, G., & Grant, L. (2014). Supporting emotional resilience and recovery in social workers: Management competencies. *Proceedings of the Work-Family Research Network Conference*, New York, June.

Kinman, G., & Wray, S. (2016, in press). *Work and Wellbeing in Higher Education*. London: University and College Union.

Kinnunen, U., Rantanen, J., de Bloom, J., Mauno, S., Feldt, T., & Korpela, K. (2015). The role of work–non-work boundary management in work stress recovery. *International Journal of Stress Management*, available at http://psycnet.apa. org/psycinfo/2015-42701-001/

Kivimäki, M., Head, J., Ferrie, J.E., Hemingway, H., Shipley, M.J., Vahtera, J., & Marmot, M.G. (2005). Working while ill as a risk factor for serious coronary events: The Whitehall II study. *American Journal of Public Health*, 95(1): 98–102.

Kossek, E.E., & Lautsch, B.A. (2007). *CEO of Me: Creating a Life That Works in the Flexible Job Age*. Upper Saddle River, NJ: Prentice Hall.

Kossek, E.E., Lautsch, B.A., & Eaton, S.C. (2005). *Flexibility Enactment Theory: Implications of Flexibility Type, Control, and Boundary Management for Work-Family Effectiveness*. Mahwah, NJ: Lawrence Erlbaum Associates Publishers.

Kossek, E.E., Pichler, S., Bodner, T., & Hammer, L.B. (2011). Workplace social support and work–family conflict: A meta–analysis clarifying the influence of general and work–family specific supervisor and organizational support. *Personnel Psychology*, 64(2): 289–313.

Lauzun, H.M., Major, D.A., & Jones, M.P. (2012). Employing a conservation of resources framework to examine the interactive effects of work domain support and economic impact on work–family conflict. *The Psychologist-Manager Journal*, 15(1): 25–36.

Leinonen, J.A., Solantaus, T.S., & Punamäki, R.L. (2002). The specific mediating paths between economic hardship and the quality of parenting. *International Journal of Behavioral Development*, 26(5): 423–435.

Leslie, L.M., Manchester, C.F., Park, T.Y., & Mehng, S.A. (2012). Flexible work practices: A source of career premiums or penalties? *Academy of Management Journal*, 55(6): 1407–1428.

Lewis, S., Anderson, D., Lyonette, C., Payne, N., & Wood, S. (2016). Public sector austerity cuts in the UK and the changing discourse of work–life balance. *Work, Employment and Society.* doi: **10.1177/0950017016638994**

Lunau, T., Bambra, C., Eikemo, T.A., van der Wel, K.A., & Dragano, N. (2014). A balancing act? Work–life balance, health and well-being in European welfare states. *The European Journal of Public Health*, 24(3): 422–427.

Macy, J.T., Chassin, L., & Presson, C.C. (2013). Predictors of health behaviors after the economic downturn: A longitudinal study. *Social Science & Medicine*, 89: 8–15.

Major, D.A., & Germano, L.M. (2006). The changing nature of work and its impact on the work-home interface. In F. Jones, R. Burke & M. Westman (eds) *Work-life Balance: A Psychological Perspective*: 13–38. New York: Psychology Press.

Malach-Pines, A., & Zaidman, N. (2013). The mark of recession in the high-tech industry: High stress and low burnout. In A. Alexander-Stamatios & C. Cooper (eds) *The Psychology of the Recession on the Workplace*: 89–100. Cheltenham: Edward Elgar Publishing.

Mauno, S., & Ruokolainen, M. (2015). Does organizational work–family support benefit temporary and permanent employees equally in a work–family conflict situation in relation to job satisfaction and emotional energy at work and at home? *Journal of Family Issues.* doi: **10.1177/0192513X15600729**

McDowall, A., & Lindsay, A. (2014). Work–life balance in the police: The development of a self-management competency framework. *Journal of Business and Psychology*, 29(3): 397–411.

Middleton, C.A. (2008). Do mobile technologies enable work–life balance? In D. Hislop (ed) *Mobility and Technology in the Workplace*: 209–224. London and New York: Routledge.

Mortimer, J.T., Zhang, F.L., Hussemann, J., & Wu, C.Y. (2014). Parental economic hardship and children's achievement orientations. *Longitudinal and Life Course Studies*, 5(2): 105–128.

Norman, H., Elliot, M., & Fagan, C. (2014). Which fathers are the most involved in taking care of their toddlers in the UK? An investigation of the predictors of paternal involvement, *Community, Work & Family*, 17(2): 163–180.

O'Driscoll, M., Brough, P., & Kalliath, T. (2006). Work-family conflict and facilitation. In F. Jones, R. Burke & M. Westman (eds) *Work-life Balance: A Psychological Perspective*: 117–142. New York: Psychology Press.

Park, Y., Fritz, C., & Jex, S.M. (2011). Relationships between work-home segmentation and psychological detachment from work: The role of communication technology use at home. *Journal of Occupational Health Psychology*, 16(4): 457–467.

Poppleton, S., Briner, R.B., & Keifer, T. (2008). The role of context and everyday experience in understanding work-non-work relationships: A qualitative diary study of white and blue-collar workers. *Journal of Occupational and Organizational Psychology*, 81(3): 481–502.

Powell, M., Dawson, J., Topakas, A., Durose, J., & Fewtrel, C. (2014). Staff satisfaction and organisational performance *Health Service Delivery*, 2(50), available at http://www.ncbi.nlm.nih.gov/books/NBK263759/

Querstret, D., & Cropley, M. (2012). Exploring the relationship between work-related rumination, sleep quality, and work-related fatigue. *Journal of Occupational Health Psychology*, 17(3): 341–353.

Reilly, P.A. (1998). Balancing flexibility—meeting the interests of employer and employee. *European Journal of Work and Organizational Psychology*, 7(1): 7–22.

Rocha, C., Hause Crowell, J., & McCarter, A.K. (2006). Effects of prolonged job insecurity on the psychological well-being of workers. *The Journal of Sociology and Social Welfare*, 33(3): 9–28.

Rudman, L.A., & Mescher, K. (2013). Penalizing men who request a family leave: Is flexibility stigma a femininity stigma? *Journal of Social Issues*, 69(2): 322–340.

Schieman, S., & Glavin, P. (2008). Trouble at the border? Gender, flexibility at work, and the work-home interface. *Social Problems*, 55(4): 590–611.

Schieman, S., & Young, M. (2011). Economic hardship and family-to-work conflict: The importance of gender and work conditions. *Journal of Family and Economic Issues*, 32(1): 46–61.

Schlachter, S., Cropley, M., & Avery, R. (2016). The organisational context of ICT use for work-related purposes during non-work time. *Proceedings of the British Psychological Society's Division of Occupational Psychology Conference*, Nottingham, January 2016: 229–231. British Psychological Society, Leicester, available at http://www.bps.org.uk/events/conferences/division-occupational-psychology/conference-app-abstract-book

Sensky, T., Salimu, R., Ballard, J., & Pereira, D. (2015). Associations of chronic embitterment among NHS staff. *Occupational Medicine*, 65(6): 431–436.

Shoss, M.K., & Penney, L.M. (2012). The economy and absenteeism: A macro-level study. *Journal of Applied Psychology*, 97(4): 881.

Solantaus, T., Leinonen, J., & Punamäki, R.L. (2004). Children's mental health in times of economic recession: Replication and extension of the family economic stress model in Finland. *Developmental Psychology*, 40(3): 412–429.

Sonnentag, S., Binnewies, C., & Mojza, E.J. (2010). Staying well and engaged when demands are high: The role of psychological detachment. *Journal of Applied Psychology*, 95(5): 965–976.

Spink, A., Cole, C., & Waller, M. (2008). Multitasking behavior. *Annual Review of Information Science and Technology*, 42(1): 93–118.

Stuckler, D., Basu, S., Suhrcke, M., Coutts, A., & McKee, M. (2011). Effects of the 2008 recession on health: A first look at European data. *The Lancet*, 378(9786): 124–125.

Tekin, E., McClellan, C., & Minyard, K.J. (2013). *Health and Health Behaviors during the Worst of Times: Evidence from The Great Recession* (No. 19234). Washington, DC: National Bureau of Economic Research.

Towers, I., Duxbury, L., Higgins, C., & Thomas, J. (2006). Time thieves and space invaders: Technology, work and the organization. *Journal of Organizational Change Management*, 19(5): 593–618.

Van Wanrooy, B., Bewley, H., Bryson, A., Forth, J., Stokes, L., & Wood, S. (2013). *Employment Relations in the Shadow of Recession: Findings from the 2011 Workplace Employment Relations Study*. Houndsmill, Basingstoke: Palgrave MacMillan.

Wagenaar, A.F., Kompier, M.A., Taris, T.W., & Houtman, I.L. (2013). Temporary employment, quality of working life and well-being. In A. Alexander-Stamatios & C. Cooper (eds) *The Psychology of the Recession on the Workplace*: 117–139. Cheltenham: Edward Elgar Publishing.

Warr, P. (1987). *Work, Unemployment, and Mental Health*. Oxford University Press.

Washburn, C., & Christensen, D. (2008). Financial harmony: A key component of successful marriage relationship. *The Forum for Family and Consumer Issues*, 13(1), available at https://ncsu.edu/ffci/publications/2008/v13-n1–2008-spring/Washburn-Christensen.php

3 Employer Support for Work–Life Balance in Recession

Findings for Britain from the Workplace Employment Relations Survey

Lucy Stokes and Stephen Wood

Flexible working and family-friendly practices aimed at supporting employees' work–life balance have come to the forefront of employment policies in many countries in the past two decades. As employers have voluntarily introduced such policies and practices, which we treat generically in this chapter as work–life balance (WLB) provisions, governments have both reflected this development and sought to encourage it further by passing legislation that provides rights for employees to have access to these supports. Legislation has been particularly concerned with encouraging employers to help mothers through the transition to parenthood, the return to work and subsequent child care. This was closely tied to concerns to reduce gender inequality and primarily aimed at encouraging the participation of mothers in the labour market. Subsequently, the work–family agenda has been extended, firstly to paternity leave and other ways of helping both parents become more involved with childcare, and then to the provision of help for all employees with caring responsibilities. Although the Nordic countries led the way in this respect, among the liberal market economies, the UK government has been at the forefront of such trends.

Legislating in this area and encouraging family-friendly practices was in particular a major element of the Labour government's employment agenda following its election in 1997 (Department of Trade and Industry, 1998). In general, employment legislation was seen as a means of encouraging and supporting good practice whilst providing a 'minimum infrastructure of decency and fairness around people in the workplace' (Department of Trade and Industry, 1998: 3). In the specific case of family-friendly policies, the aim was to stimulate a work culture that would reflect a new relationship between work and family life, the expectations being that good employers would go beyond minimum statutory requirements and that organisations should benefit if they adopt the new culture, for example through the performance and retention of core staff.

The programme of the various successive Labour Governments included enhancing maternity provisions, introducing parental leave, a right to take time off to deal with emergencies, and a right to flexible working, initially for carers, but extended by the Coalition government to all workers in 2014. The evidence from comparing the results from the 2004 Workplace Employment Relations Survey (WERS), a nationally representative survey of British workplaces and their employees, with those from the 1998 WERS, was that the adoption of flexible working and family-friendly practices was increasing but the majority of workplaces were using only those practices that were subject to legislation (Kersley et al., 2006), and the adoption was more prevalent in large private firms and the public sector (Wood et al., 2003). By 2004, many forms of flexible working practices, such as job-sharing, term-time only working, compressed hours and the opportunity to work from home, remained confined to less than a third of workplaces.

This chapter is concerned with what has happened to such trends following the recession that was precipitated by the financial crisis of 2008 and the subsequent austerity programme of the Government to address a public sector debt crisis in 2010. If the increasing availability of flexible working and family-friendly practices was largely a response to legislation or broader normative pressures, we might expect no great change in their adoption, although their use by employees might be affected by, for example, the increasing job insecurity generated by recessionary pressures. However, insofar as some of the trend, particularly in practices not subject to legislation, reflects employers positively evaluating their utility, we might expect some reappraisal of their costs and benefits. On the one hand, employers may respond to a less favourable economic climate by cutting back on such provision where they see this as costly, for example, in the case of financial help with childcare. Employers may also see less need to provide practices to retain staff in a period when employees have reduced labour market opportunities. On the other hand, some forms of flexible working, such as working from home, may have the potential to reduce costs (see Lyonette et al. in Chapter 4), and practices which allow flexibility in hours worked may help employers to adjust the size of the workforce to cope with changes in demand for their products or services. More generally, employers may see the provision of practices as still important for staff recruitment and retention, especially if they have an eye on the post-recession period and are keen to preserve their human capital.

Existing evidence suggests that employers had tended to cut back on WLB practices in the recession in the early 1990s in the UK (Dex and Smith, 2002) and Sweet et al. (2014) showed a decline in the availability of flexible working arrangements in the USA between 2006 and 2009, i.e. immediately following the 2008 recession. Human resource managers, via a post-2008 Chartered Institute of Personnel and Development (2012) survey, expressed some concern that the development of flexible working practices might be constrained by the recession. In national political circles, there was some renewed emphasis on the costs of WLB practices adding to business burdens (e.g. Beecroft, 2011). Yet, equally, there were suggestions that these practices, and particularly flexible working practices, could help employers manage the impact of the recession, by, for example, encouraging some workers to reduce their hours. One commentator even went so far as to imply that the recession could be a catalyst for a qualitative change in the provision of WLB practices, as she wrote: "Traditional nine-to-five working practices won't dig us out of this deep recession. It is time to embrace 'flexibilism' in the workplace" (Hobsbawm, 2009).

From the employees' perspective, WLB policies may become more important in recessions. Flexible working practices may, for example, enable them to work longer hours to offset the effects of wage freezes. If such practices help to improve the integration of employees' work and personal lives (for example, by reducing commuting times), they may also provide more time to recover from the demands of work and perhaps even offset any increased energy depletion associated with intensified demands. Allied to this, whether managers are supportive, particularly of employees' WLB needs, may become increasingly important as organisational changes affect employees' lives, finances and job security. Such supportive management may be especially important where the WLB practices do not exist, as it can act as a substitute for these by facilitating informal practices that aid the integration of work and personal life (Bagger and Li, 2014), or, where formal practices do exist, it may encourage their use. However, faced with recessionary pressures, there is a risk that managers may become less supportive. For more on managers and the pressures faced during austerity in the public sector, see Lyonette et al. (Chapter 4).

Against this background, this chapter will address four issues:

1. The extent of change in the provision of WLB practices following the recession.
2. Changes in management's attitudes towards the WLB of their employees through recession.
3. The extent to which use of WLB practices was affected by employees' recessionary experience.
4. The extent to which employees' work–life conflict was affected by their experience of recession.

We tackle these issues through an analysis of the data from the 2011 Workplace Employment Relations Survey, conducted when the economy was coming out of recession (although the government's austerity programme was still being implemented), combined with data from the 2004 WERS, which provides the benchmark for assessing any change. The recession and austerity programme had adverse effects in both private and public sector workplaces, but the effects were more pronounced in the public sector (van Wanrooy et al., 2013). We therefore explore differences between the sectors throughout the chapter. We first introduce the surveys before reporting the results of our analysis and their implications for how, if at all, the recession has affected WLB practice. The remainder of the paper is organised in four sections, mirroring our four issues.

The Workplace Employment Relations Survey

The Workplace Employment Relations Survey (WERS) comprises a series of six surveys which aim to provide a nationally representative account of the state of employment relations and working life inside British workplaces. The survey collects data from managers, employees and employee representatives in workplaces with five or more employees across the economy, with the exception of mining, agriculture and domestic service.

We use data from the 2011 and 2004 surveys, both from the management survey (which involves interviewing the most senior manager with responsibility for employment relations, human resources or staff in participating workplaces), and a self-completion questionnaire survey of employees, which was completed in workplaces included in the management survey (Department of Trade and Industry, 2004; Department for Business, Innovation and Skills, 2013). In the 2011 survey, interviews were conducted with managers in 2,680 workplaces, compared with 2,295 workplaces in 2004, with a response rate of 46 per cent in 2011 and 64 per cent in 2004.

The employee-level data for the 2011 WERS were collected through a self-completion questionnaire distributed to up to 25 randomly selected employees at the majority of workplaces where the management interviews were undertaken (81 per cent in 2011 and 86 per cent in 2004). The response rate stood at 50 per cent among all sampled employees in 2011 and 54 per cent in 2004. Weights to correct for the sample design and any observable non-response biases are applied throughout the analysis reported in this chapter.

We examine change over time by comparing results from the 2004 and 2011 surveys, but in addition we use the panel component of the survey which includes all workplaces that were surveyed in both years. Using the panel means we can isolate change within workplaces over time, and hence overcome the problem that changes observed through the cross-sectional comparison may reflect changes both within workplaces and in the composition of the workplace population.

Our analysis of WLB practices considers both flexible working arrangements as well as family-friendly practices. Our measures of flexible working arrangements are provided by the management survey, which asked managers, "Do you have any of the following working time arrangements for any employees at this workplace?" Six arrangements were included in both the 2004 and 2011 surveys: the option to reduce working hours, flexi-time, working from home, compressed hours, job-sharing and term-time working. To capture family-friendly provision, managers were asked whether any employees at their workplace were entitled to each of the following practices: provision of a workplace nursery, financial help with childcare, financial help with care of older adults, a specific period of leave for carers of older adults, or a specific period of paid parental leave.

Employees were also asked about practices in their workplace and whether they had used them, as they were asked: "In the last 12 months, have you made use of any of the following arrangements, and if not, are they available to you if you needed them?" The practices are paid emergency leave, flexi-time, the chance to reduce working hours, compressed hours, working from home, job sharing and term-time working. This measure is only available for 2011.

Our primary measure of management's attitudes to helping employees with their work–life balance is based on an employee's assessment, as respondents were asked the extent to which they agreed (on a five-point scale ranging from strongly agree to strongly disagree) that managers at their workplace "understand about employees having to meet responsibilities outside work". We define management to be understanding of employees' WLB needs if the employee strongly agrees or agrees with the above statement.

In addition, there is a measure of managers' attitudes in the management survey, which asks managers the extent to which they agreed, again on a five-point scale, with the statement, "It is up to individual employees to balance their work and family responsibilities". This measure should be taken to be the manager's view of the employees' responsibilities and not necessarily that of the employer: it may well be that as employers provide WLB practices, which are indicative of taking some responsibility for the employee's WLB, they consider that employees now have the ultimate responsibility for achieving WLB.

WERS provides through the employee survey measures of the two dimensions of work–nonwork conflict which can be used as proxies for WLB. The first, work-to-nonwork conflict, is measured based on asking employees the extent to which they agree with the statement, "I often find it difficult to fulfil my commitments outside of work because of the amount of time I spend on my job". The second is nonwork-to-work conflict, measured by employees' responses to a similar question: "I often find it difficult to do my job properly because of my commitments outside of work". Our analysis focuses on distinguishing between those with high levels of each form of conflict, identified as those who strongly agree or agree that they experience difficulties, from those reporting limited or no conflict. The questions on conflict were not included in the 2004 WERS and thus we cannot assess change over time.

The 2011 WERS allows us to explore the impact of the recession in three ways. First, examining change between the 2004 and 2011 surveys provides some insight into changes that have taken place during that period. However, because the recession began in the middle of the period between the 2004 and 2011 surveys, we cannot directly evaluate the recession's effect through observing changes from 2004 to 2011, as any changes might be due to factors before the recession in 2008. Nonetheless, any changes in this period may be suggestive of recessional effects, given that the economic crisis was probably the most telling event in this period, as employment relations legislation and institutions were relatively stable (van Wanrooy et al., 2013: 2–5). Conversely, if observations are stable between the two surveys, this would suggest that there has been no generalised effect of a national recession.

Second, the 2011 WERS included specific questions on the impact of the recession on the workplace (in the management survey) and on actions taken to combat it that directly affected employees, such as wage freezes or work reorganisations. These allow us to explore variation across workplaces and employees. The impact of the recession was measured by asking managers, ". . . can you tell me to what extent your workplace has been adversely affected by the recent recession?" In our analysis we concentrate on differentiating workplaces that were most affected by the recession, defined as those where the respondent gauged that it affected their workplaces a great deal or quite a lot, from those who were affected moderately, just a little or not at all.

Third, the employee survey includes a question about the actions taken in the light of the recession that affected the individual respondent. It asked employees, "Did any of the following happen to you as a result of the most recent recession, whilst working at this workplace?" Employees were asked to tick all that applied to them from the following list: "My workload increased", "My work was reorganised", "I was moved to another job", "My wages were frozen or cut", "My non-wage benefits (e.g. vehicles or meals) were reduced", "My contracted working hours were reduced", "Access to paid overtime was restricted", "I was required to take unpaid leave", "Access to training was restricted". A response of "I was not working at this workplace during the recession" was also included to allow for recent recruits. An index of the extent to which the employee experienced recessionary action was created, based on the total number of the above actions that applied to the employee. We term this the employees' recessionary experience.

The Extent of Change in the Provision of WLB Practices Following the Recession

Flexible Working Practices

The extent to which the prevalence of flexible working practices changed between 2004 and 2011 varied between practices. Based on the proportion of workplaces offering these arrangements for any employees at their workplace, the most commonly available arrangement in both years was the option to reduce working hours, available in over half of workplaces, followed by flexi-time, available in around one-third of workplaces (Table 3.1). There

Table 3.1 Availability of flexible working arrangements, 2004 and 2011, cell per cent

	All workplaces		Private sector		Public sector	
	2004	*2011*	*2004*	*2011*	*2004*	*2011*
Reduce working hours	62	<u>56</u>	60	<u>54</u>	76	75
Flexi-time	35	34	34	32	43	49
Working from home	26	<u>30</u>	24	<u>29</u>	35	42
Compressed hours	11	<u>19</u>	10	<u>17</u>	21	<u>36</u>
Job-sharing	25	<u>17</u>	19	<u>11</u>	67	<u>53</u>
Term-time working	14	16	9	12	49	51

Base: all workplaces with 5 or more employees. Figures are based on responses from 2,292 (2004) and 2,662 (2011) workplace managers.

Source: van Wanrooy et al. (2013: 113).

Note: an underlined figure indicates a statistically significant change between 2004 and 2011, at the five per cent level of significance.

was an increase in the availability of working from home and compressed hours between 2004 and 2011, but the option to reduce working hours and job-sharing became less common, and there was no significant change in the availability of flexi-time or term-time working. Similar trends are found in the panel of workplaces surveyed in both 2004 and 2011, although the increase in workplaces offering home working was insignificant.

Formal flexible working practices are more common in the public sector and in larger organisations (*cf* Lewis, 2003; Wood et al., 2003), although informal methods may be used in smaller organisations. The trends over time in the prevalence of flexible working practices were similar in both sectors, with the exception that the decline in the option to reduce working hours was found only in the private sector. The percentage of private sector workplaces offering this arrangement fell from 60 per cent in 2004 to 54 per cent in 2011, and remained available in around 75 per cent of public sector workplaces.

Trends over time varied with workplace size. Whereas there was no change in the availability of flexi-time in aggregate, among larger workplaces there had been a rise in the percentage offering this arrangement from 43 per cent to 59 per cent among workplaces with 100 or more employees. Furthermore, the declining prevalence of both the option to reduce working hours and job-sharing was concentrated among smaller workplaces and had not changed to a statistically significant extent among larger workplaces.

Overall, it does not appear that a significant proportion of workplaces cut back their provision of flexible working arrangements in response to recession. If the declining prevalence of the option to reduce working hours and job-sharing were a response to recession, it could be expected that any reductions in their availability would be concentrated in those workplaces hit hardest by recession. There is some support for this conjecture, as within the panel of workplaces the decline in the proportion of workplaces allowing employees to reduce their working hours occurred only in those workplaces which were adversely affected by recession (falling from 69 per cent in 2004 to 55 per cent in 2011). In contrast, this remained unchanged (at 61 per cent) in those workplaces less affected by the recession. For job-sharing, however, there were no clear differences in the trend over time by the extent to which the workplace was affected by recession. Similarly, for those practices that had become more common between 2004 and 2011, no identifiable differences in the trend were apparent according to the extent to which the workplace was affected by recession. There is, therefore, little evidence to suggest that employers increased or reduced their provision of flexible working arrangements as a response to recession.

To add to our confidence in this conclusion, costs were not cited as a major constraint on providing flexible working arrangements. If they were, we might have expected that employers would have reduced their provision of these in the recession. When asked, "what are the constraints in providing flexible working arrangements for employees at this workplace?" cost was cited by only one in ten workplaces. Other constraints were more commonly reported: flexible working was considered to be incompatible with the nature of the work or operating hours by 53 per cent of managers, sizeable proportions cited pressure on other employees and managers (30 per cent) and lack of demand from employees (19 per cent).

Family-Friendly Provision

Very few workplaces offer a workplace nursery (3 per cent in 2011), but there had been a significant increase in the proportion of workplaces providing financial help with childcare, rising from 5 per cent in 2004 to 31 per cent in 2011 (Table 3.2). This financial help could consist of childcare vouchers or loans, subsidised childcare places not located at the workplace, as well as repayable contributions to fees for childcare. There may have been a substantial increase in the use of childcare voucher schemes, where typically employees sacrifice part of their salary in exchange for childcare vouchers, reducing the tax and national insurance contributions payable, as this was stimulated by legislative changes in 2005 (Seely, 2014). However, childcare vouchers were not specifically mentioned in the question asked in 2004, and it is possible that the observed increase partly reflects this change in question wording.

There was a rise in the percentage of workplaces offering a specific period of leave for carers of older adults, in addition to time off for emergencies, rising from six per cent in 2004 to eight per cent in 2011. However, there was no increase in the provision of financial help with the care of older adults, which is in fact extremely rare, as it is available in less than one per cent of

Table 3.2 Family-friendly provision, 2004 and 2011, cell per cent

	All workplaces		Private sector		Public sector	
	2004	2011	2004	2011	2004	2011
Workplace nursery or nursery linked with workplace	2	<u>3</u>	1	<u>2</u>	8	7
Financial help with child care	5	<u>31</u>	4	<u>29</u>	13	<u>47</u>
Financial help with the care of older adults	0	1	0	1	0	0
A specific period of leave for carers of older adults	6	<u>8</u>	4	<u>6</u>	18	22
A specific period of paid parental leave	–	10	–	8	–	27

Base: all workplaces with 5 or more employees. Figures are based on responses from 2,284 (2004) and 2,638 (2011) workplace managers.

Notes
1. The 2004 survey did not include the response option for a specific period of paid parental leave
2. The number 0 represents less than 0.5 per cent, including none.
3. An underlined figure indicates a statistically significant change between 2004 and 2011, at the five per cent level of significance.

workplaces. Similar trends were observed through the panel of workplaces as there was a rise in the percentage of workplaces offering financial help with childcare (rising from 8 per cent to 35 per cent) and the provision of a specific period of leave for carers of older adults also became more common (rising from 6 per cent to 12 per cent).

The increase in the proportion of workplaces offering financial help with childcare occurred across workplaces of all sizes, but was particularly strong amongst larger workplaces. It may be the case that larger workplaces find it easier or less costly to administer childcare voucher schemes. It may also be the case that larger firms are more concerned with maintaining a reputation as a good employer. The increase occurred in both the private and public sector.

The provision of a specific period of leave for carers of older adults was also more common among larger workplaces and the increase in the availability of this was significant only for larger workplaces, with no change among smaller workplaces. Such leave remained more common in the public sector than in the private sector. However, it was only in the private sector where a significant increase was observed. Leave for elder care was also more commonly offered in workplaces where more than half of the workforce were female, but there was no significant relationship between gender composition and the availability of financial help with childcare. This may well reflect the fact that women are more likely than men to be caring for an older adult, and thus employers in workplaces with high proportions of female employees may be responding to the needs of their workforce. In contrast, financial help with childcare is likely to be of relevance to male and female parents.

Analysis of the panel data showed that the increase in the provision of financial help with childcare was greater in those workplaces least affected by the recession. The proportion of workplaces with such a practice rose from 9 per cent to 40 per cent among workplaces less affected by the recession, which compares with an increase from 7 per cent to 30 per cent in workplaces most adversely affected by the recession. The recession may thus have had a dragging effect on the uptake of financial help for childcare.

Changes in Management's Attitudes towards the WLB of their Employees

Between 2004 and 2011, there was a small rise in the percentage of employees who felt that managers at their workplace were understanding of employees' WLB needs, increasing from 60 per cent in 2004 to 62 per cent in 2011. This represented a continuation of the trend observed between 1998 and 2004; among workplaces with 10 or more employees (workplaces with fewer than 10 employees were not included in the 1998 WERS), the percentage of employees who perceived managers to be understanding of their responsibilities outside work stood at 55 per cent in 1998, rising to 58 per cent in 2004 and to 61 per cent in 2011.

However, these global figures mask important differences between sectors and by gender. The increase in the percentage of employees thinking that their managers were understanding of WLB needs occurred only in the private sector (Table 3.3), whereas the percentage fell slightly in the public sector. This fall was, nonetheless, concentrated amongst female employees (declining from 65 per cent in 2004 to 61 per cent in 2011, compared with a constant 53 per cent for men). The increase in the private sector in the proportion seeing managers as understanding was across both genders (rising from 57 per cent to 61 per cent among men and from 63 per cent to 66 per cent among women).

Employees in small- and medium-sized workplaces (and in smaller organisations) were more likely to perceive managers as understanding of their WLB needs, reflecting perhaps the way that small employers are more likely to favour informal methods either to help WLB (Lewis et al., 2015) or more generally (Forth et al., 2006). This remained the case in 2011: around two-thirds (68 per cent) of employees in workplaces with fewer than 50 employees thought that managers understood their responsibilities outside work, compared with 58 per cent of employees in workplaces with 100 or more employees (Table 3.3). Nonetheless, an increase in the proportion feeling that managers understood their needs between 2004

Table 3.3 Employees perceiving managers to be supportive of their WLB needs, 2004 and 2011, cell per cent

	2004	2011
All employees	60	<u>62</u>
Private sector	59	<u>63</u>
. . . Male employees	57	<u>61</u>
. . . Female employees	63	<u>66</u>
Public sector	61	<u>58</u>
. . . Male employees	53	53
. . . Female employees	65	<u>61</u>
Workplace size		
. . . fewer than 50 employees	69	68
. . . 50–99 employees	61	59
. . . 100 or more employees	52	<u>58</u>

Base: all employees in workplaces with 5 or more employees. Figures are based on responses from 21,501 (2004) and 21,327 (2011) employees.

Note: an underlined figure indicates a statistically significant change between 2004 and 2011, at the five per cent level of significance.

and 2011 was apparent only in larger workplaces, and then only within the private sector.

The extent to which managerial attitudes were perceived to be favourable to WLB needs was lower in public sector workplaces most adversely affected by the recession than those less affected, but this was not so in private sector workplaces. In the public sector, such management attitudes were perceived in 54 per cent of workplaces adversely affected, compared with 62 per cent in other workplaces; in the private sector the figures were not significantly different: 62 per cent and 64 per cent, respectively. In contrast, in both sectors but in a similar vein, employees who had experienced some change as a result of recession were less likely to view managers as understanding of their responsibilities outside work; furthermore, the percentage of employees agreeing that managers were understanding decreased with the number of recessionary actions the employee had experienced (Figure 3.1). More than two-thirds (69 per cent) of employees who experienced no recessionary action agreed that managers were understanding about their WLB needs, compared with just over half (55 per cent) of employees who experienced at least one recession-related change.

The proportion of managers agreeing that WLB was the individual's responsibility rose from 66 per cent in 2004 to 77 per cent by 2011, with this increase also apparent within the panel of workplaces. This increase reversed the trend observed in WERS between 1998 and 2004 among workplaces

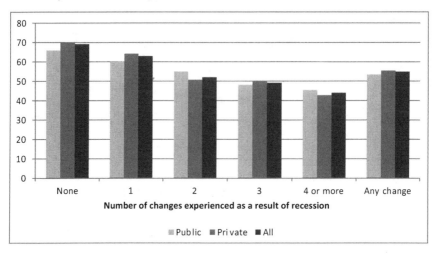

Figure 3.1 Employees perceiving managers to be supportive of their WLB needs, cell per cent

Base: all employees in workplaces with 5 or more employees, excluding employees not at the workplace during recession. Figures are based on responses from 18,594 employees.

with 10 or more employees, as the proportion declined from 84 per cent in 1998 to 66 per cent in 2004, before rising to 75 per cent in 2011. It may be, as suggested earlier, that the increase in the individualistic perspective reflects an increased perception among managers that with greater provision of flexible working arrangements, employees now have greater responsibility for achieving WLB. There is some evidence to support this, as within panel workplaces, the percentage of managers perceiving WLB to be the responsibility of the individual showed a statistically significant increase in workplaces where provision of flexible working arrangements had increased, but showed no statistically significant rise where such provision had remained stable or declined (van Wanrooy et al., 2013). Alternatively, it could reflect declining support for WLB practices, perhaps as managers see them increasingly as a luxury in the light of the recession and public sector debt. There was, however, no relationship between whether managers view the responsibility for WLB as resting with themselves and our measure of how employees view the supportiveness of managers.

The increase in the proportion of managers viewing WLB as the responsibility of the individual occurred in both the private and public sectors, but the rise was greater in the public sector. Among panel workplaces, the increase was, however, statistically significant only for public sector workplaces. The recession or austerity programme may then have affected both the perceptions of public sector employees about how managers treat them and the views of managers on the degree to which employees are responsible for their WLB.

The Extent to Which the Use of WLB Practices Was Affected by Employee's Recessionary Experience

WLB practices may not be available to all employees within a workplace, and even where available, employees may not always be aware of their existence or make use of them, even when they are relevant to them. Flexi-time and home working were the most widely used flexible working practices, with 30 per cent of all employees using flexi-time and 17 per cent using working from home (at least for part of their time) (Table 3.4). The least used was job sharing (5 per cent). Half (50 per cent) of all employees used at least one practice.

Men were less likely than women to use all the particular practices, with the exception of working from home, as 19 per cent of male employees reported the use of working from home, compared with 16 per cent of female employees, a statistically significant difference. All arrangements were more commonly used by employees with dependent children. Few differences in usage were apparent by age, with the exception of reducing working hours, which was more commonly used by employees aged 60 or more, and use of job-sharing was lower among employees aged under 20. Reduced working hours and compressed hours were both more commonly used by private sector employees, whereas term-time working and paid emergency leave were more commonly used in the public sector. There were no differences in usage of flexi-time, home working or job-sharing by sector.

Table 3.4 Use of flexible working arrangements, according to employees' experiences of recession, cell per cent

	All	Public sector			Private sector		
		Experienced recessionary action	None	All	Experienced recessionary action	None	All
Paid emergency leave	12	18	18	18	11	11	10
Flexi-time	30	42	<u>26</u>	37	27	28	27
Reduce working hours	9	9	<u>12</u>	10	8	10	9
Compressed hours	9	10	8	9	9	9	9
Working from home	17	15	<u>10</u>	13	19	<u>13</u>	19
Job sharing	5	5	<u>7</u>	5	4	5	4
Term-time working	7	15	<u>29</u>	19	3	4	3

Base: all employees in workplaces with 5 or more employees, excluding those who did not know whether an arrangement was available to them. Figures are based on responses from at least 15,141 employees. Employees who were not at the workplace during recession are also excluded from the base for the columns for employees experiencing recessionary action.

Note: an underlined figure indicates a statistically significant difference between employees who experienced recessionary action and those who did not.

Some differences in usage were apparent according to whether employees had experienced recessionary action, but not relative to the intensity of the recessionary effect on the workplace. Employees in the public sector who had experienced recessionary action were less likely to have made use of job-sharing, the chance to reduce working hours and term-time working than employees who had not experienced such action (Table 3.4). It may be that employees were less willing to make use of such flexible working practices where they had been affected by recession. In contrast, flexi-time and home working were more commonly used by public sector employees who had experienced recessionary action. Among private sector employees, those employees who reported experiencing recessionary action were also more likely to have used the option to work from home, but no differences in usage were apparent for any of the other flexible working arrangements. The adoption of practices such as flexi-time and home working might, in some cases at least, be part of the recessionary action.

The Extent to Which Employees' Work–Life Conflict Was Affected by Their Experience of Recession

Just over one quarter (27 per cent) of employees had high work-to-nonwork conflict, with almost half (48 per cent) reporting little or no conflict. A much smaller proportion (4 per cent) of employees reported high nonwork-to-work conflict. The majority of employees (79 per cent) had little or no such conflict. Controlling for hours worked and other job, employee and workplace characteristics, both forms of conflict were higher among employees in the private sector and among those with caring responsibilities.

There was no significant difference in the proportion of employees with high levels of both forms of work–life conflict, according to the extent to which their workplace was adversely affected by recession. However, the level of both types of conflict is related to the number of recessionary actions an employee experienced. Among employees who had experienced at least one action, one-third had a high level of work-to-nonwork conflict, compared to 19 per cent of employees who experienced no recessionary action. Furthermore, the percentage of employees reporting work-to-nonwork conflict increased with the number of recessionary actions they experienced (Figure 3.2, left-hand panel). The prevalence of nonwork-to-work conflict also showed some increase according to the number of actions experienced, although this was smaller in magnitude; five per cent of employees who experienced at least one recessionary action had high nonwork-to-work conflict compared to three per cent of employees who experienced no such action, a statistically significant difference (Figure 3.2, right-hand panel).

Among employees experiencing recessionary action, work-to-nonwork conflict was lower where employees used flexible working arrangements. More generally, the use of flexible working practices was associated with lower work-to-nonwork conflict, but this is insignificant when the autonomy that employees had in their job is controlled for. Further multivariate

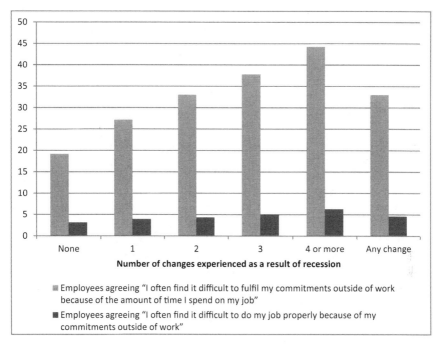

Figure 3.2 Work–life conflict, according to number of changes employee experienced in recession, cell per cent

Base: all employees in workplaces with 5 or more employees, excluding employees not at the workplace during recession. Figures are based on responses from 19,017 employees.

analysis has shown this reflects the way such practices increase job autonomy which in turn reduces conflict (Wood et al., 2016). In the case of nonwork-to-work conflict, such conflict was higher among those who used flexible working arrangements. This may reflect employees making use of such practices in order to manage the demands they face outside of work.

Both public and private sector employees were less likely to report work-to-nonwork conflict where management was considered supportive, regardless of whether they had experienced recessionary action. Nonwork-to-work conflict was also lower among employees who perceived their managers to be understanding of WLB. These findings provide further support for the importance of managers' attitudes, and not just the provision of formal practices, in supporting employees to balance their work and outside commitments.

Conclusions

Using a representative sample of British workplaces, we have shown that the availability of many WLB practices remains limited. The most commonly available practices are those that enable employees to adjust their working hours. In contrast, help with caring responsibilities for older adults remains relatively rare. Nevertheless, the majority of employees view their managers as understanding that they have needs outside of the workplace, although this does not necessarily coincide with managers seeing employers as having prime responsibility for employees' WLB. Only a minority of employees experienced high levels of work-to-nonwork conflict and even fewer had high levels of nonwork-to-work conflict.

The proportion of workplaces offering home working and compressed hours increased between 2004 and 2011, whereas there was a decrease in arrangements for reducing working hours and job-sharing. Any changes did not appear to be related to the intensity of the recession, with the exception of the decline in arrangements for reducing working hours which was the only practice where change was related to the extent to which the workplace was adversely affected by the recession. There were some differences in employees' use of practices according to whether they had experienced recessionary action; home working was more commonly used by such employees and may have played a role in managing the recession, not least as it may help reduce estate costs (see Lyonette et al. in Chapter 4).

In common with existing evidence showing that any increase between 2004 and 2011 in the proportion of employees perceiving management to be supportive was largely confined to private sector employees (van Wanrooy et al., 2013), the proportion of private sector employees who perceived their managers to be understanding of WLB increased. It remained stable among male public sector employees and fell among female public sector employees. This may in part reflect the effects of austerity within public sector workplaces, as some managers altered their attitudes or employees had direct experience of changes in managerial behaviour. Yet in both the public and private sectors, employees who experienced recessionary action were less likely to consider managers supportive of their WLB needs.

Overall, the recession does not appear to have had a significant effect on the practices offered by employers, or the attitudes of managers in the private sector. Matching the latter differentiation between sectors, lower take-up of job-sharing and reduced working hours by employees experiencing recessionary action was confined to the public sector. This is consistent with the idea that employees may be less willing to make use of such arrangements in a harsher economic climate, particularly perhaps for practices that make employees less visible to the employer. Flexi-time was more commonly used by public sector employees experiencing recessionary action; this could potentially be used to better match working hours to the demands of the job and so its use may not be as likely to generate concerns over job security among employees.

Employees experiencing recessionary action were more likely to report high work–nonwork conflict. This applied for both private and public sector employees but because the extent of recessionary action was greater in the public sector, public sector employees were disproportionately affected.

Nevertheless, levels of work-nonwork conflict remained higher among private sector employees.

The research has two main limitations. First, no 2004 benchmark is available for the use of practices or work–nonwork conflict. We are thus unable to know if employees have reduced their usage of WLB practices and we have no direct means of testing whether work-to-nonwork conflict is higher or lower post-recession. Second, managers were asked only whether practices were available to *any* employee within their workplace, and so it is not possible to ascertain whether employers may have changed the proportion of employees within the workplace for whom the practices were provided. Nor are we able to identify in detail the way the practices were being used and the rationale behind their use.

The overall conclusion of the study is that in the private sector the recession has had little effect on management practice, but actions taken by managers in the light of recessionary pressures have had some effect on employees' work-to-nonwork conflict. Such conflict remained higher among private sector employees. The public sector has also seen relatively little change in formal provision, but managers' attitudes towards WLB have become less supportive over this period (both as reported by managers and as perceived by employees). Reduced employee use of certain flexible working arrangements was also confined to the public sector. Differences in trends between sectors, particularly in management attitudes, may reflect some impact of the austerity programme in the public sector. Given the importance of supportive management to employees, it is important to monitor and understand more fully any trend towards less favourable attitudes on the part of managers towards employees' WLB. It may reflect a more instrumental attitude to WLB, a theme which is taken up by Lyonette et al. in Chapter 4.

Acknowledgements

The authors would like to thank Alex Bryson and John Forth for their helpful comments. We acknowledge the Department for Business, Innovation and Skills, the Economic and Social Research Council, the UK Commission for Employment and Skills, the Advisory, Conciliation and Arbitration Service and the National Institute of Economic and Social Research as the originators of the 2011 Workplace Employment Relations Study data, and the Department of Trade and Industry, the Economic and Social Research Council, the Advisory, Conciliation and Arbitration Service and the Policy Studies Institute as the originators of the 2004 Workplace Employment Relations Survey, and the UK Data Archive at the University of Essex as the distributor of the data. The National Centre for Social Research was commissioned to conduct the survey fieldwork on behalf of the sponsors. None of these organisations bears any responsibility for the authors' analysis and interpretations of the data.

References

Bagger, J., & Li, A. (2014). How does supervisory family support influence employees' attitudes and behaviors? A social exchange perspective. *Journal of Management,* 40(4): 1123–1150.

Beecroft, A. (2011). *Report on Employment Law.* London: Department for Business, Innovation and Skills.

Chartered Institute of Personnel and Development. (2012). *Flexible Working Provision and Uptake.* London: Chartered Institute of Personnel and Development.

Department for Business, Innovation and Skills. (2013). *Workplace Employee Relations Survey, 2011.* [Computer file] Colchester, Essex: UK Data Archive, February 2013. SN: 7226, available at http://dx.doi.org/10.5255/UKDA-SN-7226-7

Department of Trade and Industry. (1998). *Fairness at Work.* London: Department of Trade and Industry.

Department of Trade and Industry. (2004). Workplace Employee Relations Survey, 2004; Cross-Section Survey, 2004 and Panel Survey, 1998–2004, Wave 2. [Computer file] 5th Edition. Colchester, Essex: UK Data Archive, January 2014. SN: 5294, available at http://dx.doi.org/10.5255/UKDA-SN-5294-2

Dex, S., & Smith, C. (2002). *The Nature and Pattern of Family-friendly Employment Policies in Britain.* Bristol: Policy Press.

Forth, J., Bewley, H., & Bryson, A. (2006). *Small and Medium-sized Enterprises: Findings from the 2004 Workplace Employment Relations Survey.* London: Department of Trade and Industry.

Hobsbawm, J. (2009). A new 'ism'. *The Guardian, Work Section,* 14th February 2009.

Kersley, B., Alpin, C., Forth, J., Bryson, A., Bewley, H., Dix, G., & Oxenbridge, S. (2006). *Inside the Workplace: Findings from the 2004 Workplace Employment Relations Survey.* London: Routledge.

Lewis, S. (2003). The integration of work and personal life: Is post industrial work the new leisure? *Leisure Studies,* 22(4): 343–355.

Lewis, S., Stumbitz, B., Miles, L., & Rouse, J. (2015). *Maternity Protection in SMEs: An International Review.* Geneva: International Labour Organization.

Seely, A. (2014). *Tax Relief for Childcare.* House of Commons Library, Standard Note SN19, available at http://researchbriefings.parliament.uk/ResearchBriefing/Summary/SN00019

Sweet, S. Besen, E., Pitt-Catsouphes, M., & McNamara, T. (2014). Do options for job flexibility diminish in times of economic uncertainty? *Work, Employment and Society,* 28(6): 882–903.

van Wanrooy, B., Bewley, H., Bryson, A., Forth, J., Stokes, L., & Wood, S. (2013). *Employment Relations in the Shadow of Recession: Findings from the 2011 Workplace Employment Relations Study.* Houndsmill, Basingstoke: Palgrave MacMillan.

Wood, S., Daniels, K., & Ogbonnaya, C. (2016). *Work–Life Balance Supports, Job Control, Work–Nonwork Conflict, and Well-Being.* Mimeo, School of Management, University of Leicester.

Wood, S., de Menezes, L., & Lasaosa, A. (2003). Family-friendly management in the UK: Testing various perspectives. *Industrial Relations,* 42(2): 221–250.

4 Work–Life Balance and Austerity

Implications of New Ways of Working in British Public Sector Organisations

Clare Lyonette, Deirdre Anderson, Suzan Lewis, Nicola Payne and Stephen Wood

An already diminished public sector continues to face the demand for greater budget cuts, following the UK election of the Conservative government in May 2015 and its pledge to maintain its post-recession austerity programme, developed during the previous Coalition government of 2010–2015. Consequently, organisations are seeking ways to sustain service delivery with even fewer resources, for example, by reducing staff numbers or, as will be highlighted in this chapter, by the strategic use of flexible working arrangements (FWAs).

For many years, the British public sector has provided employees with opportunities for flexible working to increase individual autonomy in time and place of work (Gregory and Milner, 2009b), often offered as part of an overarching work–life balance (WLB) agenda. Whether or not FWAs do in fact support employee WLB is a point for debate, as discussed in other chapters (for example, Kinman and McDowall, Chapter 2). While the availability of FWAs as a whole increased prior to the 2008 recession (Kersley et al., 2006; Busby and James, 2011), analysis of data from the 2011 Workplace Employment Relations Survey (WERS; van Wanrooy et al., 2013) revealed some shifts in the availability of different types of FWAs, including increased homeworking and compressed hours and reduced job-sharing and part-time working (Stokes and Wood, Chapter 3). Nevertheless, it is unclear how the WLB agenda has been affected by the financial crisis.

In this chapter, we examine whether FWAs are under threat, or whether in fact they have been used to help public sector organisations manage the effects of the Government's austerity policies, by focusing on British local councils. Councils have statutory responsibilities for governing local services, including planning, housing, social services, education, environmental health and transport, and are especially relevant to this research as they are the most deeply affected by austerity cuts and among the most visible and publicly accountable public services (Den Dulk and Groeneveld, 2012). We also ask whether or not FWAs can maintain their benefit to employees, as well as to employers, in challenging economic times. In so doing, we distinguish between 'traditional' FWAs (such as flexitime, reduced hours and job sharing, which are usually assumed to be employee-led) and 'evolved'

FWAs (the widespread, employer-led strategic use of remote working as part of wider workplace change initiatives to cut costs and maintain service delivery). We highlight the importance of the development of enhanced IT systems over several years within the public sector and consider whether this has impacted on the capacity of local government organisations to confront the 2008 economic crisis and subsequent austerity measures. The chapter begins by outlining the development of FWAs in the British public sector, specifically from the New Labour administrations of 1997 onwards and the factors that have driven these initiatives. This is followed by a description of qualitative research undertaken with a sample of HR directors and managers from 12 local councils in Britain, focusing on whether or not FWAs have been used to manage austerity and perceptions of the impacts of the austerity programme on both employees and managers, as well as on service delivery. We use the term FWAs in our reporting—although participants often used the terms WLB policies and practices—as we question whether or not these flexible working initiatives are indeed supportive of WLB. Finally, we discuss some implications of these developments and impacts for the triple agenda of individual employee WLB and well-being, workplace effectiveness and social justice.

The Implementation of Flexible Working Arrangements in Britain

There is evidence that FWAs and supportive organisational cultures can enhance employee well-being (Redman et al., 2009; Beauregard, 2010; Butts et al., 2013), while also benefiting organisations (Rapoport et al., 2002; Lewis and Cooper, 2005), and can thus potentially address a dual agenda of supporting employees and employers (The Work Foundation, 2016). However, their effectiveness in this regard depends on how they are implemented (Kim et al., Chapter 10), which in turn may reflect the reasons why they are introduced in the first place and the shifting pressures on organisations as contexts change (Lewis et al., 2016).

The adoption of FWAs is typically explained in terms of both institutional drivers (including legal and normative environments, equality arguments and pressures from women employees) and economic considerations (Applebaum et al., 2002). However, the absence of strong evidence of a link between FWAs and enhanced performance (de Menezes and Kelliher, 2011), coupled with empirical support for institutional factors (Goodstein, 1994; Wood, 1999; Wood et al., 2003), has meant that priority has been given to an institutional approach in explaining the adoption of such initiatives (e.g., Kossek et al., 1994). Organisations continue to be concerned with maintaining legitimacy as a result of normative, legal and societal pressures, including increased female labour force participation and high levels of public attention to WLB issues (DiMaggio and Powell, 1983; Goodstein, 1994), as well as public visibility. For example, the relatively high level of formal FWAs in public sector organisations across Europe, supplementing legislation, has been attributed to their visibility in relation to government standards, the pressures to recruit and retain staff, especially women returners, as well as the absence of a profit drive. Institutional pressures were found to be the major drivers for this trend, with little evidence of the effects of economic drivers (Den Dulk and Groeneveld, 2012). However, we might expect economic drivers of FWAs to be growing in importance in the British public sector as a result of the 2008 recession and associated austerity cuts.

In the British context, development of legislation has meant that the coercive, and not simply the normative, power of social pressures has played a role in increasing the adoption of some policies. As outlined by Stokes and Wood in Chapter 3, employment legislation developed by the Labour Governments of 1997–2010 attempted to balance fairness and economic concerns: for example, the introduction of formal FWAs was discussed in terms of both fairness *and* from an economic perspective, implying mutual benefit (e.g. Department of Trade and Industry, 1998). A key illustration of this is the legislation on the right to request flexible working, which employers can refuse to grant if it adversely affects their business. The focus on a broad notion of fairness suggests the awakening of a triple agenda, that is, to seek policies that benefit both employees and employers in socially just ways. Since the 2008 recession, however, there has been a renewed focus on the costs of FWAs and, as the 2010–2015 UK Coalition Government's labour market policy developed, there was a rebalancing of the fairness–economy relationship, with an increasing focus on economic concerns. Consequently, for example, legislation has extended parental leave and the right to request flexible working from parents of young children to all employees, but doubts remain among some employers and policy-makers about the costs involved, particularly in small businesses (e.g., Beecroft, 2011). Nevertheless, intermediary organisations such as the Chartered Institute of Personnel and Development (2012) remain convinced of the mutual benefits of FWAs and imply that they could be functional in recession and austerity.

Running alongside this 'rebalancing' of the fairness–economy relationship has been a long-standing focus on reforms of the public sector, or New Public Management (NPM), facilitated by technological advances. For example, in a Cabinet Office report from 2005, 'Transformational Government: enabled by technology', the then Prime Minister, Tony Blair, set out his vision "to seize the opportunity provided by technology to transform the business of government" (2005: 2). Within this vision, it was argued that "technology has a major part to play in the solutions to each of three major challenges which globalisation is setting modern governments—economic productivity, social justice and public service reform" (ibid). Mr Blair added that "this strategy has the potential for real transformation of public services . . . there is a real appetite for change and modernisation within the public services themselves" (2005: 1). Whether or not there was such an appetite for change, the report demonstrates that three years before the onset of the 2008 global recession, plans were well under way to transform the public sector to make it more streamlined and effective via the use of technology. A year later, Dunleavy and colleagues highlighted a new 'post-NPM' era of 'digital-era governance' (DEG), which advances the "digitalisation of administrative processes" (2006: 467). The Varney Report (2006) further highlighted the continued need for public sector reform, citing the successful implementation of more online services such as NHS Direct Online and car tax renewals, and calling for further changes to "mak[e] the most of technological changes" (2006: 3).

We have seen in Chapter 3 that employees experiencing recessionary actions had higher levels of work–nonwork conflict and that in the public sector such employees were less likely to use certain FWAs. Recent research (Lewis et al., 2016) has demonstrated that public sector discourses of WLB can be sensitive to changing economic contexts. For example, despite a continuing discourse of mutual benefits to employee and employer, there is also a distinct shift towards greater emphasis on the economic interests of employers during austerity. This chapter complements these recent findings by examining how councils use—and build upon—FWAs during a time of austerity and whether or not FWAs can maintain their benefit to employees, as well as employers, in challenging economic times.

The Qualitative Study

Semi-structured interviews were conducted with HR directors and managers in 12 local councils across Scotland and the North, Midlands and South of England, to explore their organisational experiences of, and perspectives on, WLB and austerity. We chose to interview HR professionals because they are responsible for developing and implementing FWAs on a formal basis and therefore have a distinctive vantage point, although this means that we are relying on their accounts to highlight concerns around the impact on employees and line managers. All the councils are large, visible and have a high proportion of women employees.

Semi-structured interviews asked participants to look back at the initial discussions and developments of WLB policies and practices over time, which in most cases pre-dated the participants' employment in the organisation. As a result, it is assumed that accounts reflect interpretations embedded in the organisation's history and culture and used in communications with employees. Questions included how WLB or similar issues were discussed in their organisation in the past and present, and at what level; formal WLB policies; why policies were adopted; how they were implemented in practice and any perceived implementation constraints; recent changes in WLB policies and their perceived future; and whether WLB considerations had any influence on the way the cuts were handled. Interviews were carried out by the authors in 2011–12 and lasted between

60 and 90 minutes. All interviews were digitally recorded and fully transcribed and NVivo was used to assist with data organisation and analysis. Thematic analysis was used to interpret the qualitative data.

Below, we first discuss two themes that emerged in relation to the use of FWAs in public sector austerity. Firstly, we identified ambivalence about 'traditional' FWAs: these are considered to be embedded within the practices of the councils but HR professionals have reservations about their sustainability in the longer-term. Secondly, 'evolved' FWAs or new ways of working are being embraced to manage austerity. We then discuss two further themes relating to some of the HR professionals' concerns about the impact of changing approaches to flexible working on a) employees and b) line managers and service delivery.

Ambivalence about Traditional FWAs

Most HR managers maintained, on the one hand, that FWAs were sufficiently embedded to withstand the pressures of austerity and indeed could be of some benefit to both the employer and to employees in facing these pressures, at least in the immediate future. For example, FWAs were viewed as being among the few benefits currently available to existing staff, helping to maintain employee commitment and engagement through the worst of the recession. On the other hand, some HR managers acknowledged the potential vulnerability of FWAs over the longer term, especially if the need for further austerity cuts increases. For example, one HR Director told us that FWAs in his council would probably remain for the rest of the year but, after that, they may come under review. He went on to elaborate on the reasons why:

> *I think what the council is probably saying at the moment is 'we have a good range of practices already in place, we have to focus now on delivering the savings and reorganising the services'. So actually, the sort of the positive work on work–life balance will probably go into a bit of a hiatus now, in my view (Council 1).*

The view that FWAs were potentially vulnerable in the future was primarily because of their focus on individual concessions. Participants shared concerns that there had been an over-emphasis in the past on individual rights and the needs of staff, rather than on service delivery needs:

> *There is a fine balance between supporting the needs of our staff and delivering our services to the high standard that's expected of us (Council 6).*

Participants also reported that some line managers, who are under pressures of their own to cut costs and maintain service delivery, continued to be sceptical about the benefits of FWAs and considered them to be employee benefits with associated costs, unaffordable in the current economic climate. This could result in implementation gaps between formal policy and actual practice, manifested in managers' reluctance to support staff needs. Within these examples, FWAs were still being linked to WLB outcomes:

> *I guess my concern is the extent to which managers who are under pressure to make cost reductions, but . . . sustain services, may start to see some of these things as 'nice to have' and therefore, possibly, can no longer afford, rather than at the core of what we offer as an employer. One of the things that I do think that we need to try and protect is that sense of being an employer which offers staff a good work–life balance (Council 3).*

A large majority of the HR professionals saw FWAs as providing opportunities for adjusting costs in the current economic context, especially to avoid redundancies. FWAs were being actively promoted within the context of the threat to jobs, encouraging people to cut hours, and packaged as enhancing WLB. Again, tensions were evident in the ability to exploit traditional FWAs such as part-time working in a period of austerity, as the participants were aware of employees' fear of redundancy. The anticipation of reduced redundancy pay in the future thus undermined attempts to make savings:

> *People are afraid at the end of the day that if they opt for part-time hours there's no guarantee that we can't make them redundant next year, and their redundancy pay would be lower and their pension would obviously be affected, and other benefits (Council 12).*

However, participants reported that savings from the use of traditional FWAs were limited, particularly when dealt with on a case-by-case basis. On the other hand, there was a growing acknowledgement by almost all participants that the greatest savings could be made through what we have called evolved FWAs, the widespread and strategic use of remote working as part of wider initiatives to cut costs, while at the same time maintaining service delivery.

New Ways of Working Are Evolving and Are Embraced to Manage Austerity

All 12 councils had implemented some form of mobile working programme, variously defined as "smarter", "modern" or "new". These involved a combination of remote working (from home or other dispersed locations such as coffee bars or 'hubs'), hot-desking, the implementation of new IT systems, job analysis and redesign, and restructuring within parts of the organisation, such as the centralisation of certain services. In several cases, these programmes had been developed prior to the recession to cut costs:

> *I think the single biggest change that happened was the major IT infrastructure investment that they put in place from 2001 onwards, and that suddenly enabled people to work from home and access all the core systems they needed as well. It was at that point, a range of other complementary policies started to come in to place, such as term-time working and compressed hours. We used the opportunity to pilot things and then build policy and the overarching WLB strategy around that (Council 1).*

The programmes were also justified by participants as not only maintaining, but actually improving, service delivery, supporting the arguments put forward for reform of the public sector over many years, with the use of increasing digitalisation (Dunleavy et al., 2006).

> *As long ago as about 2006 the council was doing a project called project N, about . . . mobile working. And we used some technology, tablet PCs, for workers to get out and visit clients. And that whole kind of re-engineering of that service, of the way people worked, reduced process time from 6 weeks to 4 hours. The residents, the clients, absolutely loved the service because instead of getting a faceless letter from the council they actually got a visit . . . And it completely revolutionised the way we worked (Council 7).*

Before the recession, such programmes had been designed to enhance employee flexibility and choice, as well as helping employers to cut costs (the 'mutual benefits' agenda). However, the austerity cuts spurred the emergence and greater use of involuntary flexibility, such as enforced remote working, which had an explicit focus on essential cost-savings, going against the discourse of individual choice which used to be central to discussions of WLB (Lewis et al., 2016). Remote working practices were increasingly foregrounded as the most effective means of saving money, as fewer people in offices meant fewer resources being used (e.g., heating, lighting) and fewer desk spaces required, and also allowed councils to sell off existing property. Others were streamlining their office space and relocating staff in shared accommodation with partner organisations in explicit efforts to save money. The mutual benefits of these evolved FWAs were acknowledged, but in many cases were increasingly side-lined in favour of employer need:

> *. . . there aren't enough desks for everybody [laugh] so we have hot desking theoretically to a greater or lesser extent but I mean theoretically if everybody came in at the same time there wouldn't be enough desks because we've actually then been able to sell some of the buildings*

that we owned or, and also stop renting additional space and obviously that's a money-saving idea, so it's kind of, it's based on a business need I suppose but actually is also seen as something which is of benefit to staff (Council 8).

Some participants went on to acknowledge that this discourse of mutual benefits was being used to justify ways of making cuts through enforced flexibility, by using the language of support for employee choice and WLB, representing a 'reconstructed' meaning of mutual benefit, e.g., flexibility was increasingly employer-led but the mutual benefits agenda was still being referred to in order to make it more palatable to employees. This is further discussed by Lewis and colleagues (2016).

The Impact on Employees

Despite persistently referring to the mutual benefits of evolved FWAs, there were some worries expressed about the potential consequences for employees. This is of particular concern, as selling off resources such as office space means that there is unlikely to be a reversal of such enforced remote working practices in this sector. The HR professionals acknowledged some resistance from employees to these evolved FWAs, although they largely dismissed this as inevitable resistance to change:

. . . With any big change like this you always get people who resist and, you know, people put a lot of their own personal energy and emotion into their desk space; you'll see people with pictures of their children all over their desk and their own little knickknacks on their desk and they don't like those being taken away; you get people who like a particular desk near the window and when it's suddenly all hot desking, you know it's first come first served; so there's a whole series of resistance, people don't necessarily like having to carry their equipment around with them even though we provide them with the tools to be able to do that (Council 9).

The same participant later voiced some concerns, however, about employees losing the social engagement aspect of work:

. . . hot-desking breaks down some of those little social networks because you're used to sitting next to the same people and chatting and then suddenly it's somebody different next to you every day so that is a big adjustment for a lot of people. People need that social environment, social interaction, they need the personal physical attachment to places and we're breaking some of those down (Council 9).

Although resistance was acknowledged, the mutual benefits of flexibility argument used by the HR professionals continues to suggest the potential for enhanced employee WLB, even during austerity. However, while evolved FWAs were being used to cut costs and help reduce the number of redundancies necessary, some staff in all organisations were still being made redundant as part of managing austerity. Thus, at the same time as this increase in remote working, there was also a decrease in staff. Consequently, a number of participants expressed concerns about the impact on 'survivors' of the redundancies who were continuing to face job insecurity as well as work intensification, with additional cuts forecast. For example, there were concerns about employees reverting back to presenteeism (where remote working was not enforced) in efforts to be seen as committed and loyal:

> *I definitely have a feel . . . an increasing sense of presenteeism is being built into the organisation. Absence levels were always historically low in [the council], but we could see that, where areas were being restructured or areas which were likely to be restructured, there was definitely an increasing longer-hours culture building again, for there were some concerns around personal well-being and health and safety of the workforce beginning to flag up, and I think that's going to become a more problematic outcome, and that would be a direct result of the cuts because people will become more uncertain, potentially more fearful about their work (Council 1).*

This was confirmed by other participants who reported that staff members were coming into work, even when sick, rather than risk being seen as weak or uncommitted to the organisation:

> *I think that's a negative because I think what's happening there is that's a fear factor; people are fearful of taking time off in case it somehow identifies them as weaker than others and when any cull comes it's the weak ones who go so I think that's a negative and I'm not comfortable with that happening. If you're unwell, don't come to work! I don't want people dragging themselves in when they're not fit to come in (Council 6).*

As staff reductions meant that remaining employees were working longer hours in order to get the work done, participants observed that employees' WLB and well-being could ultimately be undermined by these unmanageable and unsustainable workloads:

> *. . . we've reduced the number of posts by about 10% of the workforce, I think, and, yes, we are pretty well delivering the same number of services. In other words, staff are busier, much, much, much busier, so work–life balance has taken a tumble and staff are having to work harder (Council 4).*

> *. . . well it's interesting because while we've been encouraging people to have a work–life balance, in some senses for the few staff that are*

going to be left I'm not sure how they're going to manage that if their workloads are going to increase. So the ideals and the reality are two different things, aren't they? . . . there's going to be fewer workers doing more work, you know, we're going to see a society where we have a massive number of people unemployed or working for nothing and then we're going to have the ones who are in work being so grateful that they're in work that they'll work flat out (Council 10).

While some HR professionals raised concerns about employees, others were less sympathetic and reverted to the rhetoric of New Public Management as a justification for reduced staff numbers and increased workloads for remaining staff, well aware that the culture of fear in an insecure job market would mean that staff were more likely to accept what was being asked of them:

We're looking for introducing more innovative work practices, lean systems thinking, transformation practices to try and improve our process so we don't need as many people to deliver them. So does that mean people are working harder? Probably yes. I mean that's part of our strategy with our performance management framework to eliminate any potential waste from our system including non-productive time. So yeah, the expectation is that people will need to work harder and they realise that the alternative is not particularly a good one (Council 9).

The Impact on Line Managers and Service Delivery

The impact of such flexible working practices and reduced staff numbers affects not just the employees mentioned above but also the line managers having to cope with new ways of working and new ways of managing staff. The fourth WLB Survey of Employers (BIS, 2014) showed that in around one-third of establishments, decisions about flexible working requests were the responsibility of line managers or supervisors. The crucial role of line managers in supporting flexible working or instilling a culture of presenteeism is widely acknowledged (e.g., McCarthy et al., 2013) and can, in some cases, be more important to an employee's overall well-being than the provision of formal FWAs (e.g., Allen, 2001; Behson, 2005). As highlighted earlier, HR professionals referred to continued managerial preferences for a more traditional style of management, in the face of increasing flexibility and the dispersion of staff:

There are two areas of resistance (to mobile working) I'd say at the moment, one is from line managers, particularly middle management layers, where they don't like the loss of control that they've perceived from people not being office-based. So not physically being able to watch people and observe them working and so on is challenging for them (Council 9).

Of course, line managers are employees, too, with increasing work demands, as well as family and other non-work responsibilities (Ford and Collinson, 2011), and the difficulties for managers were highlighted by many participants. Some participants maintained that flexible working had helped with such difficulties, while also acknowledging increasing responsibilities:

> . . . *where managers were taking on functions they hadn't previously managed, or who were having to work with teams who were geographically spread around, the fact that we had that approach to flexible working and people not always having to be, you know, people working in almost virtual teams at times, that had helped culturally prepare people for changing the way managers were working (Council 1).*

There were many reports of the requirement for managers to be retrained to enable them to manage virtual teams. Some appeared to be embracing that challenge and managing to make it work:

> . . . *the managers need quite a lot of education and support about different ways of managing that they are managing more by results and performance and less by being directly visible with the employees. . . . Some enlightened managers really, really make it work and they're good then as sort of champion managers, advocate managers (Council 7).*

On the other hand, the HR professionals often referred to the difficulties for managers in trying to continue to deliver services under the austerity programme. Concerns about sustaining service delivery are problematic, given that 'new' ways of working programmes were partly justified as not only maintaining, but actually improving, service delivery:

> *And I think that we are, by and large, seeking to squeeze more out of a smaller resource base and I don't think that, whilst I'm sure managers have considered the implications for the staff who remain and the impact of trying to spread work more across a smaller number of people, I think they've been under quite a lot of pressure themselves to achieve savings targets and to continue to deliver services of the same number and the same quality but with fewer staff (Council 3).*

It is such concerns that prompted managers to question the sustainability of FWAs if roles are required to change radically, as a result of redundancies and restructuring:

> *Yes, I think, as saving these 450 posts this year and as pressures build, managers will be less inclined to have people working so flexibly in some parts of the organisation. Indeed, they may even want to review how flexible working arrangements are within their teams, because the*

team design itself may have to be fundamentally different. So of course people who have flexible working now are doing so on the basis of the role they're currently doing with a level of team resource around them that enables that to work, but if team resource reduces, the manager may have to revisit the flexible working arrangements (Council 1).

Conclusions

In this chapter, we explore HR professionals' perceptions of change in public sector use of FWAs before the recession, during the recession and in subsequent austerity. Chapter 3 uses quantitative data to assess possible effects of the recession on the use of FWAs in the public and private sectors. We have used qualitative data in this chapter to examine evolved FWAs in more depth in British public sector local councils. We have highlighted an increasing focus, built up over a number of years, on enhanced IT, which was developed to streamline the public sector and cut unnecessary waste. Our findings demonstrate how evolved FWAs, significantly enabled by such technological advances implemented in advance of the 2008 recession, are being used in the management of austerity. Homeworking was one of the few FWAs which had increased during the recession (Stokes and Wood, Chapter 3), and we demonstrate how hot-desking and remote working emerged as the only real identifiable FWA that resulted in a clear financial benefit to employers. This was being increasingly promoted to all employees, and even enforced, justified within a mutual benefits discourse (Lewis et al., 2016). Nevertheless, the mutual benefits focus was increasingly—and explicitly—being sidelined in favour of the employer-led, business case focus, further justified by the growing effects of the austerity cuts. However, HR professionals had observed that pockets of resistance emerged from both line managers and other employees who valued the social interaction involved in coming to work. Meanwhile, there were also indications that the sustainability of some traditional FWAs such as reduced-hours working may be vulnerable in the longer-term. The HR professionals believed this was partly as a result of the increasing concerns of employers and managers around service delivery and also as a result of employees being either unwilling or unable to take up FWAs in the face of job insecurity.

Despite potential resistance on the part of some employees to the enforcement of remote working and the associated reduction in social engagement, it is possible that changes such as widespread remote working may provide benefits in the longer-term if the majority of staff are enjoying greater flexibility and as a result, a better WLB. Indeed, a Work Foundation report (2016) highlights the increased use of mobile working and the associated benefits for individual employees. FWAs such as remote working during recession and austerity may also herald more enlightened practices post-recession, with potential consequences for widespread acceptance of flexible working by men and women and greater gender equality both within the workplace and at home. This is an empirical and policy question for the future. However, in the public sector, alongside the rise in remote working, there has been a corresponding increase in job losses and, consequently, more pressure on 'survivors' to deliver the same services with fewer staff. Although our findings could not explore this in great detail due to our reliance on the accounts of HR professionals, this suggests that employees were in fact less likely to achieve a WLB, findings supported by the WERS data on the differences between public and private sector employees reported in Chapter 3. Kinman and McDowall also reflect upon some of the negative impacts of FWAs on WLB in Chapter 2. Further research with public sector employees would provide greater insights into the consequences of evolved FWAs for individuals.

Our research participants also reported that many line managers were struggling to manage virtual teams working from home or in remote workspaces, although many were making attempts to make this new form of management work in practice. The increasing pressures placed on managers in the public sector have been previously reported (Ford and Collinson, 2011) and were certainly further highlighted in the reports in our research. Again, the reliance on HR managers in this research meant that we were unable to gauge the true impact of remote working on line managers trying to maintain the same level of service delivery with a reduced workforce.

The more negative aspects of increased remote working have also been raised recently (highlighted by Kim et al., Chapter 10), and CEOs of some high profile organisations appear to be bringing their employees back into the workplace and reducing opportunities for greater work flexibility. For example, senior management in large US organisations such as Yahoo have argued that collaboration is important during austerity, increasing the need for staff to be working closer together and to be present in their offices in order to increase productivity. This may or may not provide a temporary solution to the impact of austerity and further (optional or otherwise) remote working seems likely in the future. In the case of the British public sector, however, selling off resources such as office space means that there is not likely in the immediate future to be a reversal of enforced FWAs. The decisions made during austerity are therefore likely to have long-lasting effects on employees and on line managers and are very unlikely to be merely a reversible test case.

In the face of increased pressures among remaining employees working harder and, in many cases, without the support and camaraderie of friends and colleagues when working remotely, the corresponding impact on individual well-being and service delivery is also of concern. Indeed, the long-standing association between flexible working and WLB is called into question by our findings. Assessed in terms of the triple agenda, evolved FWAs serve the interests of employers, potentially enhancing workplace effectiveness. However, while widespread remote working may provide some benefits, enforced remote working that does not take account of employees' needs or perspectives may be detrimental to individual employee WLB and well-being. In such cases, the pursuit of social justice seems to have been swept aside as a consequence of austerity programmes.

References

Allen, T.D. (2001). Family supportive work environments: The role of organisational perceptions. *Journal of Vocational Behaviour*, 58(3): 414–435.

Appelbaum, E., Bailey, T., Berg, P., & Kalleberg, A.L. (2002). Shared work-valued care: New norms for organizing market work and unpaid care work. *Economic and Industrial Democracy*, 23(1): 125–131.

Beauregard, T.A. (2010). Introduction: The import of intrapersonal and interpersonal dynamics in work performance. *British Journal of Management*, 21(2): 255–261.

Beecroft, A. (2011). *Report on Employment Law*. London: Department for Business, Innovation and Skills.

Behson, S.J. (2005). The relative contribution of formal and informal organisational work-family support. *Journal of Vocational Behavior*, 66(3): 487–500.

Busby, N., & James, G. (eds). (2011). *Families, Care-giving and Paid Work: Challenging Labour Law in the 21st Century*. Cheltenham: Edward Elgar.

Butts, M.M., Casper, W.J., & Yang, T.S. (2013). How important are work-family support policies? A meta-analytic investigation of their effects on employee outcomes. *Journal of Applied Psychology*, 98(1): 1–25.

Cabinet Office. (2005). *Transformational Government: Enabled by Technology*. ISO: The Stationery Office.

Chartered Institute of Personnel and Development. (2012). *Flexible Working Provision and Uptake*, available at http://www.cipd.co.uk/binaries/5790%20Flexible%20Working%20SR%20(WEB2).pdf

De Menezes, L.M., & Kelliher, C. (2011). Flexible working and performance: A systematic review of the evidence for a business case. *International Journal of Management Reviews*, 13(4): 452–474.

Den Dulk, L., & Groeneveld, S. (2012). Work–life balance support in the public sector in Europe. *Review of Public Personnel Administration*, 32(4): 353–381.

Department for Business, Innovation and Skills. (2014). *The Fourth Work-Life Balance Employer Survey 2013*. BIS Research Paper No. 184. Department for Business, Innovation and Skills, London.

Department of Trade and Industry. (1998). *Fairness at Work*. London: Department of Trade and Industry.

DiMaggio, P.J., & Powell, W.W. (1983). The iron cage revisited: Institutional isomorphism and collective rationality in organizational fields. *American Sociological Review*, 48(2): 147–160.

Dunleavy, P., Margetts, H., Bastow, S., & Tinkler, J. (2006). New public management is dead: Long live digital-era governance, *Journal of Public Administration Research and Theory: J-PART*, 16(3): 467–494.

Ford, J., & Collinson, D. (2011). In search of the perfect manager? Work-life balance and managerial work. *Work, Employment and Society*, 25(2): 257–273.

Goodstein, J.D. (1994). Institutional pressures and strategic responsiveness: Employer involvement in work–family issues, *Academy of Management Journal*, 37(2): 350–382.

Gregory, A., & Milner, S. (2009b). Work-life balance: A matter of choice? *Gender, Work and Organization*, 16(1): 1–13.

Kersley, B., Alpin, C., Forth, J., Bryson, A., Bewley, H., Dix, G., & Oxenbridge, S. (2006). *Inside the Workplace: Findings from the 2004 Workplace Employment Relations Survey*. London and NewYork: Routledge.

Kossek, E., Dass, P., & De Marr, B. (1994). The dominant logic of employer-sponsored work and family initiatives: Human resource managers' institutional role. *Human Relations*, 47(9): 1121–1149.

Lewis, S., Anderson, D., Lyonette, C., Payne, N., & Wood, S. (2016). Public sector austerity cuts in the UK and the changing discourse of work–life balance. *Work, Employment and Society*. Online first: 1-16.

Lewis, S., & Cooper, C.L. (2005). *Work-life Integration: Case Studies of Organisational Change*. Chichester: John Wiley & Sons.

McCarthy, A., Cleveland, J., Hunter, S., Darcy, C., & Grady, G. (2013). Employee work-life balance outcomes in Ireland: A multilevel investigation of supervisory support and perceived organizational support. *International Journal of Human Resource Management*, 24(6): 1257–1276.

Rapoport, R., Bailyn, L., Fletcher, J., & Pruitt, B. (2002). *Beyond Work-family Balance: Advancing Gender Equity and Workplace Performance*. New York: John Wiley & Sons.

Redman, T., Snape, E., & Ashurst, C. (2009). Location, location, location: Does place of work really matter? *British Journal of Management*, 20(Supplement 1): S171–S181.

Van Wanrooy, B., Bewley, H., Bryson, A., Forth, J., Stokes, L., & Wood, S. (2013). *Employment Relations in the Shadow of Recession: Findings from the 2011 Workplace Employment Relations Study*. Houndsmill, Basingstoke: Palgrave MacMillan.

Varney, D. (2006). Service Transformation: A Better Service for Citizens and Businesses, a Better Deal for the Taxpayer. London: HMSO.

Wood, S. (1999). Family-friendly management: Testing the various perspectives, *National Institute Economic Review*, 168(1): 99–116.

Wood, S., de Menezes, L., & Lasaosa, A. (2003). Family-friendly management in the UK: Testing various perspectives. *Industrial Relations*, 42(2): 221–250.

The Work Foundation (Part of Lancaster University). (2016). *Working Anywhere: A Winning Formula for Good Work?* London: The Work Foundation Alliance.

5 Regulating Work and Care Relationships in a Time of Austerity

A Legal Perspective

Nicole Busby and Grace James

Recent austerity measures in the UK have led to labour market deregulation alongside cuts to welfare provision. Such reforms have resulted in reduced protection for the large numbers of women workers who combine low paid, precarious work with high levels of care-giving. Furthermore, cuts to public services risk upsetting the finely tuned arrangements on which those who provide care alongside paid work depend. This chapter considers the impact of austerity on the legal and policy framework surrounding the reconciliation of paid employment and unpaid care. The chapter aims to explore the relationship between gender and care in order to identify the limits of the current framework for addressing the needs of those who provide unpaid informal care alongside paid work.

The resulting analysis will highlight how, despite political claims to the contrary, budget cuts and the reduction in access to legally enforceable rights have detrimentally affected many women's work–life balance (WLB) by negatively impacting on employment prospects, personal well-being and social and economic security throughout the life course—from the years of family formation to retirement. The negative effects of care-giving have always impinged on women's life experiences. However, many of the gains made to gender equality through incremental improvements to law and policy over several decades are now lost or threatened due to the changes wrought in the name of austerity. As well as the obvious effects on individuals, such slippage has wider long-term implications as a failure to care for the carer impacts on all aspects of society, on families and employing organisations and also threatens economic success.

Our focus on the paid work/unpaid care equation which is central to most women's lives does not mean that we wish to exclude carers who do not or cannot undertake paid work alongside their care commitments. We certainly do not consider such individuals as less worthy subjects of labour law than those who engage in paid work, but our overriding aim is to explore the effects of state attempts to rebalance the relationship between paid work and welfare and the place of law and policy in achieving this. Taking a life-course trajectory, the chapter will identify specific pressure points where improvements to the law and policy framework could alleviate the many difficulties experienced by worker/carers. By highlighting the effects of the austerity agenda at different stages in the life course, we aim to illustrate the often devastating individual and cumulative effects of a failure to prioritise and protect gender equality from the programme of budget cuts and deregulation. Our central argument is that gender equality should be protected against political expediency, especially in times of economic downturn. The chapter concludes by considering how such protection could be guaranteed in the future.

Women's Lives, Carers' Lives: Gender, Unpaid Care and Labour Law

In all industrialised societies, unpaid care for family members and other dependent individuals is overwhelmingly provided by women, whether they engage in paid work or not (Busby, 2011). However, the traditional labour law framework has never accommodated such work, adopting a marketised conceptualisation of 'labour' which encapsulates most forms of paid work but which excludes work which is unpaid and consequently viewed as being of no market value (Busby, 2011). Furthermore, such unpaid work attracts specific legal protection only insofar as it impacts on the individual's ability to perform paid work and is not explicitly accounted for in the regulatory regime and so remains hidden from view (Busby, 2011; Fudge, 2013). The assumptions that underpin this approach have always been flawed (Busby, 2011; Fudge, 2016) but appear particularly incongruous in the contemporary workplace, where the protection of WLB is the focus of much attention. Despite the adoption of a more holistic approach to workers' well-being through the development of 'family friendly' policies which are intended to facilitate family responsibilities and associated requirements, legal protection is still largely focused on the 'paid employment' part of the equation, so that workers who also provide unpaid care are viewed as 'the other' in contrast to the normative paradigm, i.e. the full-time, permanent, unencumbered (male) worker.

In the UK, the rationale underpinning law's provision has been slow to catch up with social changes such as the post-war rise in women's labour market participation, the growth in the number of lone parent families and other less 'traditional' family forms. Thus, the resulting law and policy framework takes a heteronormative approach to balancing personal and paid work responsibilities. By viewing those who provide high levels of unpaid care alongside paid employment as exceptions to the norm, the law seeks to provide remedial measures which are primarily aimed at enabling such workers to remain in the labour force through, for example, anti-discrimination laws, maternity rights and protection for part-time workers. These generally depend on a high degree of market regulation. Such employment rights have been incrementally bolstered by associated welfare measures and tax credits and the provision of public services which, in various combinations depending on personal circumstances, are aimed at providing individuals and their dependants with an adequate standard of living. Whilst such a welfare/work mix may be capable of facilitating a necessary degree of flexibility for individual care arrangements, its reliance on economic and social policy does not provide any guaranteed protection, leaving worker/carers vulnerable and particularly susceptible to changes in political ideology.

The sweeping changes introduced by the UK's Coalition Government (2010–2015) and carried forward by the current Conservative Government in the name of austerity are the specific focus of this chapter. Driven by a neo-liberal agenda, many of the changes enacted are, on their face, 'gender blind' as they were not specifically targeted at women or those who perform unpaid care. However, their impacts reveal unintended consequences which could have been avoided if equality impact assessments had been carried out and alternative courses of action considered. Some of these measures are indicative of a deregulatory approach to employment law, such as the increase in the unfair dismissal qualifying period from one to two years introduced in April 2012 (see Employment Rights Act 1006, amended s. 92(3) (2)). The impact of this amendment will be felt by those women who work in precarious and unprotected areas of the labour market who will find it difficult to build up the longer service requirement due to the demands of balancing care commitments with paid work. The Coalition Government's non-enactment of certain provisions under the Equality Act 2010 has had similarly disproportionate effects on groups of women workers. The 'new approach' to equality (May, 2012) led to the shelving of the Act's fledgling attempt to address intersectionality (Crenshaw, 1991) by enabling actions based on two grounds of discrimination to be brought (s.14) and the prohibition of third party harassment (s.40) as the estimated annual costs to businesses of £350m were deemed too high (HM Treasury, 2011). However, no account was taken of the personal and financial costs to the individual resulting from a loss of employment because you happen to be black and a woman (*Bahl v The Law Society and others* [2004] IRLR 799) or subjected to workplace discrimination by an individual who happens to be outside of your employment contract (*Burton and Rhule v De Vere Hotels* [1996] IRLR 596).

Furthermore, the socio-economic duty (s. 1) which would have required public bodies to assess their approach to inequalities caused by class factors encouraging improvements in, for example, health and education outcomes in more deprived areas was also abandoned. Announcing this decision, Home Secretary and (then) Equalities Minister Theresa May stated,

> Even as we increase equality of opportunity, some people will always do better than others . . . I do not believe in a world where everybody gets the same out of life, regardless of what they put in. That is why no government should try to ensure equal outcomes for everyone.
>
> (May 2010)

The overt rejection of equality of results is not new to the UK's law and policy framework, which has always aimed at the achievement of formal equality through the provision of equal treatment. However, this explicit retreat to the traditional position from what appeared, at least ostensibly, to be the beginnings of an alternative means of overcoming inequalities, surely amounts to a retrograde step. In addition, the withdrawal of the means of challenging breaches of the Equality Act and other employment protection provisions through the assertion of statutory rights has severely threatened workers' access to justice. In the remainder of this chapter, we will consider the effects of these and other measures on WLB and, in particular, the regulation of paid work and unpaid care relationships.

Pregnancy and Maternity

For many women, the gendered implications of care-giving for labour market participation are often directly experienced for the first time when they are pregnant or have recently given birth. It is a time when women need to leave the labour market for a period of time, in order to give birth, physically recover and, if they choose to, care for the newborn during his/her first year. UK employment laws provide fairly generous leave entitlements for mothers. Available under S71–75 ERA 1996 and regulations 4–12A of the Maternity and Parental Leave etc. regulations 1999 (SI 1999/3312), employees are entitled to a maximum period of 12 months leave. To those who qualify, leave is paid for nine months: earnings related for the first six weeks at 90% of her weekly earnings and then payable at the national statutory maternity pay (SMP) rate, or 90% of average earnings if that is less, for 33 weeks, leaving three months unpaid. New mothers report taking an average 9–10 months of leave, with those working in certain sectors taking more (manufacturing industries) and others less (education) (see EHRC/BIS, 2015: 33). Those who do not qualify for SMP may claim maternity allowance. Interestingly, given the core focus of this book, New Labour, when they came to office in 1997, had intended to extend the payment of SMP to a full year, but this was shelved due to economic instability caused by recession, reflecting the vulnerability of such social policies to economic hardship (see Rubery and Rafferty, 2013).

Recent legislation has been extended to include those who have a baby through a surrogacy arrangement (The Children and Family Act 2014). It also allows parents to share care-giving responsibilities during this initial period (see Mitchell, 2015). Laws are also in place to protect working women from unfavourable treatment during pregnancy and maternity leave. The Equality Act 2010 s.18 prohibits unfavourable treatment because of pregnancy or illness suffered as a result of it or because of seeking to exercise or having exercised one's entitlement to maternity leave. Protection lasts from when the pregnancy begins to until the end of maternity leave (the 'protected period'), and if the treatment is unfavourable, it is likely to be automatically unfair, contrary to the Employment Rights Act 1996 (ERA) S.99. EU legislation also provides protection (see The Equal Treatment Directive 76/207/EEC (now, Recast Directive 2006/54/EC) and the Pregnant Workers Directive 92/85/EEC). A body of EU case law has been developed over the years, extending the rights and protection to mothers, albeit in a disjointed way that has often been criticised for failing to promote more equal parenting (see for example, Caracciolo et al., 2001; McGlynn, 2001; Busby and James, 2016).

Despite this fairly robust legal framework, tens of thousands of women annually experience pregnancy and maternity related discrimination at work. A recent investigation headed by the Equality and Human Rights Commission (EHRC) and the Department for Business, Innovation and Skills (BIS) estimates that as many as 54,000 women are annually dismissed, made compulsorily redundant while others are not, or are treated so poorly that they feel they have to leave their jobs (EHRC/BIS, 2015). Many, around 100,000 women a year, experience harassment and negative comments relating to pregnancy and flexible working from employers and colleagues and a third felt unsupported by their employer at some point when pregnant or returning to work, whilst one in ten were discouraged from attending antenatal appointments. This confirms equally disappointing figures from a previous investigation (see Equal Opportunities Commission (EOC, 2005) and underscores the fact that very little is being done to effectively tackle the problem (see James, 2009). Indeed, the only current method of challenging this unlawful behaviour is through individual legal action—a means of legal enforcement that has always been flawed (see Dickens, 2012) but which, as will be highlighted below, has been severely restricted as a result of recent measures. In the remainder of this section we demonstrate how an already fragile system for enforcing employment law rights and protections is now severely flawed, making it incredibly difficult for this group of claimants to access justice following pregnancy and maternity related discrimination. Tens of thousands of women annually experience pregnancy or maternity related discrimination, and in what follows we discuss three key ways in which austerity-focussed reforms have detrimentally affected their ability to pursue a legal action against offending employers.

First, certain funding cuts have made it very difficult for any claimants to access legal advice when they suspect that their treatment at work is unlawful. The availability of free legal advice for employment related disputes has always been precarious, but cuts to advisory services and the abolition of nearly all civil legal aid in 2013 has crippled the system. Approximately £320 million was cut from the legal aid budget, with further cuts, of approximately £220 million annually, planned until 2018 (Bowcott, 2013; Legal Aid, Sentencing and Punishment of Offenders Act, 2013). The EHRC, an important provider of information and advice for claimants who have suffered discrimination, has had its budget cut from £70 million to £17.1 million, and many providers of free legal advice are closed or struggling to stay open and /or meet demand (Bowcott, 2013). At Maternity Action, a charity, "demand for telephone advice consistently outstrips . . . capacity" (Maternity Action, 2012: 4).

The importance of legal advice at this initial stage is beyond doubt. It is key in helping individuals navigate the law to determine whether their personal experience might have some resolution in law (see McDermont and Busby, 2012). For claimants who are pregnant or have recently given birth and are therefore caring for a newborn, it can mean the difference between raising grievances and accessing justice or not. In addition, legal advice can help an individual to understand the true scope of her claim—for example, including a claim for unfair dismissal where relevant (see James, 2009).

The second hurdle that these claimants now face, as a result of recent measures introduced by the Coalition government to reduce the number of claims being taken to employment tribunals, is compulsory early Advisory, Conciliation and Arbitration Society (ACAS) conciliation. Since May 2014, all potential claimants are required to notify the ACAS of any disputes and, having done so, will be contacted by a conciliation officer whose primary role is to "act as broker" (see Dickens, 2012: 37), rather than advisor, and to help the parties resolve the dispute and agree to a binding settlement where relevant, without going to tribunal. Time limits for bringing claims to tribunals are paused for a calendar month in the first instance and a further 14 days if both parties consent. Only if no settlement can be reached will a certificate be issued allowing a claim to be lodged at tribunal.

During the first year of operation, 83,000 cases were dealt with by early conciliation and 63% of these did not proceed to tribunal—and of those that did, the majority of cases were settled prior to full tribunal hearing (ACAS, 2015). In many ways, this new procedure is fulfilling its mandate and keeping the tribunal's case load down. However, the process is fairly formal and its ability to deliver an effective service to individuals has been questioned (McDermont and Busby, 2012). In addition, it elongates the timeframe and, for those claimants who are pregnant or have recently given birth, can present an additional stress, especially as they will receive no support from ACAS in terms of evaluating or articulating their claim within the legal framework. Interestingly, research suggests that claimants spend an average of 27 hours on the dispute (ACAS, 2015): a considerable time commitment for most claimants, but a potentially mammoth undertaking for women with newborn babies. It is ironic that the law insists that a woman take two weeks compulsory maternity leave for health and safety reasons (ERA, 1996: S.72), yet we remain 'blind' to the potential impact of childbirth and care-giving upon *her* ability to access justice in this context. As discussed elsewhere, the process was not designed with pregnant and new mothers in mind, which epitomises their invisibility in this context,

the very act of treating these claimants as though they are the same as all other claimants privileges an assimilation model that has proved to be inadequate in terms of the standards we set through legislation relating to pregnancy. Yet it is, oddly, considered an acceptable approach in terms of the mechanics of the law.

(James, 2009: 101; see also James, 2007)

The third measure to severely hamper potential claimants' ability to access justice was also introduced under the Coalition government. In 2013, employment tribunal fees were introduced, designed to reduce the number of vexatious claims that were thought to be overburdening the tribunal system (although no sound evidence was ever presented to support this claim) and to remove the cost burden 'from hardworking taxpayers' (Shailesh Vara, Justice Minister, quoted in 'Employment tribunal fees a 'victory' for worst employers', *Financial Times*, 28th July 2014). The level of fee is determined by the type of claim: Type A claims are the fairly straight forward cases and require an issue fee of £160 and a hearing fee, if needed, of £230. Type B claims are the more complex cases and impose an issue fee of £250 and a hearing fee of £950. If, in due course, the claimant wants to appeal the decision a further fee of £400 is charged to lodge the case at the Employment Appeal Tribunal (EAT) and an additional £1,200 is charged for the hearing (Employment Appeal Tribunal Fees Order 2013 SI2013/1893). The fees apply to all claimants unless they qualify for remission, which analysis suggests very few households do (TUC, 2013 cited in Dunstan, 2013: 10).

Evidence suggests that a large number of claimants are, since the introduction of fees, unwilling to register an action at an employment tribunal. There was a 79% drop in the number of applications lodged from October to December 2013, compared with the same period in 2012 (Ministry of Justice, 2014) and there has been a gradual ongoing reduction ever since (ACAS, 2015 and Ministry of Justice, 2015). Interestingly, within a year of the introduction in July 2013 of employment tribunal fees for claimants, sex discrimination claims had fallen by 91%. Recent ACAS research found that 45% of claimants whose cases did not result in a settlement decided against submitting a claim to an employment tribunal and 26% of those stated that fees were the reason for not doing so (ACAS, 2015).

When these fees are placed in the context of a significant rise in the cost of living, widespread pay freezes, cuts to social security benefits (such as child benefit) and plans for further significant cuts to welfare expenditure, the decline in tribunal claims is unsurprising. As the Chief executive of the Citizen's Advice Bureau (CAB), Gillian Guy, put it when calling on the government to review its policy on tribunal fees,

the risk of not being paid, even if successful, means for many the employment tribunal is just not an option. The cost of a case can sometimes be more than the award achieved and people can't afford to fight on principle any more.

(Gentleman, 2014)

For a potential claimant discriminated against because of pregnancy or maternity leave, the fees are an even greater deterrent as she faces additional costs associated with a new baby, including baby merchandise, the prospect of leave without pay and concerns about future employment and childcare costs (in relation to the latter, see Family and Childcare Trust, 2015). Indeed, as highlighted by Maternity Action during initial consultations, the fees impact on the number seeking redress through the tribunal system—a number which is already very low—but also significantly reduces the deterrent effect of the law which could result in increased incidence of discrimination (Maternity Action, 2012).

Overall, these recent modifications to the dispute resolution system have had a huge impact on all those who face disputes at work and the impact on pregnant and new mothers at work is specific to them. Very few women who experience pregnancy- and maternity-related discrimination at work actually pursue a legal action. According to 2005 research, about 71% of those who experience problems of this nature at work take no action (formal or informal) at all (EOC, 2005). Whilst we ought not to assume that litigation is necessarily the best or most rational route for all women who experience discrimination, especially given the potential stress and financial implications, it is fundamentally important that we provide these women with a realistic means of legal redress and begin to research and address the reasons and rationale for this 'litigation gap' (James, 2009). In 2005, the EOC inquiry concluded that

> The current law protecting pregnant women and women who have been pregnant operates remedially. A woman who is wronged by any failure to comply with the law must take enforcement action. The majority do nothing. No government or other body intervenes on a woman's behalf and there is currently no duty upon employers to demonstrate compliance with the law. There is therefore little incentive for employers to comply with the law and little deterrent for them not to comply. As a result most pregnancy discrimination is going unchallenged and unmonitored.
>
> (EOC, 2005: 91)

Ten years later, we are still failing to adequately support the growing number of women who are treated unlawfully at this critical point in their life-course. The impact on worker/carers is significant, as illegal workplace practices and behaviour are no longer subject to the requisite degree of scrutiny and too often go unchallenged and unpunished, enabling and encouraging bad practice to flourish.

Informal Care Provision and Women's Employment

The difficulties outlined above in relation to the assertion of what are, after all, statutory rights, are not confined to the period preceding and following childbirth. Most women continue to provide unpaid care far beyond the years of childbearing. Many move from one care commitment to another, from caring for children to caring for elders, and women's paid work experience is profoundly affected by this 'second shift' (Hochschild and Machung, 1989). It is estimated that over 6.5 million people currently provide care for adults who are ill, frail or disabled, and that figure is predicted to rise substantially in coming years (Carers UK, 2012; James and Spruce, 2015). Women are more likely than men to be carers for elderly dependants and more likely to be dual-carers, caring for their children and elderly dependants (Agree et al., 2003). Women more often provide such care at the point in their life course when it "is likely to have the most significant impact on their careers and earning power" (Carers UK, 2013: 57). As a result of their disproportionate share of care commitments, women are far more likely than men to be reliant on the welfare state, whether they are 'in work' (i.e. paid employment) or not, so that state intervention has been central in improving women's lives on their own terms and, in this respect, has been identified as a "key plank of second wave feminism" (Conley, 2012: 16). However, the advent of the austerity agenda in 2010 has seen a whole raft of supportive measures swept away by the incoming tide of budget cuts based on the 'cut fast, cut deep' approach to fiscal management, which favours disinvestment by the state over revenue raising through taxation.

Following the general election in 2010, the Coalition Government's Emergency Budget claimed that deficit reduction would be achieved at a ratio of 77:23, that is, roughly 77% through cuts in spending and 23% through higher taxes (Osborne, 2010). However, subsequent analysis by the Institute of Fiscal Studies (IFS) calculated that by 2013 the ratio was actually 85:15 in favour of cuts (Paul Johnson, Director of the IFS quoted in 'IFS analysis of spending review highlights tax shortfall', the Guardian 27th June 2013). The Coalition's strategy has required large-scale cuts to social security and tax credits as well as to public service provision. Evidence, drawn from a range of sources, has shown that the cumulative impact of this strategy has been detrimental to gender equality in terms of income, services and jobs (Institute of Fiscal Studies, 2011; Women's Budget Group, 2011; House of Commons' Library, 2013).

The effects of such an approach to deficit reduction have been particularly harsh for those women who have, or have had, high levels of care commitments, such as lone mothers or single female pensioners. Since June 2010, the House of Commons Library has calculated the source of Treasury revenue both from cuts in expenditure and changes in direct taxation. This analysis, which highlights the impact of each measure on an individual's income and then calculates the gender split of that measure, has consistently found that around three-quarters of Treasury income comes from women, despite the fact that their incomes tend to be lower than men's. By the 2013 Budget, this data showed that, since 2010, a total of

£11,454m (79%) had been raised from women, compared with £2,956m (21%) from men (House of Commons' Library, 2013).

The Women's Budget Group has analysed how the changes to indirect taxation have affected the incomes of different types of households as a proportion of their income, finding that increasing VAT had a particularly harsh effect on the incomes of lone mothers, workless households with children and women living on their own. An interesting comparison can be drawn between this policy and the Chancellor's fuel duty tax giveaway, which benefited single men and households with male earners the most, and women lone parents and single female pensioners the least (Women's Budget Group, 2011). Tax (break) incentives have little impact on women's lives, as nearly 4 million people earn too little to pay tax, 73% of whom are women (Women's Budget Group, 2011: 3). Research by the IFS, commissioned by the Fawcett Society, analysed and projected the cumulative impact of tax and benefits changes between 2010–11 and 2014–15, finding that lone mothers are set to lose the most as a proportion of their net income when compared with all other types of household (Institute of Fiscal Studies, 2011).

While there is no suggestion that worker/carers are necessarily the intended targets of the austerity cuts, the particular ideology on which the current strategy is founded is worthy of consideration. As outlined at the start of this chapter, labour law's failure to acknowledge unpaid care provision as 'work' has left it outside of the law and policy framework. As well as leaving many worker/carers without adequate employment protection, this exclusion has resulted in a lack of recognition of the contribution made by such labour, which goes far beyond the immediate recipient of care, as it is also of undeniable benefit to employers, the state and society as a whole. Employers benefit directly because, for every (male) worker who is able to comply with the normative paradigm of the unencumbered worker, there is likely to be one or more (female) carers providing varying degrees of support for children, elders and others. The state benefits in obvious ways through the sharing of the 'burden' of care, by which the free labour provided enables resources to be allocated elsewhere. In fact, it can be argued that, without the effort expended by carers in nurturing and supporting others, capitalism would founder (Busby, 2011). The benefits to society are, thus, manifold as, through the giving of their time, and emotional and physical support, carers make an intrinsic and critical contribution to the very fibre of what binds individuals together (Herring, 2013). However, rather than being recognised as an asset, the sense of solidarity and interconnectedness that lies at the heart of the care relationship poses the greatest threat to any sustained state support for worker/carers. This is because of the general shift away from what is deemed to be state dependency towards a greater emphasis on the free market as provider. Neo-liberalism's focus on individual autonomy is detrimental to care relationships and the mechanisms and frameworks that support them. Although by no means a new development, the high value attributed to individualism has been fast-tracked by the austerity agenda.

The provision of care is often dependent on the existence of a personal relationship, or affective dimension by which we are all bound together in mutual ties of love and affection (Kittay, 1999). This personal requirement makes care impossible to commodify so that it is difficult to place within a market structure. However, care also entails a task-centred approach encompassing less profound, more mundane but equally crucial and demanding 'body work', which incorporates the cleaning, the feeding, the assistance with bodily functions and the administration of medication (Stewart, 2013). This work is crucial but is grossly undervalued even where it *is* performed in return for payment (Pennycook, 2013). Even without austerity, it is women who disproportionately bear the costs of care, be it through the 'motherhood penalty', which results in lower earnings and reduced job security throughout pregnancy and beyond, through the precariousness of paid work and consequent impacts on individual WLB in employment, or through the likelihood of living—and supporting others—in poverty due to gendered pay gaps or reduced pension entitlement in old age. It is revealing that the exponential growth of the paid care sector in recent years has not been accompanied by an improvement in pay and other conditions for care workers who continue to be among the most precarious workers in the UK and elsewhere (Pennycook, 2013). That the majority of such workers are female migrants is, perhaps, unsurprising but this fact also points to a number of interrelated solutions, which will be set out in the concluding section.

Conclusions

This chapter has explored the impact of austerity policies on work/care relationships. As our analysis has shown, the provision of unpaid care exacts a high price from women throughout their working lives, from experiences of pregnancy discrimination and the motherhood penalty through to retirement with many poorly served by length of service-based or final salary pension arrangements. Such experiences pre-date the current austerity agenda but recent policy choices have undoubtedly led to a reduction in the levels of employment protection available as well as in other areas of state support with negative impacts on WLB.

In closing, we offer some suggested solutions to the individual problems outlined here, which together provide an alternative strategy to the current austerity agenda. These proposals offer an alternative feminist response capable of guarding against the reversal of gains made in gender equality on the grounds of political ideology. They do this by challenging the notion of 'austerity', at least in its current conceptualisation which characterises those who depend on state support (in its various guises) as a means of providing for themselves and their dependents as somehow irresponsible and/or feckless and thus part of a 'problem' that needs to be eradicated (Busby, 2014).

The first and most important solution is a general recognition of the social benefits and economic contribution of care-giving, whether it is paid for or unpaid and provided alongside paid work or not. As well as being accompanied by a comprehensive system of publicly funded and affordable childcare and other types of respite suited to the needs of carers and recipients, such recognition should be supported by accessible statutory rights which can be effectively enforced. As the consideration of pregnancy and maternity has shown, without access to justice, bad employment practices, including discrimination, flourish. However, legal solutions which aim to compensate victims for the effects of such practices are not enough. In isolation, such redress does nothing to challenge the root causes of inequality and neither does it help to 'normalise' the personal characteristic or condition underlying the disadvantage (Busby, 2013). Alongside its traditional reactive approach, law should act as an agenda-setter, capable of challenging stereotyping and stigma by establishing and supporting alternative normative behaviours. In order to achieve this in the current context, gender equality and access to justice must be guaranteed rather than open to the threat of future political expediency.

Furthermore, the currently dormant provisions of the Equality Act outlined at the start of this chapter should be enacted and the rationale which originally underpinned the development of the Act (Hepple, 2015) reasserted and extended so as to provide a focus on the achievement of equality of results rather than opportunities. Such an approach would recognise the historical disadvantage suffered by women carers and the persistent and pernicious effects of this on employment and other life experiences. The impact of the cumulative effect of a range of personal characteristics on women's lived experiences should be addressed and, rather than the narrow focus on dual discrimination originally provided by the Act, the concept should be broadened out to encompass the concept of intersectionality. All policies aimed at reducing state involvement in social provision should be gender impact-assessed and alternative measures taken where necessary. Finally, and crucially, employers and the state must take whatever measures are necessary to achieve a shift away from women's current position as the primary providers of care towards a more equal allocation of responsibility so that men are encouraged and enabled to share equally in shouldering the burdens and reaping the benefits of care-giving.

References

ACAS. (2015). *Research Paper: Evaluation of Early ACAS Conciliation 2015*, available at http://www.acas.org.uk/media/pdf/5/4/Evaluation-of-Acas-Early-Conciliation-2015.pdf

Agree, E., Bissett, B., & Rendall, M. (2003). Simultaneous care for parents and care for children amongst midlife British women and men. *Population Trends*, 112(2): 29–35.

Bowcott, O. (2013). Cash-strapped law centres turn clients away as legal aid cuts bite. *The Guardian*, 18th September 2013, available at http://www.theguardian.com/law/2013/sep/18/law-centres-clients-legal-aid

Busby, N. (2011). *A Right to Care: Unpaid Care Work in European Employment Law*. Oxford: OUP.

Busby, N. (2013). Labour law, family law and care: A plea for convergence. In J. Wallbank & J. Herring (eds) *Vulnerabilities, Care and Family Law*: 181–198. Oxford: Routledge.

Busby, N. (2014). Unpaid care, paid work and austerity: A research note. *Feminists@ Law*, 4(1): 1–12.

Busby, N., & James, G. (2016). Regulating working families in the European Union: A history of disjointed strategies. *Journal of Social, Welfare and Family Law*, 37(3): 295–308.

Caracciolo Di Torella, E., & Masselot, A. (2001). The ECJ case law on issues related to pregnancy and maternity: An attempt of classification. *European Law Review*, 26(3): 239–260.

Carers UK. (2012). *Facts about Carers 2012*. London: Carers UK, available at http://www.carersuk.org/media/k2/attachments/Facts_about_carers_Dec_2012.pdf

Carers UK. (2013). *Carers and Family Finances Inquiry*. London: Carers UK.

Conley, H. (2012). Economic crisis, austerity and gender equality—the UK case. *European Gender Equality Law Review*, 2: 14–19.

Crenshaw, K. (1991). Mapping the margins: Intersectionality, identity politics, and violence against women of color. *Stanford Law Review*, 43(6): 1241–1299.

Dickens, L. (ed). (2012). *Making Employment Rights More Effective: Issues of Enforcement and Compliance*. Oxford: Hart Publishing.

Dunstan, R. (2013). *Overdue: A Plan of Action to Tackle Pregnancy Discrimination Now*. Maternity Action, available at http://www.maternityaction.org.uk/wp/wp-content/uploads/2013/12/Overdue.pdf

EHRC/BIS. (2015). *Pregnancy and Maternity-Related Discrimination and Disadvantage First Findings: Surveys of Employers and Mothers*. BIS Research Paper No. 235, available at https://www.gov.uk/government/uploads/system/uploads/attachment_data/file/448162/BIS-15–447-pregnancy-and-maternity-related-discrimination-and-disadvantage.pdf

The Employment Rights Act 1996. http://www.legislation.gov.uk/ukpga/1996/18/contents

EOC. (2005). *Greater Expectations: Final Report of the EOC's Investigation into Discrimination Against New and Expectant Mothers in the Workplace*. Manchester: EOC, available at http://www.maternityaction.org.uk/wp/wp-content/uploads/2013/09/eocpregnancydiscrimgreaterexpectations.pdf

Family and Childcare Trust. (2015). *Childcare Cost Survey 2015*, available at http://www.familyandchildcaretrust.org/childcare-cost-survey-2015

Fudge, J. (2013). From women and labour to putting gender and law to work. In M. Davies & V. Munro (eds) *The Ashgate Research Companion to Feminist Legal Theory*: 321–329. Farnham: Ashgate.

Fudge, J. (2016). A new vocabulary and imaginary for labour law: Taking legal constitution, gender, and social reproduction seriously. In D. Brodie, N. Busby & R. Zahn (eds) *The Future Regulation of Work*: 9–26. London: Palgrave Macmillan.

Gentleman, A. (2014). Priced out of court: Why workers can't fight employment tribunals. *The Guardian*, Sunday 17th August 2014.

Hepple, B. (2015). *Equality: The New Legal Framework* (2nd Ed.). Oxford: Hart.

Herring, J. (2013). *Carers and the Law*. Oxford: Hart.

HM Treasury. (2011). *Plan for Growth*, available at https://www.gov.uk/govern ment/uploads/system/uploads/attachment_data/file/221514/2011budget_growth. pdf

Hochschild, A., & Machung, A. (1989). *The Second Shift: Working Families and the Revolution at Home*. New York: Penguin.

House of Commons' Library. (2013). *Estimating the Costs of Tax and Benefit Changes by Gender*, 19th November 2013.

The Institute of Fiscal Studies. (2011). *The Impact of Tax and Benefit Reforms by Sex: Some Simple Analysis*, available at http://www.ifs.org.uk/bns/bn118.pdf

James, G. (2007). Law's response to pregnancy/workplace conflicts: A critique. *Feminist Legal Studies*, 15(2): 167–188.

James, G. (2009). *The Legal Regulation of Pregnancy and Parenting in the Workplace*. London: Routledge.

James, G. and Spruce, E. (2015). Workers with elderly dependants: Employment law's response to the latest care-giving conundrum. *Legal Studies: The Journal of the Society of Legal Scholars*, 35(3): 463–479.

Kittay, E.F. (1999). *Love's Labor, Essays on Women, Equality and Dependency*. New York: Routledge.

The Legal Aid, Sentencing and Punishment of Offenders Act 2013. http://www. legislation.gov.uk/ukpga/2012/10/contents/enacted

Maternity Action. (2012). *Maternity Action Response to the Ministry of Justice Consultation CP22/2011 Charging fees in Employment Tribunals and Employment Appeal Tribunals*, available at http://www.maternityaction.org.uk/sitebuildercon tent/sitebuilderfiles/maternityactiontribfees2012.pdf

May, T. (2010). *Equality Strategy Speech*, available at https://www.gov.uk/gov ernment/speeches/theresa-mays-equality-strategy-speech Accessed 20th August 2015.

McDermont, M., & Busby, N. (2012). Workers, marginalised voices and the employment tribunal system: Some preliminary findings. *Industrial Law Journal*, 41(2): 166–184.

McGlynn, C. (2001). European Union family values: Ideologies of 'family' and 'motherhood' in European Union law. *Social Politics*, 8(3): 325–351.

Ministry of Justice. (March 2014). *Tribunal Statistics Quarterly: October to December 2013*, available at https://www.gov.uk/government/uploads/system/uploads/ attachment_data/file/289342/tribunal-stats-oct-dec-2013.pdf

Ministry of Justice. (June 2015). *Tribunal and Gender Recognition Statistics Quarterly*, available at https://www.gov.uk/government/uploads/system/uploads/attachment_ data/file/434176/tribunal-gender-statistics-jan-mar-2015.pdf

Mitchell, G. (2015). Encouraging fathers to care: The Children and Families Act 2014 and shared parental leave. *Industrial Law Journal*, 44(1): 123–133.

Osborne, G. (2010). *Emergency Budget Statement*, 22nd June 2010, available at http:// www.publications.parliament.uk/pa/cm201011/cmhansrd/cm100622/debtext/ 100622-0004.htm#10062245000001

Pennycook, J. (2013). *Does It Pay to Care? Under-payment of the National Minimum Wage in the Social Care Sector*. London: Resolution Foundation.

Rubery, J., & Rafferty, A. (2013). Women and recession revisited. *Work, Employment and Society*, 27(3): 414–432.

Stewart, A. (2013). Legal constructions of body work. In C. Wolkowitz, R. Cohen, T. Sanders, & K. Hardy (eds) *Body/Sex/Work: Intimate, Embodied and Sexualised Labour: Critical Perspectives on Work and Employment*: 61–76. Basingstoke: Palgrave Macmillan.

Trades Union Congress (TUC) (2013). *At What price Justice? The Impact of Employment Tribunal Fees*. London: TUC.

Women's Budget Group. (2011). *The Impact on Women of the Budget 2011*, available at http://www.wbg.org.uk/index_7_282363355.pdf

6 Trade Unions and Work–Life Balance

The Impact of the Great Recession in France and the UK

Susan Milner

Work–life balance (WLB) relates to working time flexibility, support for childcare, and formal leave policies for parents and stands at the heart of changes in the nature and regulation of employment at all levels, within the workplace and beyond (Moen, 2011). In particular, its close relationship with the regulation of working time makes it a key issue for employment relations. Advocacy of WLB by employers (individually and collectively) and trade unions has been found to be effective in establishing workplace provision and influencing governments to take supportive measures (Hein, 2005). Such advocacy responds to employers' interests by helping to increase employee engagement, reduce absenteeism, and retain skilled workers; it also fits unions' need to recruit new members and promote an equality agenda: a triple agenda of supporting employee WLB, workplace effectiveness and social justice. Consequently, collective bargaining between employers and employee representatives has been actively promoted as a tool for innovation in WLB policy and practice (EU, 2008; Tiraboschi and Caragnano, 2013).

However, collective bargaining on WLB has been slow to develop in many countries, and its extent and effectiveness vary markedly across countries. Moreover, the economic crisis since 2008 has had the general effect of weakening collective bargaining as a way of regulating workplace employment relations and reducing the proportion of employees covered by it. On average, the proportion of employees covered by collective bargaining fell by an average of 4.5% between 2008 and 2013, across 48 countries where comparable figures were available (Visser et al., 2015). However, whilst the extent of bargaining as a way of determining wages has undoubtedly been reduced since the onset of economic crisis, it has been suggested that its role in establishing WLB measures and regulating working time may have increased, perhaps as a way of compensating for lower wages or as a way of saving jobs (OECD, 2012; Weiler, 2013). In other words, whilst the quantity of agreements may have dropped, qualitative changes in the nature of bargaining may favour the development of agreements on WLB issues.

In order to assess the impact of the economic crisis on trade unions and collective bargaining on WLB, this chapter examines two country case studies, France and the UK, which were previously studied comparatively in the pre-crisis period (Gregory and Milner, 2009a). Both countries share similarities in terms of size and economic power, are highly open to international trade and investment and suffered heavily in the financial crisis, but present contrasting institutional features and are therefore classed as different social and employment regime types (Gallie, 2011; Boje and Ernaes, 2012). Comparing these two countries therefore allows us to identify key drivers of change since 2008.

Economic Crisis, Employment and Labour Market Change in France and the UK

In France, the early recession in late 2008 was shallower than in Germany and other Eurozone countries, and the economy recovered in 2010, but fell back into recession in 2013. At the same time, the French state contracted less than many other Eurozone countries, with governments rhetorically rejecting austerity policies whilst practising policies aimed at reducing public sector employment. Governments of both right and left resisted wholesale cuts to welfare, apart from pension reform, with spending on health and family benefits remaining relatively high by OECD standards.

Women's employment rate continued to rise in France, even during the economic downturn, partly linked to increased part-time working (Eurostat, 2015a, b; Minni, 2015). Part-time working is not generally seen in France as a WLB measure but as a form of employer-led flexibility, which is likely to trap women in low-paid, insecure employment. For this reason, it has been criticised by trade unions, who prefer reduced full-time working hours.

The 2008–2009 recession had the effect of reducing disparities between men and women at the lower end of the scale as more men saw their working time, including overtime, cut, and their pay squeezed: in the private sector, the discrepancy in working hours between men and women dropped from 16% to 13% between 2008 and 2010, and the gender pay gap fell from 35% to 28% (Morin and Remila, 2013). However, the overall gender pay gap has remained roughly stable over the last decade or so, at 15.1% in 2013, with a rise in 2007–2008, after which it reverted to previous levels (Eurostat, 2015c), indicating persistent vertical and horizontal segregation and a strong motherhood penalty. Nevertheless, the motherhood penalty has less impact in France than in the UK for the second and third child, due to higher levels of public investment in childcare and stronger workplace rights, leading to higher proportions of female full-time rather than part-time employment (Grimshaw and Rubery, 2015).

Since the financial crisis, concerns about changes in working time linked to the weakening of the 35-hour-week legislation have been expressed by trade unions. Unions representing professional and management staff report longer working hours without reference to weekly limits and consequent deterioration of WLB (Ugict-CGT, 2012, 2015). Perceptions of job insecurity and work intensification have grown in France since 2008, particularly in the public sector. Labour market changes since 2008 have therefore accentuated existing pressures on WLB, particularly for women who continue to carry a disproportionate double burden of paid and unpaid work. An Ipsos survey carried out for *Elle* magazine in 2015 indicated that the proportion of French women finding it difficult to achieve WLB in their workplace was increasing year on year, as was the proportion claiming they had to forego promotion for childcare reasons (Ipsos, 2015).

In the British case, recession in 2008–2009 and then, less severely, in 2011–2012 was coupled with austerity, particularly after 2010. By the end of 2013, the economy displayed signs of recovery which lasted into 2015, but the rate of growth then started to show signs of fragility. Meanwhile, as in France, public debt continued to rise, from a rather lower starting point: gross government debt increased from 51.8% of GDP in 2008 (68.1% in France) to 76.4% in 2010, 85.8% in 2012 and 89.4% in 2014 (compared to 95% in France) (Eurostat, 2015d), despite the most severe public spending cuts of any European country after 2010. Based on government spending review data, the public services union Unison (2014) estimated that £11.3 billion had been cut from government grants to local councils, and that 250,000 women's jobs had been lost in local government.

Although unemployment did not rise as much as in previous recessions, feelings of job insecurity rose, pay was squeezed, and job intensification and stress increased, particularly for women (Gallie et al., 2012). Women's employment rate has been above the EU average for some time, standing at 76.2% at the end of 2014 (for 20–64 year olds) (Eurostat, 2015a). However, as in France, the rate of increase in the female employment rate slowed down after 2008 (Penfold and Foxton, 2015) and under-employment has risen (Rubery and Rafferty, 2013; TUC, 2015a).

Unlike in France, part-time employment constitutes an important means of achieving worklife balance in the dominant British 'modified male bread-winner model' (Crompton et al., 2007). After 2008, the relatively high proportion of women working part-time remained roughly stable and now constitutes 25.3% of total employment (Eurostat, 2015b). The gender pay gap remains stubborn, although it has been falling slowly but steadily since 1997. For full-time employees it fell to 9.4% in 2014 but stands at 19.1% overall, the sixth largest gender pay gap in the EU (Eurostat, 2015c).

A high level of female part-time working reflects a gendered pattern of polarised working time, which sees full-time-employed fathers working among the longest hours in the EU (Cabrita and Galli da Bino, 2013; Cabrita 2015). The Trades Union Congress (TUC) reports that the number of people working excessive hours (over 48 per week) has risen by 15% since 2010, with workers in education, health and social work, mining and quarrying, accommodation and food services and information technologies particularly affected (TUC, 2015b).

Casualisation has come to the forefront of trade union campaigns. According to government statistics which may under-estimate the scale of the practices, around one in ten employees are agency workers (1.5 million) or work on zero-hours contracts (1.4 million). A survey of members of the shopworkers' union Usdaw highlighted the increased financial insecurity and accelerating erosion of time autonomy experienced by retail employees since 2008, in a sector which is among the most prolific users of zero-hours contracts. The report claims that since 2008, employers are more likely to expect employees to make adjustments to their caring responsibilities in order to be available for paid employment, rather than the other way round (Usdaw, 2015: 19; see also TUC, 2015a).

More generally, as in France, surveys indicate increased difficulties of combining work and family after 2008, with negative impacts for businesses as well as employees. The proportion of British employees feeling that their WLB is unhealthily skewed towards work has risen steadily (Hay, 2015; Working Families/Bright Horizons, 2015).

Trade Unions and the Impact of Crisis in France and the UK

WLB policies and practices result from a variety of pressures, which are common across developed economies but shaped by contextually specific institutional, social, political and economic forces (Lewis et al., 2008; Mätzke and Ostner, 2010; Den Dulk et al., 2012). Regarding the role of trade unions in WLB, three interlinked sets of factors have been identified as comprising the opportunity structure in which they operate: increasing proportions of women within union membership; the policy environment and the role of the state; and formal and informal institutions of employment relations (Gregory and Milner, 2009a; Ravenswood and Markey, 2011; Williamson, 2012).[1]

Increased Female Union Membership

Early research in this field focused on the gender of union leaders and negotiators or what Briskin (2006, 2014) termed 'bargaining equity': it argued, based on the experience of women campaigning within unions, that WLB and other related issues would not come to the forefront of union agendas while their leadership, policy-making and negotiation structures remained predominantly male. Of course, employer associations are also gendered organisations and their leadership structures are at least as male-dominated as those of trade unions, if not more so (Guichet, 2015). However, more attention has been paid to trade unions because of a discrepancy between the ideology of gender equality underpinning their policy and action and the gender imbalance in leadership structures (Gombrell-McCormick and Hyman, 2013). Change in European countries is slow (Briskin, 2014), but there are signs of change due to increased female membership and specific measures such as quotas and training (ETUC, 2014).

In the UK, the proportion of women members is rising, and since 2010 they form the majority, as union density has fallen more sharply for men than for women (BIS, 2015: 7). In France, however, women still account for fewer than half of union members, in a country with exceptionally low union density (estimated at around 8% overall, and 7.5% for women). In both countries, the main confederations and some federations, particularly those representing the public sector and sectors with large female work-forces, have adopted formal parity policies which, particularly since 2000, have been implemented more vigorously than previously (Heery and Nash, 2011; Milner and Gregory, 2014; Guichet, 2015). It is expected, therefore, that WLB issues will gradually achieve greater prominence in both coun-tries, although more slowly in France than in the UK.

The Policy Environment and the Role of the State

Trade unions act on different levels, depending on the opportunities that are open to them within the workplace, at a sectoral level and at a national level (Den Dulk et al., 2014). A key component of the opportunity structure is the public policy environment and the WLB benefits it offers to employees in the form of welfare, family support and protective measures such as organisa-tion and limitation of working time. If unions have the opportunity to lobby governments to provide such benefits, they are likely to focus on activity at the national level. If such lobbying opportunities are closed to unions, they may seek to win members by providing similar types of benefits themselves or pushing employers to provide them at the company level (Ewing, 2005). Due to their weakness at the company level, French trade unions have tradi-tionally chosen to exert influence over national policy. British unions, on the other hand, have prioritised workplace action and indeed, in the context of decreased policy influence after 1979, have oriented their renewal strategies to grassroots organising, as well as community campaigning (Wright, 2011).

In the British case, WLB policy—whilst broadly influenced by EU initiatives—has assumed its own path, with a prominent emphasis on choice and flexibility (see Milner, 2010). The dominant approach since the 1990s has been to extend employees' right to request flexible working and to encourage parents to share leave, whilst retaining weak financial incen-tives for them to do so. In this respect, the Conservative–Liberal Democrat coalition government (2010–2015) not only continued but expanded previ-ous Labour policy. However, the low rate of statutory leave pay limits the take-up. The TUC, which had joined with leading family campaign chari-ties to lobby successfully for the extension of the right to request flexible working, therefore argues that accessing rights in the current economic cli-mate will be increasingly difficult (TUC, 2014a). The discrepancy between a policy discourse of flexibility and the reality of relatively low availability of employer-friendly flexibility, compared to other European countries (see Vargas and Boehmer, 2015), suggests that the 'agency gap' (Hobson, 2011) may be widening in the UK.

Childcare has also become a focus for policy debate in the UK, as childcare costs are the highest in Europe in times of squeezed incomes (Working Families, 2015). The TUC welcomed the initiative announced by the coalition government to introduce tax credits for childcare but argued that it would help wealthier parents more than low-income families (TUC, 2014c). Noting that average costs had risen by some 30% since 2010, the 2014 TUC women's conference passed a resolution arguing that lack of affordable childcare represented the major obstacle to female employment in the UK (TUC, 2014d). Although the TUC's hopes for a Labour government to take forward its campaign on childcare were dashed in 2015, the issues of childcare and elder care remain prominent in public debate.

The policy environment in France has adopted similar discourses of choice and flexibility, although within the context of competing concerns with fertility rates and gender equality (Milner, 2010). Its distinguishing features have traditionally been a high rate of public expenditure on family policy and childcare support, generous parental leave (which has been criticised for its long duration, however, meaning that although it assists low-income households, it tends to reinforce gendered assumptions about care and contributes to further labour market disadvantage of low-income mothers), a high level of public provision for early years (3–4 years) but with gaps for younger children and geographical unevenness in coverage, average childcare costs and a relatively limited role for employers in the provision of workforce WLB measures (Adéma and Thévenon, 2008).

The period since 2008 has seen two major public policy debates in France relating to WLB, first under the centre-right Sarkozy presidency (2007–2012) and later under president Hollande's socialist administration. The first relates to working time. President Sarkozy argued that in economic crisis France could not retain the 35-hour week and, whilst stopping short of repealing the law, introduced fiscal incentives for overtime which the incoming socialist government reversed. In 2014, however, the new finance minister publicly stated that the 35-hour week damaged businesses, particularly smaller firms, in times of economic downturn, although the government also made clear that it would not repeal the law, which is popular with French voters. Instead, it encouraged a wider process of labour law reform as a way of encouraging businesses to use collective bargaining to gain more working time flexibility. An example of this is businesses' use of a 2013 law which allows them to negotiate competitiveness pacts to regain control of working time arrangements on economic grounds (see Lehndorff, 2014). In line with trends since the 1980s, working time stands at the forefront of proposed changes to protective legislation, as outlined in the controversial 2016 draft bill reforming France's labour law.

French trade unions themselves are divided in their response to these changes. The CGT not only defends the existing 35-hour-week legislation but in October 2015 launched a new campaign to reduce working time further, to 32 hours a week, as a means of creating jobs and generating productivity gains (CGT, 2015). However, the CGT is isolated in making this demand. The CFDT, the confederation which most strongly promoted the 35-hour week, now argues in favour of a different approach focused not on weekly working time limitation but on a lifecourse approach to WLB, through the use of individual time accounts. Moreover, in collective bargaining the CFDT has adopted a more flexible approach to Sunday working. Although initially all the major confederations formed a united front to challenge the draft bill on labour law reform, the CFDT indicated more willingness to negotiate with government on key points of the legislation. The changed policy environment on working time in the context of economic crisis has, therefore, sharpened divisions between unions.

The second main focus of WLB policy since 2008 is reform of parental leave. France's long parental leave was reformed in 2004 to increase benefits for the first six months in an attempt to incentivise shorter leave and thereby reduce the amount of time spent by mothers out of the labour market. In 2009, president Sarkozy announced the need to shorten parental leave and increase the benefit level, but change proved slow and by the 2012 elections he had not enacted the plan. As a way of reassuring trade unions and family associations which had protested against the proposal to cut parental leave, the Sarkozy administration pledged new funds for childcare and relaxed the rules on numbers of children per childminder or in nursery settings, but critics highlighted the shortfall in funding needed to create the promised extra places (Fagnani and Math, 2011). A Senate report in 2015 noted that the proportion of under-threes in formal childcare had fallen by two-thirds over a decade (Pellevat, 2015).

In 2014, parental leave was reformed again. The new shared child-rearing benefit came into effect from January 2015 and is available to fathers and mothers of children born or adopted after that date, for a maximum of six months if one parent takes leave or 12 months if shared equally between two parents. Parents on leave receive a flat-rate benefit of around 390 euros a month for full leave. As with the earlier reform, the government's stated intention to make the take-up of parental leave more gender-equal (97% of leave-takers are women) was interpreted by commentators as simply a way of saving money as the family benefits fund sank further into deficit (see e.g. Leclair, 2014). It is too early to assess the impact of the change, but experts expect fathers' take-up to be limited (Fagnani et al., 2015).

The CGT argues that since 2008 governments have attempted to recommodify family policy, that is, shift responsibility from the state to individual households (CGT, 2012). Instead, it campaigns for increased state spending on family policy in order to achieve high replacement rates for parental leave, and invest in childcare provision for under-threes (CGT, 2011). The CFDT also calls for better-paid parental leave, but rather than new funding it calls for resources to be switched away from family allowances for second and further children and invested instead in childcare provision (Cabanal, 2014).

In summary, this comparison of the changes in the policy environment in France and the UK since 2008 shows similar challenges and opportunities for trade unions wishing to promote WLB: decreased investment in childcare and formal support for shared parental leave, coupled with insufficient levels of replacement benefit to reverse pressures on women to withdraw from the labour market after childbirth. In addition, in the French case, the crisis has led to the erosion of working time limitation. Overall, these changes have opened up the possibilities for diversification of working time schedules within the workplace, particularly for parents, but also widened the agency gap, especially for lower-income parents, and exacerbated gendered career tracks. Although trade unions have attempted to ally themselves with family advocacy groups to lobby for increased investment in leave and childcare, they have struggled to make their voice heard. In the French context, formal opportunities for unions to influence policy through national-level bargaining exist, but these have tended to accentuate divisions between union confederations over attitudes to flexibility. As we will see below, similar divisions have also influenced local-level bargaining.

Employment Relations Institutions and Practices

Despite the rhetoric of a 'European social model', member states have always demonstrated strong differences in employment relations institutions and practices (Jepsen and Serrano Pascual, 2006). Variation increased after the 'big-bang' enlargement of 2004 and since the beginning of the economic crisis (Bechter and Brandl, 2015). The post-2008 crisis has amplified existing trends, especially decentralisation of collective bargaining, rather than ushering in new changes (Broughton and Welz, 2013).

In the UK, the sharp decline in union density and bargaining coverage seen in the 1990s slowed after 2000, down to 25% and 27.5% in 2014 (but only 16% in the private sector), respectively (BIS, 2015). Single-employer (decentralised) bargaining is the main form of bargaining in the private sector, where, according to WERS data from 2011, it covered 19% of employees; in the public sector, where pay and conditions were traditionally set through national-level bargaining, many employers have withdrawn from national bargaining (van Wanrooy et al., 2013). The UK's liberal market economy may therefore be seen as having pioneered a trend of erosion and decentralisation of collective bargaining which has become more widespread across Europe as a result of the economic crisis (Emery, 2015). Consequently, decentralisation of bargaining in the British case is not in itself likely to reduce the scope for WLB measures to be negotiated, but the diminished extent of bargaining indicates a shrinking opportunity structure.

France exhibits markedly different features, as we would expect when comparing a statist coordinated economy and a liberal market economy. There is an extremely large gap between the low level of union density (8%) and high level of bargaining coverage (98%), which is explained not just by the enduring importance of sectoral bargaining but also the state's ability and willingness to extend collective agreements across a sector or region (Visser, 2013). On paper at least, multi-employer sectoral bargaining appears to have bucked the European trend and remained stable over the last decade in terms of the number of agreements and proportion of employees covered. On the other hand, it has been accompanied by ever-greater use of single-employer (decentralised) bargaining, and the mechanisms for coordinating the two levels are weak (Bechter and Brandl, 2015). French unions are relatively recent converts to workplace bargaining and have tried to shore up sectoral bargaining as a way of protecting themselves from local-level negotiations where they are generally weaker and, they argue, there is a less developed culture of trust and compromise (Combrexelle, 2015: 41–42). Consequently, given the under-investment by unions and some companies, particularly smaller companies and those in harder to organise sectors such as construction, leisure and hotels and catering, a common criticism of collective bargaining is that is has been 'hollowed out', that is, emptied of real content by purely formal rituals designed to show legal compliance.

Rather than being driven by employers or trade unions, collective bargaining in France has above all been promoted by the state through a mixture of sanctions (binding requirements to report, subject to infringement proceedings and potential fines) and incentives (tax and social security credits for companies which negotiate). As well as a general statutory requirement to engage in bargaining (applying to all private-sector companies where a trade union representative is present, although other representatives may bargain under certain conditions) which has existed since 1982, on wages, working time and working conditions, specific measures to encourage bargaining on working time were introduced in the 1999 and 2000 Aubry laws which set a maximum weekly working time of 35 hours. The prominence of working time as a state-sponsored means of reorganising the bargaining system opened up a space for bargaining on WLB (Gregory and Milner, 2009b).

More recently, the same logic was applied to gender equality, which was defined as an area of responsibility for social partners to negotiate at sectoral and company levels. The Génisson law in 2001 established a duty on private companies to put in place measures to achieve gender equality, including primarily through collective bargaining. Lack of responsiveness to this duty, other than under threat of sanctions or in order to access financial incentives, was attributed to trade union inaction, as well as employer foot-dragging (Laufer, 2003; Le Feuvre, 2006). A 2006 law, enacted under the centre-right administration, made it mandatory for companies to bargain on gender equality, conduct a gender pay audit and put in place an action plan. In 2010, specific incentives and sanctions were introduced, the former for small companies, the latter for larger firms. Legislation on workplace equality was further strengthened by a law passed in January 2014 which, according to the largest union, the CGT, represented 'some progress', including the obligation for sectoral level bargaining to examine the gender impact of wage policies and structures, and the establishment of the first financial penalties on companies which have not put in place their gender equality plan. The government also showed its willingness to issue formal warnings and follow up with prosecutions.

Gender equality was in 2015 integrated into a wider set of requirements for companies to negotiate and provide an information database comprising indicators on employee health and well-being, under the heading of 'quality of working life', which was the subject of a national-level intersectoral agreement in 2013 (Ministère du Travail, 2013, 2015). The government argued that it offers a more systematic approach to tackling inequalities and to pursuing a triple agenda of business effectiveness, employee well-being and societal equity (Oziel, 2015). However, the approach has also been criticised by feminists who fear that 'mainstreaming' of gender could dilute employers' bargaining and reporting commitments, and the CGT union rejected the 2013 agreement as inadequate (CGT, 2013). To date, 'quality of working life' agreements remain limited to a few large companies with significant state ownership, such as Areva, Thales and La Poste (see below). In France, then, the key driver of change concerns the relationship between collective bargaining and the law.

Collective Bargaining on WLB in the Crisis

In France, employers' reluctance to provide work-family benefits, formerly identified as a characteristic of France's social policy model, has given way more recently to high-level initiatives led by large companies in the private and public sectors. In 2008, management consultant Jérôme Ballarin launched a Businesses' Charter for Working Parents, which gained the support of 500 companies, led by L'Oréal, which in 2008 became the first to sign a collective agreement based specifically on the charter and focusing on home working and adjustment of working hours to family responsibilities (L'Oréal, 2008). Annual 'barometers' of WLB in companies published by Ballarin's observatory show that the proportion of employees expressing concerns about working time WLB have been rising steadily, to 93% in 2015; however, a majority say their employer does not do enough for WLB, although the proportion has decreased, from 75% 2012 in to 61% in 2015 (OPE, 2015a). Meanwhile, 59% of employers stated that WLB was an important priority for them in 2015, up 14 points from the previous year (OPE, 2015b).

Presenting this report, the OPE drew attention to the collective agreement on quality of working life, signed in 2013 between La Poste and four trade union confederations: FO, CFDT, CGC-CFE and CFTC. The agreement, following an employee consultation exercise in 2012, focused on health and safety but included new arrangements for part-time working for older workers, and opened up further negotiations on support for working parents; the main immediately applicable measure relating to WLB was the extension of home working (La Poste, 2013). The CGT refused to sign the agreement, arguing that it did nothing to improve the quality of working life for employees or address the quality of services (FAPT-CGT, 2013). In 2015, a further agreement was signed, this time placing WLB within a gender equality perspective which also focused on recruitment and promotion. As well as promoting 'chosen' part-time work, that is, employees' right to request a change from full-time to part-time employment, subject to rosters, the agreement contains a number of employee-friendly WLB measures: the right to 'switch off' technologies at the end of the working day, the principle that meetings should be held as far as possible at times to enable parents to be able to attend easily, the principle that journeys should not be harmful to work-family arrangements of parents, particularly single parents, and special protection for mothers, parents of disabled children and single parents (La Poste, 2015). This time, the agreement was signed by all unions present, including the CGT and the 'autonomous' unions.

The defence electronics company Thales has also been conspicuously active in adopting agreements on gender equality for its French workforce, dating back to 2004 when it signed one of the first agreements following the 2001 Génisson law (see above), including rights for part-time workers and flexible calculation of hours and time off in lieu (Thales, 2004). Overall, the number of agreements dealing with gender equality has risen steadily at sectoral and especially at company level (Ministère du Travail, 2015). Agreements on gender equality have also increasingly included specific provision for WLB measures.

A study of equality agreements in 2007–2008 found that WLB measures were included only in a small minority of cases and concluded that they were 'rare' (Rabier, 2009). Six years later, a similar study noted an increase after 2011 in the number of agreements dealing with WLB, included in a third of the sample, mostly covering awareness-raising measures to encourage parents to access leave and upholding the principle of non-discrimination against part-time workers (Garner and Recoules, 2014). A further evaluation report noted in 2012 that, although 'almost all' company-level agreements now included WLB provisions, most provisions remained weak and require commitment by management to put them into practice (Brunet and Dumas, 2012). The postal workers' agreement therefore appears particularly far-reaching and innovative in its proactive approach, not just towards protecting maternity and taking parents' needs into management practice, but also in establishing the 'right to switch off' (Lapprand, 2015). The right to 'switch off' is also included as part of a fundamental right to employee WLB in the 2016 draft labour law reform bill.

In the private sector, the France Télévisions agreement on gender equality, signed in 2007, has also been singled out by unions as offering good provision for WLB. It stipulates that team meetings must be held within school hours and that if training sessions fall outside those times, employees should receive compensation to pay childcare costs (France Télévisions, 2007). However, unions have highlighted the difficulties in implementing many of the rights established in the agreement, caused by job obligations to travel and to work in the evenings (Cuny, 2011: 53). A new agreement was signed in 2014 by the CGT, CFDT, FO and the journalists' union, to include new maternity protection, recognition of the needs of single parents, the need to plan travel requirements in advance, and payment of parental leave (France Télévisions, 2014).

There has been comparatively less systematic data collection on WLB agreements in the UK, due to the absence of statutory oversight. Where data are collected, they focus primarily on wage developments and, to a lesser extent, working time (e.g. LRD, 2015). A key priority of union activity has been to bargain working time reductions in order to reduce the number of people working in excess of 48 hours and improve employee WLB (Exell, 2006), although, as noted earlier, the post-crisis period has seen this gain reversed. However, some signs of negotiated gains for employees on working time have been evident as a trade-off for low pay rises in the context of low inflation. A study of 469 pay deals after 2011 showed that longer leave entitlement, linked to qualifying periods of service, was included in around 45% of agreements (LRD, 2015: 15).

Several agreements in the 2014–2015 pay round included entitlements to make leave more flexible or to make overtime pay more flexible (LRD, 2015: 16–17). For example, at BAe Systems Submarines, bargaining resulted in the removal of a requirement for employees to take weekly blocks of annual leave (LRD, 2015: 16). The agreement must be seen in the context of an intense union campaign for jobs in a sector which has seen several site closures and mass redundancies (Waddell and Golds, 2013). A further trend identified in the 2014–2015 pay round was extensions to holiday pay linked to overtime, carried out in the previous year. As well as being driven by the need to trade increased leave (a form of employee-determined flexibility) for employer-driven flexibility through unpaid overtime, this development was encouraged by European Court of Justice rulings relating to the Working Time Directive upholding the voluntary nature of overtime (LRD, 2015: 17).

Paternity leave has also become a more frequent bargaining issue (LRD, 2015: 16). The Cooperative Banking Group increased paid paternity leave from two to a maximum of four weeks in 2014. The Unifi union (since 2004 merged into Unite the Union which signed this agreement) has been active in pursuing partnership agreements with the main high street banks, including some such as Lloyds where previously the union was not recognised (Unite, 2015). Such partnerships typically include a range of bargaining and consultation issues, including working time and rights for parents alongside pay. Union strategy predated the financial crisis (see e.g. Woolnough, 2003; Gregory and Milner, 2009a), but has intensified in the context of branch closures and mass layoffs since 2008. Elsewhere, Usborne Publishing also increased its childcare allowance paid to mothers and fathers on leave by £20 to £280 a month per child per family (LRD, 2015: 16). Again, this agreement is the latest in a series of deals reached between the Unite union and management, following an earlier settlement which raised maternity pay (Unite, 2011). Similarly, an earlier agreement with Michelin to extend paternity leave pay to ten days (Unite, 2011) was succeeded in the 2014–2015 round by an increase to two weeks at full pay (LRD, 2015: 16).

Thus, despite the economic crisis which has cast a shadow over employment relations (van Wanrooy et al., 2013; see also Stokes and Wood, Chapter 3), British unions have in some cases successfully pursued deals for their members on working time and parental leave (TUC, 2014b). Spurred on by limited changes to statutory provision which make it easy for businesses to offer more, and in some cases triggered by legal rulings on working time, some companies have been willing to trade employee-friendly flexibility and family-friendly measures for pay moderation. However, this trend still accounts for a minority of workplaces and many unions report that in hard economic times, the struggle to preserve jobs makes it harder for WLB measures to get onto the agenda (Rigby and O'Brien-Smith, 2010; TUC, 2014b).

Conclusion

We have seen in this chapter that trade unions are active in campaigning for WLB in France and the UK, surveying their members to assess the impact of economic crisis on their ability to manage their life inside and outside work, informing their members of their rights, and lobbying the government for supportive legislation, particularly around working time, the situation of low-income workers and parental leave. Partly, this agenda for union activity (still relatively new compared to their traditional role in pay bargaining, and still unevenly pursued by unions) has developed as a result of long-term internal change: increased female membership, policies to support more balanced gender representation, recruitment strategies and new approaches to partnership in the workplace or concession bargaining, which have been promoted in times of economic crisis as a way of compensating for very low wage rises or as a way of saving jobs. Partly, the union agenda has been influenced by changes in the legal and policy environment, particularly limited but still important changes to parental leave, and a policy concern with the gender pay gap.

However, unions' ability to influence policy-makers and to introduce or enforce employee rights in the workplace has been adversely affected by changes since 2008. Although in both countries the weakening of collective bargaining and more difficult conditions for recruitment of union members are longer-term trends which were more marked in earlier decades, the cumulative effect has been to reduce unions' influence in the public sphere and their leverage in negotiations with employers in harsh economic times. A key difference here relates to the institutional framework for collective bargaining in France and the UK: French unions have stronger institutional rights in the policy sphere, and collective bargaining is actively promoted by statutory obligations which the current French administration has sought to enforce by legal proceedings. As we have seen, there is evidence that collective bargaining in some large companies has been able to develop a progressive WLB agenda, which has also influenced the development of legal rights. Despite this legal protection, however, French unions are weak in the workplace outside of the largest and state-owned firms. The shift away from statutory to bargained rights is, therefore, likely to reinforce gaps in coverage between larger and smaller firms, and is currently the subject of fierce conflict between many unions and the government.

In both countries, employers' willingness to offer WLB has grown but very slowly and unevenly; in this respect, there has been some convergence of practice between the two countries. Some companies are active in improving on legislative provision, but these are mainly, although not exclusively, larger firms, concentrated in key sectors. The shift in collective bargaining towards more 'qualitative' issues such as WLB is therefore likely to leave significant sections of the workforce exposed to negative effects of the post-2008 crisis without compensatory rights, although it may also provide a space for innovation and learning.

Note

1 This opportunity structure differs somewhat from that outlined in Gregory and Milner (2009a), which placed more emphasis on trade union agency and less emphasis on external structures and institutions. The structure has been adapted following work by other authors cited in this section, which highlighted structural factors and the importance of domestic context.

References

Adéma, W., & Thévenon, O. (2008). Les politiques de conciliation du travail et de la vie familiale en France au regard des pays de l'OCDE. *Recherches et Prévisions*, 93(September): 51–72.

Bechter, B., & Brandl, B. (2015). Developments in industrial relations in European Union. In *Industrial Relations 2014*: 17–40. Brussels: European Union.

Boje, T. P. and Ernaes, A. (2012). Policy and practice: the relationship between family policy and women's labour market participation in Europe. *International Journal of Sociology and Social Policy*, 32 (9/10): 589–605.

Briskin, L. (2006). *Equity Bargaining—Bargaining Equity*. University of York, Centre for Research on Work and Society. Working Paper 2006–01. University of York, York.

Briskin, L. (2014). Strategies to support gender equality bargaining *inside* unions: Representational democracy and representational justice. *Journal of Industrial Relations*, 56(2): 208–227.

Broughton, A., & Welz, C. (2013). *Impact of the Crisis on Industrial Relations*. Dublin: European Foundation for the Improvement of Living and Working Conditions.

Brunet, S., & Dumas, M. (2012). *Bilan de l'application des dispositifs promouvant l'égalité professionnelle entre femmes et hommes*. Paris: Conseil Economique et Social.

Cabanal, J. (2014). *La politique familiale a besoin de sens et de cohérence*. Press release no. 361, 30 September. Paris: CFDT.

Cabrita, J. (2015). *Developments in Collectively Agreed Working Time, 2014*. Dublin: European Foundation for the Improvement of Living and Working Conditions.

Cabrita, J., & Galli da Bino, C. (2013). *Developments in Collectively Agreed Working Time, 2012*. Dublin: European Foundation for the Improvement of Living and Working Conditions.

Combrexelle, J.-D. (2015). *La négociation collective, le travail et l'emploi*. Paris: La Documentation Française.

Confédération Générale du Travail (CGT). (2011). *Droit à une politique familiale solidaire*. Fiche no. 24. Repères revendicatifs. Montreuil: CGT.

Confédération Générale du Travail (CGT). (2012). *La politique familiale en France*. Montreuil: CGT.

Confédération Générale du Travail (CGT). (2013). *Négociation qualite de vie au travail—égalité professionnelle*. Montreuil: CGT.

Confédération Générale du Travail (CGT). (2015). *Travailler toutes, travailler tous, travailler mieux, travailler moins*. Montreuil: CGT.

Crompton, R., Lewis, S., & Lyonette, C. (eds). (2007). *Women, Men, Work and Family in Europe*. Houndsmill, Basingstoke: Palgrave Macmillan.

Cuny, L. (2011). *Survey on the Situation of Work-life Balance in the Audiovisual and Live Performance Sectors in Eight European Countries*. Brussels: EuroFIA/ European Federation of Journalists.

Den Dulk, L., Groeneveld, S., & Peper, B. (2014). Workplace worklife balance support from a capabilities perspective. In B. Hobson (ed) *Worklife Balance: The Agency and Capabilities Gap*: 153–173. Oxford: Oxford University Press.

Den Dulk, L., Peters, P., & Poutsma, E. (2012). Variations in adoption of workplace work-family arrangements in Europe: The influence of welfare-state regime and organizational characteristics. *International Journal of Human Resource Management*, 23(13): 2785–808.

Department for Business Innovation and Skills (BIS). (2015). *Trade Union Membership 2014: Statistical Bulletin*. London: BIS.

Emery, L. (2015). Multi-employer bargaining in the UK—does it have a future? In G. Van Guys & T. Schulten (eds) *Wage Bargaining under the New European Economic Governance: Alternative Strategies for Inclusive Growth*: 221–258. Brussels: European Trade Union Institute.

European Trade Union Confederation (ETUC). (2014). *7th Annual ETUC 8 March survey*. Brussels: ETUC.

European Union (EU). (2008). *Communication from the Commission to the European Parliament, the Council, the European Economic and Social Committee and the Committee of the Regions: A Better Work-life Balance: Stronger Support*

108 *Susan Milner*

for Reconciling Professional, Private and Family Life. COM 2008/635 final, 3 October.

Eurostat. (2015a). *Employment Rates by Sex, Age Group 20–64*, available at http://ec.europa.eu/eurostat/tgm/refreshTableAction.dotab=table&plugin=1&pcode=t2020_10&language=en

Eurostat. (2015b). *Part-time Employment as a Percentage of Total Employment, by Age and Sex*, available at http://appsso.eurostat.ec.europa.eu/nui/show.do?dataset=lfsa_eppga&lang=en

Eurostat. (2015c). *Gender Pay Gap Statistics*, available at http://ec.europa.eu/eurostat/statistics-explained/index.php/Gender_pay_gap_statistics

Eurostat. (2015d). *General Government Gross Debt—Annual Data*, available at http://ec.europa.eu/eurostat/tgm/table.do?tab=table&init=1&language=en&pcode=teina225&plugin=1

Ewing, K. (2005). The function of trade unions. *Industrial Law Journal*, 34(1): 1–22.

Exell, R. (2006). Collective bargaining on working time: The UK. In M. Keune & B. Galgóczi (eds) *Collective Bargaining on Working Time: Recent European Experiences*: 273–288. Brussels: ETUI.Fagnani, J., Boyer, D., & Thévenon, O. (2015). 'France: Country report', in: P. Moss (ed.) *International Review of Leave Policies and Research*, available at http://www.leavenetwork.org/fileadmin/Leavenetwork/Country_notes/2015/france.pm.pdf

Fagnani, J., & Math, A. (2011). The predicament of childcare policy in France: What is at stake? *Journal of Contemporary European Studies*, 19(4): 547–561.

Fédération Nationale du Secteur des Activités Postales et des Télécommunications-CGT (FAPT-CGT). (2013). *Accord sur la qualité de vie au travail à la Poste. Tract*. Montreuil: CGT.

France Télévisions. (2007). *Accord groupe sur l'égalité professionnelle femmes-hommes*. Agreement available on the ORSE website: http://www.egaliteprofessionnelle.org/index.php?p=dialogue&r=accord-ent

France Télévisions. (2014). *Accord en faveur de l'égalité entre les femmes et les hommes*. Agreement available on CGT website: http://www.snrt-cgt-ftv.org/images/stories/textes/accords/140428aAccFTV.pdf

Gallie, D. (2011). *Production Regimes, Employee Job Control and Skill Development*. Centre for Learning and Life Chances in Knowledge Economies and Societies Research Paper no. 31. Institute for Education, Centre for Learning and Life Chances in Knowledge Economies and Societies, London.

Gallie, D., Felstead, A., Green, F., & Hande, I. (2012). *Fear at Work in Britain: First Findings from the Skills and Employment Survey 2012*. Cardiff: University of Cardiff/Economic and Social Research Council.

Garner, H., & Recoules, M. (2014). *Egalité, diversité, discriminations. Etude de 80 accords d'entreprise sur la diversité*. Document d'études no.182. Paris: DARES/Ministère du Travail.

Gombrell-McCormick, R., & Hyman, R. (2013). *Trade Unions in Western Europe: Hard Times, Hard Choices*. Oxford: Oxford University Press.

Gregory, A., & Milner, S. (2009b). Trade unions and work-life balance: Changing times in France and the UK? *British Journal of Industrial Relations*, 47(1): 122–146.

Grimshaw, D., & Rubery, J. (2015). *The Motherhood Pay Gap: A Review of the Issues, Theory and International Evidence*. Geneva: International Labour Organisation.

Guichet, C. (2015). *Les forces vives au féminin*. Paris: Conseil Économique, Social et Environnemental.

Hay Group. (2015). *Insight Employee Effectiveness Survey*. London: Hay Group UK.

Heery, E., & Nash, D. (2011). *Trade Unions and Collective Conciliation: A Secondary Analysis*. Research Paper No. 10–11. Acas, London.

Hein, C. (2005). *Reconciling Work and Family Responsibilities: Practical Ideas from Global Experience*. Geneve: International Labour Office.

Hobson, B. (2011). The agency gap in work-life balance: Applying Sen's capabilities framework within European contexts. *Social Politics*, 18(2): 147–167.

Ipsos. (2015). *Aide-toi et ta boîte t'aidera*!. Report for Elle magazine annual forum, 27 March, Ipsos, Paris.

Jepsen, M., & Pascual, A.S. (eds). (2006). *Unwrapping the European Social Model*. Bristol: The Policy Press.

Labour Research Department. (2015). *2014–15 Pay Round. Earnings Up—But They're Still Below 2009 Peak in Real Terms*. Labour Research, 140 (annual pay bargaining issue).

La Poste. (2013). *Accord-cadre sur la qualité au travail à la Poste*. Agreement available on the site of ANACT.

La Poste. (2015). *Accord social relatif à l'égalité professionnelle entre les femmes et les hommes à la Poste*. Agreement available on site of ORSE.

Lapprand, M. (2015). *Nouvel accord à la Poste: droit à la déconnexion*. Paris: Force Ouvrière, available at http://www.force-ouvriere.fr/a-la-poste-un-nouvel-accord-innovant-pour-l-egalite?lang=frLaufer, J. (2003). Entre égalité et inégalités: les droits des femmes dans la sphère professionnelle. *L'Année Sociologique*, 53(1): 143–173.

Leclair, A. (2014). Le congé parental pourrait être limité à 18 mois pour les mères. *Le Figaro*, 29 September, available at http://www.lefigaro.fr/actualite-france/2014/09/28/01016–20140928ARTFIG00152-le-conge-parental-pourrait-bientot-etre-limite-a-18mois-pour-les-meres.php

Le Feuvre, N. (2006). The enforcement of social policies: The case of the equality in employment laws in France. In A. Guichon, C. Van den Anker & I. Novikova (eds) *Women's Social Rights and Entitlements*: 82–103. Houndsmill, Basingstoke: Palgrave MacMillan.

Lehndorff, S. (2014). It's a long way from norms to normality: The 35-hour week in France. *Industrial and Labor Relations Review*, 67(3): 838–863.

Lewis, J., Knijn, T., Martin, C., & Ostner, I. (2008). Patterns of development in work/family reconciliation policies for parents in France, Germany, The Netherlands and the UK in the 2000s. *Social Politics*, 15(3): 261–286.

L'Oréal. (2008). *Accord relatif à la conciliation vie privée—vie professionnelle*. Agreement available on the ORSE site (ORSE, 2016).

Mätzke, M., & Ostner, I. (2010). Introduction: Change and continuity in recent family policies. *Journal of European Social Policy*, 20(5): 387–398.

Milner, S. (2010). 'Choice' and 'flexibility' in reconciling work and family: Towards a convergence in policy discourse on work and family in France and the UK? *Policy and Politics*, 38(1): 3–21.

Milner, S., & Gregory, A. (2014). Gender equality bargaining in France and the UK: An uphill struggle? *Journal of Industrial Relations*, 56(2): 246–63.

Ministère du Travail, de l'Emploi, de la Formation Professionnelle et du Dialogue Social. (2013). *Accord national interprofessionnel Qualité au Travail*. Accord du 19 juin. *Journal Officiel*, CC 2013/41.

Ministère du Travail, de l'Emploi, de la Formation Professionnelle et du Dialogue Social. (2015). *La négociation collective en 2014*. Paris: Ministère du Travail, de l'Emploi, de la Formation Professionnelle et du Dialogue Social.

Minni, C. (2015). *Femmes et hommes sur le marché du travail*. Dares Analyses, 17.

Moen, P. (2011). From 'work-family' to the 'gendered life course' and 'fit': Five challenges to the field. *Community, Work & Family*, 14(1): 81–96.

Morin, T., & Remila, N. (2013). *Le revenu salarial des femmes reste inférieur à celui des homes*. Insee Première, 1436.

Observatoire de la Parentalité en Entreprise (OPE, 2015a). *Baromètre de la conciliation travail-vie familiale. Volet salariés*. Paris: OPE.

Observatoire de la Parentalité en Entreprise (OPE, 2015b). *Baromètre de la conciliation travail-vie familiale. Volet employeurs*. Paris: OPE.

Organisation for Economic Co-operation and Development. (2012). *Employment Outlook 2012*. Paris: Organization for Economic Co-operation and Development.

Oziel, C. (2015). *La qualité au travail—une démarche innovante qui peine à s'imposer. Empreinte Sociale*. Novethic, available at http://www.novethic.fr/empreinte-sociale/conditions-de-travail/isr-rse/la-qualite-de-vie-au-travail-une-demarche-innovante-qui-peine-a-s-imposer-143485.html

Pellevat, C. (2015). *Les modes d'accueil des jeunes enfant: un enjeu d'égalité entre les femmes et les femmes*. Rapport d'information, 473. Paris: Sénat.

Penfold, M., & Foxton, F. (2015). *Participation Rates in the UK – 2014: Women*. London: Office for National Statistics.

Rabier, M. (2009). L'analyse du contenu des accords d'entreprise sur l'égalité professionnelle: In Ministère du Travail. Paris: La Documentation Française.

Ravenswood, K., & Markey, R. (2011). The role of unions in achieving a family-friendly workplace. *Journal of Industrial Relations*, 53(4): 486–503.

Rigby, M., & O'Brien-Smith, F. (2010). Trade union interventions in work–life balance. *Work, Employment & Society*, 24(2): 203–20.

Rubery, J., & Rafferty, A. (2013). Women and recession revisited. *Work, Employment and Society*, 27(3): 414–432.

Thalès Group. (2004). *Accord cadre relatif à l'égalité professionnelle entre les femmes et les hommes dans le groupe Thales en France*. Agreement available on the ORSE site (ORSE, 2016).

Tiraboschi, M., & Caragnano, R. (eds). (2013). *LIBRA (Let's Improve Bargaining, Relations and Agreements on Working Times and Life Balance) Final Report*. Modena: Centro Studii Marco Biagi.

Trades Union Congress (TUC). (2014a). *Flexible Working Change Welcome But It's Still Too Easy to Say No, Says TUC*. Press release, 30 June. London: TUC.

Trades Union Congress (TUC). (2014b). *TUC Equality Audit 2014*. London: TUC.

Trades Union Congress (TUC). (2014c). *Childcare Help Is Welcome But Wealthier Parents Stand to Gain the Most*. Press release, 4 June, available at https://www.tuc.org.uk/node/120319

Trades Union Congress (TUC). (2014d). *TUC Women's Conference Motion on Childcare*, available at https://www.tuc.org.uk/equality-issues/gender-equality/childcare/tuc-womens-conference-motion-childcare

Trades Union Congress (TUC). (2015a). *The Impact on Women of Recession and Austerity*. London: TUC.

Trades Union Congress (TUC). (2015b). *15% Increase in People Working More than 48 Hours a Week Risks a Return to 'burnout Britain'*, Warns TUC. Press release,

9th September, available at https://www.tuc.org.uk/international-issues/europe/workplace-issues/work-life-balance/15-cent-increase-people-working-more

Union Générale des Ingénieurs, Cadres, et Techniciens (Ugict-CGT). (2012). *Le travail des cadres dans la crise. Rapport d'enquête.* Montreuil: Ugict-CGT.

Union Générale des Ingénieurs, Cadres, et Techniciens (Ugict-CGT). (2015). *L'Ugict tire la sonnette d'alarme sur la situation de l'encadrement.* Montreuil: Ugict-CGT.

Union of Shop, Distributive and Allied Workers (Usdaw). (2015). *Is Worrying Tying You Up in Knots? Campaign briefing.* Manchester: Usdaw.

Unison. (2014). *Counting the Cost: How the Cuts Are Shrinking Women's Lives.* London: Unison.

Unite. (2011). *Equality and Family Rights: Your Guide.* London: Unite the Union.

Unite. (2015). *A New Recognition Agreement for the Banking Sector.* London: Unite the Union.

Van Wanrooy, B., Bewley, H., Bryson, A., Forth, J., Stokes, L., & Wood, S. (2013). *Employment Relations in the Shadow of Recession: Findings from the 2011 Workplace Employment Relations Study.* Houndsmill, Basingstoke: Palgrave MacMillan.

Vargas, O., & Boehmer, S. (2015). *Policies to Improve Work-life Balance.* Dublin: European Foundation for the Improvement of Living and Working Conditions.

Visser, J. (2013). *Wage Bargaining Institutions—From Crisis to Crisis.* Economic Papers 488. Brussels: European Commission.

Visser, J., Hayter, S., & Gammarano, R. (2015). *Trends in Collective Bargaining Coverage: Stability, Erosion or Decline?* Issue Brief No. 1, Geneva: International Labour Office.

Waddell, I., & Golds, J. (2013). *Navigating Excellence.* London: Unite the Union, available at http://www.unitetheunion.org/uploaded/documents/Shipbuilding%20201311-14580.pdf

Weiler, A. (2013). *Social Dialogue and Gender Equality in the European Union.* Working Paper No. 4. International Labour Office, Geneva.

Williamson, S. (2012). Gendering the bricks and mortar: Building an opportunity structure for equality bargaining. *Journal of Industrial Relations*, 54(2): 147–163.

Woolnough, R. (2003). Barclays consultation model transforms industrial relations. *Personnel Today*, 22 July 2003, available at http://www.personneltoday.com/hr/barclays-consultation-model-transforms-industrial-relations

Working Families. (2015). *Top Employers: Changing the Way We Live and Work. Benchmark Report 2015.* London: Working Families, available at http://www.workingfamilies.org.uk/wp-content/uploads/2015/09/WF_A4_16pp-Top-Employers-Benchmark_2015_FINAL_PR_03.pdf

Working Families/Bright Horizons. (2015). *Time, Health and the Family: What Working Families Want in 2014.* London: Working Families/Bright Horizons.

Wright, C. (2011). *What Role for Trade Unions in Future Workplace Relations?* London: ACAS.

7 Work–Life Balance and Class
In Search of Working-Class Work-Lives

Tracey Warren

Introduction

If we think about the sort of person who is working hard to achieve a balance between their family, personal and working lives, what type of character tends to spring to mind? Might it be a working mum negotiating the demands of child-care and running a home with those of a paid job? Certainly, any quick perusal of Internet images using 'work–life balance' (WLB) as a search term throws up multiple familiar visuals of 'working mothers'. These women are often depicted with babies or young children, sometimes juggling, whilst dressed in smart office wear. There is invariably a laptop computer in the mix. What about men and their work–lives? Well, if we add 'men' into our work–life search terms, then babies, and laptops and smart suits, again jump from the (fewer) available images. These prevalent depictions of WLB tellingly suggest that WLB is largely a matter for and a topic about women with children, who work in white-collar jobs, and for their male white-collar colleagues, albeit to a lesser degree.

This chapter offers a critique of the ideal-typical worker who stars in work–life balancing narratives: namely a working mum who is employed in a white-collar job, and in particular in a more senior position. This worker type not only dominates widespread WLB visuals but, it will be claimed, forms the bedrock of academic and policy debates on WLB, too. It will be argued that dominant academic and policy interpretations of WLB severely neglect critical social inequalities that shape our everyday WLB. The chapter focuses specifically upon class. It critiques a disregard of the working class and a privileging of middle-class troubles in the now-extensive multi-disciplinary literature that is devoted to WLB. Middle-class work–life troubles are dominated by time, in particular a work–life imbalance resulting from being time squeezed. The chapter argues that financial hardship is also a route to work–life imbalance, but that this route, and its associated class inequalities, have been neglected.

It is imperative to take class inequalities in financial hardship into account in a book that focuses upon a triple agenda for change in times of austerity via supporting employee WLB, workplace effectiveness and social justice.

Class and class inequalities had rather fallen out of fashion in the academic sociology that underpins this chapter. The 'Great Recession' helped to place class divisions firmly back on multiple agendas: popular, political and academic, and class has re-taken its place as a core focus of sociological analysis (Skeggs and Loveday, 2012; Paton, 2014; Atkinson, 2015; Savage, 2015; Tyler, 2015). To strengthen the book's focus upon employee WLB and social justice in particular, this chapter turns a class lens on WLB in austerity Britain, drawing upon my long-standing research interest in class and work inequalities.

Class Inequalities in Austere Times

The deep recession of 2008–9 in the UK and the long period of austerity that followed stimulated discussion over the potentially classed ramifications of the economic crisis. In one early classed interpretation, fuelled by high profile job loss in such sectors as banking and finance, the recession was predicted to hit middle-class workers hardest. Indeed, it was claimed soon into the crisis that this would be the first ever 'middle-class recession' (see Vaitilingam, 2009 for a discussion). In reality, the recession actually impacted the jobs of those workers employed in lower-level occupations harder still: leading to their higher levels of unemployment and, a feature of this recession in particular, underemployment too (Warren, 2015). Moreover, the long period of austerity that followed the recessionary period acted to solidify and even widen rather than narrow class gaps in people's working lives and their standards of living (Belfield et al., 2014). As it developed, austerity Britain became defined as less about senior financial workers losing their jobs and less too about the 'squeezed middle'. It became more about the intensification of precarity and insecurity impacting working-class lives (Standing, 2011; Piketty, 2014) and about deepening levels of deprivation and destitution amongst poorer households including national scandals over growing hunger and food poverty (All-Party Parliamentary Inquiry into Hunger in the United Kingdom, 2014; Dorling, 2015; Purdam et al., 2015).

This chapter was inspired by debates over the classed ramifications of times of austerity in the UK, post 2008. It asks about class and WLB. The chapter argues that working-class work–lives have been neglected in the study of WLB. It makes the case that work–life debates are dominated by the work–lives of middle-class workers and their families. Moreover, there is too heavy a focus on the specific time-based work–life challenges facing middle-class lives. Time has framed the way that WLB is defined, and this has resulted in an overly narrow remit in work–life studies. As a result, crucial work–life challenges facing many working-class workers and their families go unseen or are partially recognised. In particular, financial hardship has dropped off the WLB agenda. In times of austerity, when levels of hardship have intensified, research has largely ignored class inequalities when exploring and developing the concept of WLB.

The Ideal-Typical Worker in WLB Debates: A Middle-Class Working Mother

Sociologist Max Weber devised his influential ideal-typical approach so that he could represent a pure concept against which its actuality in everyday life may be measured: an ideal typical bureaucracy, for example, or ideal types of capitalist worker. His methodological development of the ideal-type has been used successfully many times across the study of working lives. Specifically on WLB, Mescher et al. (2010) studied multinational firms that sought to portray themselves as WLB supporters and demonstrated that an ideal-typical WLB worker, mothers with young children, dominated their corporate messages. Ransome also used ideal-types, but to critique WLB studies. He argued that the ideal-typical household that dominates WLB discourse contains "families with dependent (especially infant) children" (Ransome, 2007: 376). Yet we know that this family type represents only a minority of households in the UK (22% in 2006), and this narrowness of its focus limits WLB studies, he claimed. This chapter goes further to propose that the ideal-typical unit of analysis in WLB discourse is classed, narrowing the remit of WLB studies further still.

Looking at the level of the individual, the characteristics of the ideal-typical person who frames much WLB deliberations are undoubtedly gendered: a woman with a paid job, a mother responsible for school-aged or younger children. Influential work–life scholars have battled to challenge this overly narrow WLB stereotype, putting forward the case that men also have work–lives, as do workers without young children; and that many workers also have elder- and other-caring responsibilities as well as commitments to their friends and communities (Eby et al., 2005; Lewis et al., 2007; Özbilgin et al., 2011; Collier, 2013). Nevertheless, the employed-mother WLB ideal-type still persists.

The classed composition of the ideal-typical WLB worker is now ripe for challenge, too. The dominance in WLB discourses of the families of women, or more accurately women with children, who work in middle-class occupations has gone without a sustained critique. With notable exceptions, including from contributors to this book (Crompton and Lyonette, 2008; Fagan et al., 2008; Warren et al., 2009), WLB studies too rarely discuss working-class workers. As editor Suzan Lewis stated a decade ago (Lewis et al., 2007), the WLB problems experienced by affluent professional and white-collar workers feature instead. This is because middle-class work–lives are routinely depicted as harder, more *difficult*, to balance.

The Working Class: Harder 'Working Lives' but Easier 'Work–Lives'?

It is interesting to reflect on the way that the greater problems experienced by middle-class workers dominate the multi-disciplinary 'work–life' literature and to contrast that particular view of class inequalities with the view from the study of 'working lives' within sociology. The working lives of the working classes are rarely depicted as *easier* than those of the middle-classes. Since the birth of sociology, the interlinked overlapping sub-disciplines of the sociologies of class and of work have identified and critiqued the restricted life chances and resultant poorer working conditions and deep economic and labour market precarity that are experienced by the working classes. They have explored too the everyday negative impact on working-class people of the moral significance of class (Sayer, 2005).

One might think then that WLB amongst the working class would be an intriguing topic for researchers concerned with class inequalities, rather than the neglected one that it is currently. Might work–life be a key area where the working class actually fare as well as, and even do better than, the middle-class, given the combination of heavier work–life problems reported by the middle classes and the multiple class disadvantages that are experienced by the working class in other areas of their working lives? Might this be an area where working-class work–lives are easier, better balanced and even desirable? That would certainly be something of a coup because working-class lives and life-styles are rarely portrayed as something the middle class do, might or indeed should aspire to more generally. Of course, working-class lives have been lauded, perhaps patronised, perhaps romanticised, by the middle-class in many ways: for being more down-to-earth or simple than middle-class lives, for example; more family-centred or communal; or more gritty, edgy or 'authentic' (the latter for men in particular, argued Skeggs, 1997). However, aspirational mobilities *out of* not *into* the working class, for oneself and/or one's children, are arguably far stronger undercurrents in debates over everyday classed lives.

A clear premise in narratives of class and mobilities is the presumption of a directional desire to move up, not down, class categories, to 'better' (not 'worsen') oneself. The urge to 'escape' a working-class background, to get out, 'against the odds' (to borrow the title of the 1997 book by Marshall et al.), is assumed to be a given for those who have the ability: the so-called bright working-class kids. We can summarise this prevailing classist narrative as follows: a select few 'bright' working-class kids are able to escape the working-class destiny that their less capable classmates are doomed to endure: a destiny marked by failing working-class schools; inferior working-class jobs; sub-standard working-class houses; working-class 'sink' estates and 'no-go' working-class localities; and 'low-brow' working-class culture.

Whilst a presumed aspirational upward mobility runs through discourses of working-class lives, a keen fear of downward mobility into the working class has long underpinned the intensive class practices that many middle-class parents actively engage in on behalf of their children, such as paying for private tutoring whilst coordinating packed after-school programmes of enrichment (and academically enhancing) activities (Devine, 2004; Reay, 2005). Moreover, and reflecting the moral dimensions of class, a middle-class fear of working-class *people* is permeated with disgust at, not admiration for, multiple aspects of working-class life-styles, the (wrong) values and (bad) taste of members of the working class, as Lawler (2005) has argued. Indeed, middle-class actors who are compelled to live in working-class localities have been shown to evolve distinction strategies to set themselves apart, to distance themselves, from the working-class (Southerton, 2002). For example, in Cappellini et al.'s (2015) study of academics living in 'Brodon', the fictional name given to the locality of their university town, the respondents were keen to distance themselves both from the area and its local people ("a depressing working class area with nothing in it", "a shit place", "Oh god, I'm not from round here", (2015: 10); "the problem with Brodon people" (2015: 12).

In many ways, then, research does not portray the working-class as having particularly desirable lives, and certainly not ones that middle-class workers aspire towards themselves nor strategise for their children. So the study of WLB is intriguing because, against all this, it depicts middle-class, not working-class, work–lives as being most difficult: harder to balance, and in most urgent need of support from dedicated WLB policies. For example, "If the government wishes to affect the work–life balance of employees in Britain, the single most important change needed is to reduce long weekly working hours, and especially in the higher grade occupations" (Dex and Bond, 2005: 60).

The inequalities that impact working class 'working lives' and the belittlement of working class life-styles inspired this chapter's focus upon working class work–lives. It asks: are working-class work–lives easier, or better balanced, than middle-class? Is WLB an area where the more usual picture of class disadvantage in working lives is turned on its head? Are working-class work–lives something to desire and aspire to? This chapter addresses these key questions by exploring the work–lives of those employed in working-class occupations. It demonstrates that many in working-class jobs do indeed fare better in WLB terms when we use the dominant conceptualisation of imbalance as working too many hours. However, rather than signal an 'easier' work–life, it is argued that this result is largely an artefact of the classed way that WLB has been understood. The particular and partial way in which imbalance is conceptualised is rooted in a privileging of middle-class anxieties about time and its squeeze. The favouring of the temporal troubles that beset middle-class work–lives has meant that the type of work challenges facing many working-class workers and their families, which we know exist from any reading of a critical analysis of class and work, have been only partially recognised or gone unseen in the study of WLB. We look to the problems of financial insecurity in particular in this chapter. First, we discuss the dominance of time, not money, in work–life studies.

Work–Life Balance and Time

The dominant understanding of class inequalities in WLB is time-based. Study after work–life study demonstrates how the work–lives of middle-class women and their families are strained by the challenges involved in balancing time-greedy professional and managerial careers whilst bringing up dependent children. In the UK, one way that women in mixed-sex couples with dependent children manage work–life challenges, for themselves and their families, is by working reduced hours, at least until the children are older. This reduced-hours WLB strategy can ease the time-squeeze when it is at one of its most intense over the life-course. Nevertheless, the strategy has been criticised for reinforcing gendered roles within the home, and for trapping women in part-time jobs where, in the UK at least, there are few opportunities for advancement and it is difficult to negotiate increased hours if desired (Fagan et al., 2012). The part-time WLB strategy is far more common amongst women employed in working-class rather than middle-class occupations, as is giving up a paid job altogether to look after a child (Warren and Lyonette, 2015). Hence, dual earner, often dual full-time, middle-class couples feature far more commonly in WLB studies that are focused on time pressures and strains.

So-called chronometric temporal-based work–life imbalance is based on the actual number of hours worked (Warren, 2003), and this form of imbalance is certainly a reality for many middle-class families. This chapter is not seeking to deny or discount the negative impact that juggling too many balls for too many hours can have on everyday work–lives, to return to those Internet images of juggling working mothers. Indeed, the UK's long-hours culture creates the conditions for particularly intense time poverty amongst senior workers and hence for their temporally unbalanced work–lives.

If we look at data from *Understanding Society* (U_Soc; McFall, 2012), the largest household survey in the UK (which followed from and incorporated the *British Household Panel Survey*, the BHPS), we can see work-time by standard occupational class amongst employees in the very large sample (100,000 individuals in 40,000 nationally representative households). The most recent data available were collected 2012–13 (U_Soc Wave D).

Figure 7.1 shows how hours of labour market work (hours in first and second jobs and any over-time, paid or unpaid) varied by occupational class (amongst employees of working age). Around a third of men in senior Managerial positions were working very long weeks in their jobs (more than 48 hours), as were a quarter of men in Professional and in Process/Plant/Machine occupations. Part-time working (fewer than 30 hours a week) was more prevalent in lower-level jobs, for women in particular.

Because these data come from household surveys, we can also see how hours build up for dual-employed couples. Due to sample size constraints, mixed-sex couples are the focus. The couples with the longest weeks in the labour market were those in which both partners worked in a non-manual job: 58% worked a combined 70 or more hour week (compared with 40% of dual manual couples).

As stated, this chapter is not seeking to deny the time squeeze that can result from such long weeks in the labour market, which impacts many middle-class work–lives. Yet it does contend that time, and in particular

a. *Women*

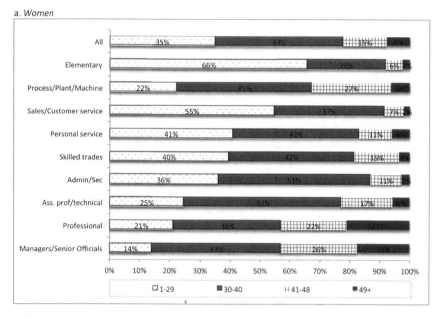

b. *Men*

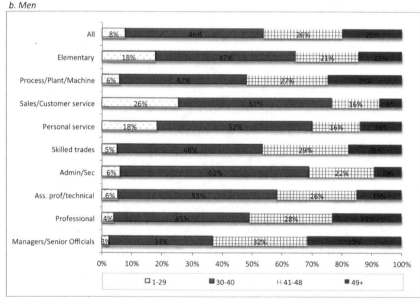

Figure 7.1 Hours of weekly labour market work[1]. Employees aged 18–64. 2012–13

Source: U_Soc Wave D
[1]Weekly hours in first and any second jobs, plus all overtime hours.
[2]Female partners aged 18–59 and male aged 18–64.

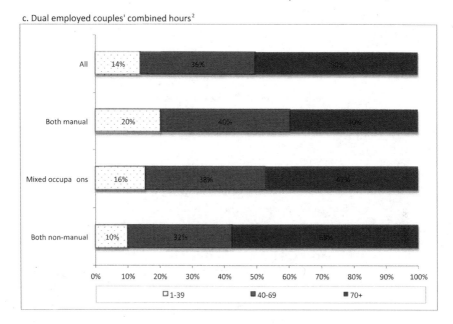

Figure 7.1 (Continued)

this chronometric measure of very long hours, dominates the understanding of WLB to such an extent that the existence of other forms of work–life imbalance have been over-shadowed (see Warren, 2003, 2015; Chatzitheochari and Arber, 2012 on short hours, time scheduling, class and WLB). In particular, the importance of the juggling ball of financial security for a balanced work–life has fallen almost completely outside research and policy that are badged under the work–life agenda. Incorporating different types of work–life imbalance into the work–life framework can provide a more holistic picture of work–life, applicable to a wider section of the population.

The Case for a Financial Foundation to a Balanced Work–Life

Outside the dedicated WLB literature, influential scholars have discussed the crucial significance of financial security in the daily lives of workers and their families. From the study of political lives, for example, Hacker et al. note: "From voting to revolting, from support for the welfare state to antagonism toward ethnic and racial minorities, economic instabilities have long been thought to shape the most fundamental aspects of political life" (Hacker et al., 2013: 41). For WLB, research from the study of time, leisure, personal finances, life quality and well-being has shaped the premise of this chapter: that financial security is surely a fundamental requirement for any work–life if it is to be deemed properly 'balanced'. The financial is key amongst the life domains that dominate the quality of life literature because it has critical ramifications for all other aspects of well-being.

Surprisingly, then, given its significance elsewhere, it is rare for research specifically on WLB to pay much, if any, attention to the financial situations of workers and their families. Reflecting back on my own pre-recession work on WLB and class, in 2005–6 I co-led a mixed-methods project that asked about policies to support work–life reconciliation among low-waged women in England. The project drew upon analysis of the BHPS and also collected in-depth interview material from female and male partners in 35 mixed-sex couples in England, all of whom had at least one child aged 7 or younger. We showed how women employed in low-waged jobs, and who had young children, were constrained in their work–life choices by limited and fragmentary social policies, such as piecemeal provision of pre-school child-care and the limited parental leave that is available in Britain (when we compare the length of leave and the level of wage compensation on offer for leave-takers with that available in other European countries). We also identified innovative policies available in the international arena around parental leave for fathers, child-care and work-time that could promote WLB. We went on to ask whether these policies were attractive and could meet the needs of working-class women and their partners in reconciling paid work and family lives.

We were heavily influenced by the dominance of time in the study of WLB. Time features throughout our published articles (Fox et al., 2009; Warren et al., 2010, 2009), but these articles underplay the findings on financial hardship that were clearly present in the interviews. When the fathers were asked about the use of and attraction of parental leave, for example, financial calculation underpinned the responses of the working-class men:

> For 90% of this population it is a financial decision yes, most people
> have got bills to pay and if they're struggling they've got to do the work.
> (Luke, manual worker, manufacturing)

> I'd use it [parental leave] if it were supported by the Government . . .
> I mean, if you were still getting 80% of your wages and everything, I
> mean you wouldn't have your travel costs, would you?
> (Gary, manual worker, manufacturing)

In addition, when asked about the potential of reducing their hours to ease work–life balancing, whether to a short full-time model (like the then French 35-hour week) or longer part-time hours (as in the Dutch Combination scenario), money concerns were cited by the men employed in manual jobs:

> Errm, I would, (like a 35 hour week) but obviously I wouldn't be able
> to make the money that I need. So unless obviously my hourly rate
> was more to make up for the loss, but I mean otherwise not really no,
> because it wouldn't really work.
> (Adam, welder, construction industry)

These men's assessments of the feasibility of any alternatives to their current work–life arrangements were clearly shaped by financial considerations, but our conclusions did not accentuate just how imperative financial security is for achieving a balanced work–life. The women interviewed also asserted the importance of finances, and of men's earnings in particular, when reflecting on the potential of policies to improve their families' work–lives:

> *If he (partner) could only work a certain amount of hours we'd struggle, we'd really struggle.*
>
> (Hayley, beauty therapist, low waged, P/T)

Finances certainly framed how those working-class couples understood work–life balance. The data were collected during years of economic growth in the UK (2005–6) and so the significance of financial in/security for working-class lives is likely to have intensified since then. As stated earlier, the recession and the subsequent period of austerity in the UK led to heightened hardship for the working class in particular. Such insidious developments as the growth in work-time underemployment including via 'zero-hours' job contracts (that do not guarantee workers any paid work at all), and the introduction of the 'bedroom tax' that cut benefit payments to those residents of social housing who had a spare bedroom, hit working-class families hardest, amidst severe cuts to welfare benefits and service provision (Atkinson et al., 2012). Later in the chapter, we look to see whether financial worries deepened during this time period. Even in 2005–6, money worries were undoubtedly denting the appeal for working-class families of innovative policies for work–life balance.

There is even more abundant evidence in the study of class and work inequalities that characteristics of the working lives of many working-class people can create economically precarious lives and/or generate severe anxieties about economic insecurity, in the short and longer terms (see Fagan et al., 2008; Skeggs and Loveday, 2012; Atkinson, 2013). Just getting by day-to-day can be a stressful challenge if jobs are low waged, hard to come by and hard to keep. Post-recession, Shildrick et al. (2012) demonstrated the strong links between poverty and insecurity that intensified in austerity Britain, especially amongst those who experience churning in the labour market: moving in and out of short-term jobs. Recurrent patterns of low paid insecure jobs and unemployment led to the normalisation of everyday hardship in 'low-pay, no-pay' Britain. The financial relief of getting a job often did little to ease the longer-term build-up of economic hardship. Shildrick et al. noted, in terms that will be very familiar to WLB scholars, that day-to-day life was a juggling act for their informants. Familiar to WLB researchers again, that juggling act impacted most heavily on the women in poor households, as studies show it had in previous periods of economic crisis (Hutson and Jenkins, 1989). It was the women who talked most about 'financial strain' in interviews: about managing, and worrying about family spending and debts and having a constantly empty purse. The women spoke longingly about the (unlikely) possibility of a holiday away from home. They recounted the hardships involved in everyday living and caring for families without the benefit of a heated home or afford-able hot water. Women's management of finances and of family emotions in economically constrained homes adds substantial burdens to their unpaid workloads (Vogler, 1994; Goode, 2009; Hall, 2016).

The next section reinforces the picture obtained from such qualitative findings by drawing on large-scale data to demonstrate the extent of classed financial hardship in austerity Britain.

Financial Hardship and Class in Austerity Britain

The chapter is concerned with financial hardship. It proposes that well recog-nised classed inequalities in 'working lives' and living standards must surely have critical ramifications for the 'work-lives' of working-class people and hence that financial security is crucial to a balanced work–life. We look to subjectively reported hardship rather than such objective measures as levels of income, savings and debt because the subjective allows individuals to reflect on their incomings and outgoings. Three waves of cross-sectional survey data are analysed: collected before the downturn began (2005–6, BHPS Wave O); in the midst of the crisis (2009–10, U_Soc Wave A); and the most recent available U_Soc wave (D, 2012–13). The data show that the proportion of employees reporting financial difficulties grew markedly in austerity Britain, with deepening problems for those working in manual jobs in particular.

In Figure 7.2, in 2005–6 around a quarter of working age employees in 'Elementary' jobs (a 'standard occupational classification' category that groups together occupations characterised by routine work that does not normally require formal educational qualifications) reported being in financial difficulties (24% of women and 29% of men), compared with 17/18% of Managers/Senior Officials. In 2009–10, in the midst of the economic crisis, the figures had rocketed up for Elementary workers (to 51/52%), rose substantially for female Managers/Senior Officials (30%), but changed only a little for male Managers/Senior Officials (22%). The class gap in financial hardship had widened substantially in the UK.

Between 2009–10 and 2012–13, overall levels of financial difficulties fell again (to a third of women and men employees in hardship by 2012–13), but not to their pre-recession levels and not all occupational groups experienced this reduction. The hardship gap between the most and least financially dis-advantaged occupational groups remained wider than it had been before the recession hit. There were still 40% or more of women and men working in Per-sonal service, Sales/Customer Service, Process/Plant/Machine and Elementary (plus women in Skilled trades) jobs reporting financial hardship in 2012–13.

We can also see how a worker's self-reported financial situation compares with any partner. In each of the three years examined, those working-age couples least likely to *both* report financial hardship were ones in which both

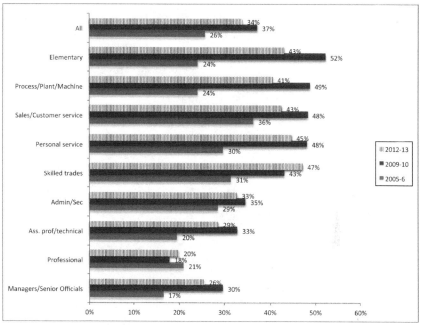

a. Women

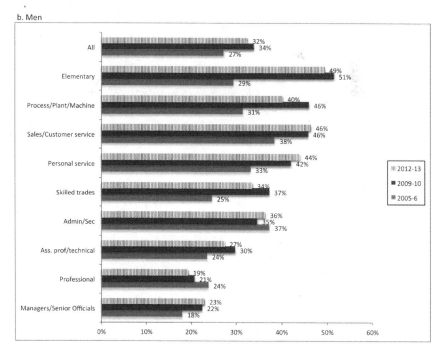

b. Men

Figure 7.2 Employees (aged 18–64) reporting 'financial difficulties/just about getting by'[1], by occupation

Source: 2005–6 (BHPS Wave O), 2009–10 (U_Soc Wave A) and 2012–13 (U_Soc Wave D)
[1]How well would you say you yourself are managing financially these days?

partners were employed in non-manual jobs. Joint financial hardship was most heavily impacting dual-manual couples whilst being in a mixed-class couple provided some buffering to the financial hardship experienced by individual manual workers. What stands out from Figure 7.3 is the doubling between 2005–6 and 2009–10 of the proportion of dual-manual couples who both reported financial hardship and, relatively speaking, remarkable stability in the perceived financial positions of dual non-manual couples both as the economic crisis impacted and as it eased.

The financial buffering that a partner in a higher-level occupation can provide mirrors the financial cushion that an employed partner can provide someone without a job. The dual-employed fared best amongst the couples, followed by male-breadwinners (Figure 7.4). If neither partner was in paid work, then perceived financial hardship was intense, and deeper still in the midst of the crisis. In 2009–10, in 64% of non (paid) working couples, both partners reported being in difficulties or just about getting by (Figure 7.4). Of course, the potential financial buffering of a partner is seen too in levels of difficulties reported by workers at different life course stages. In 2012–13, when one-third of employees overall were reporting hardship, the figures for lone parents (with a child under 16 years of age) were at 52% for women and 46% for men (figures not shown).

Discussion and Conclusions

It has been argued in this chapter that middle-class worries dominate debates around WLB to such an extent that the work–lives of the working-class have been drowned out. The study of WLB is, in effect, the study of middle-class mothers and their families. The view that work–life problems impact middle-class families most severely is a result of the particular way that imbalance has been conceptualised, as being largely about time squeeze. Studies of WLB rarely probe deeply into financial security when exploring what balance or imbalance means. Because the focus is largely on relatively affluent middle-class couples, it is not so surprising that finances do not crop up. As the findings in this chapter show, even in the depths of a very deep economic crisis in the UK, in 2009–10 only a small minority (14%) of respondents in dual non-manual couples both reported being in financial hardship. This compared with a large minority (41%) of dual working-class couples.

This chapter challenges the absence of the work–lives of the working-class from academic WLB debates. It thus contributes to the critique of the ideal-typical worker who dominates WLB discourses: the working mother with young children, by adding her class into the analysis. In reality, the ideal typical WLB worker is a mother of younger children, heterosexual in a non-separated couple, white, European, able-bodied, in a middle-class job. Despite the fact that intersectional analysis is well established, the work–life literature has been slow to engage with decades of these

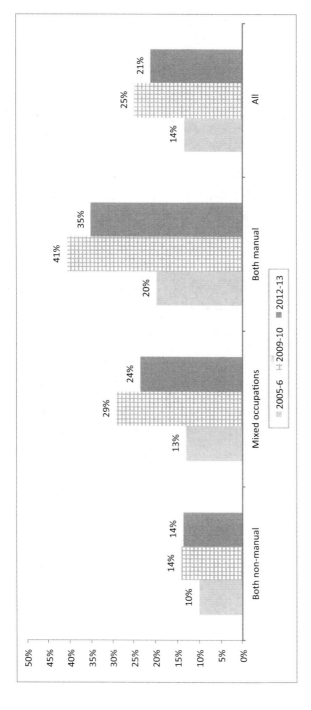

Figure 7.3 Proportion of dual-employed working[1] age mixed-sex couples who both report being in financial difficulties[2]

Source: 2005–6 (BHPS Wave O), 2009–10 (U_Soc Wave A) and 2012–13 (U_Soc Wave D)

[1] Women aged 18–59 and men 18–64.

[2] 'In financial difficulties/just about getting by'.

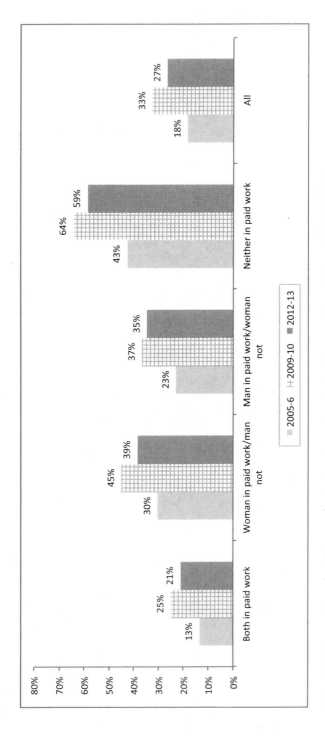

Figure 7.4 Proportion of working age[1] mixed-sex couples who both report being in financial difficulties[2]

Source: 2005–6 (BHPS Wave O), 2009–10 (U_Soc Wave A) and 2012–13 (U_Soc Wave D)
[1]Women aged 18–59 and men 18–64.
[2]In financial difficulties/just about getting by'.

debates. Accordingly, as Özbilgin et al. (2011: p.182) argued, "the conceptual development in this field has remained stunted in terms of making work–life issues relevant across divisions of social diversity, beyond gender diversity".

This chapter also challenges more fundamentally the omission of financial matters from our understanding of WLB. Financial problems, which impact working-class not middle-class lives more heavily, have somewhere along the line been deemed to fall outside the remit of 'WLB' debates. Indeed, in conferences I have been told that WLB scholars should not be criticised for neglecting financial security because WLB was actually developed to be about time and that finances are 'about something else': hence, I am asking WLB to do something it was never designed to. My response is that this disregard of the financial reflects the fact that WLB was devised by middle-class authors about the troubles that they were experiencing: it gave a tag to their 'problem without a name', to re-use Betty Friedan's (1963) identification of the unhappiness expressed by materially comfortable middle-class housewives. That would be fine if the scholars of WLB were candid about research being centred on and largely about middle-class work–life experiences. But these middle-class understandings of what is crucial to work–life balancing have been extrapolated unmodified to all work–lives. WLB masquerades as an inclusive and holistic approach that aims to promote a better understanding of work–life in general when in reality it is a concept that privileges the work–life worries of the middle-class whilst disregarding those of the working-class.

Despite its neglect in much of the study of WLB, financial security is surely a fundamental requirement for any work–life if it is to be deemed properly 'balanced', not something different to it. Financial well-being was measured in this chapter using a self-reported measure. The subjective is seen to be a strong measure of financial well-being that is different from but complements such more commonly analysed data relative income and wage levels. Nevertheless, the chapter has only begun to touch upon the key dimensions of the financial for students of WLB. Drawing upon the extensive research into economic in/security could provide a valuable way forward in the study of WLB and class. In their research, for example, Hacker et al.'s (2013) identify a number of areas of economic security that, I argue, also underpin a balanced work–life. Hacker et al. explored the 'scope' of economic insecurity: the extent to which respondents had experienced 'economic shocks'. These are grouped under four domains: employment-related financial shocks like job loss, health costs (it was a USA study), family (such as financial shocks due to divorce or bereavement) and wealth (decline in assets and savings). They identify, too, what they call households' "capacity to buffer against economic risk" (Hacker et al., 2013: 25), by exploring debt levels, financial reserves and the ability to borrow money from family members and friends. They also differentiate respondents' assessments of their own personal financial security from worries about the economy in general.

These elements, and more, of what it is to feel financially secure or at risk of or in hardship provide the economic foundations of our everyday lives and, accordingly, our work–lives. A key objective of this book is to highlight the impacts of austerity and difficult economic times on WLB. Its guiding theme is the triple agenda of supporting employee WLB, workplace effectiveness and social justice in an austerity context. The conclusion from this chapter is that to meet the challenges of this triple agenda for change, the study of WLB now must add the identification of the work–life problems of the working-class and the pursuit of solutions for working-class imbalanced lives to its core interest in middle-class chronometric temporal-based imbalance. Without this, in times of austerity and deepening hardship, we are left unable to state whether class inequalities in financial-based work–life imbalance are intensifying, and we are left incapable of proposing what policies might be suitable for supporting more balanced working-class, not just middle-class, work–lives.

Acknowledgements

This research was funded by award BR100093 from the British Academy. BHPS and Understanding Society data were made available through the UK Data Archive and were collected by the Institute for Social and Economic Research (University of Essex) and the National Centre for Social Research. Neither the original collectors of the data nor the Archive bear any responsibility for the analyses or interpretations presented here.

References

All-Party Parliamentary Inquiry into Hunger in the United Kingdom. (2014). *Feeding Britain: A Strategy for Zero Hunger in England, Wales, Scotland and Northern Ireland*. London: the Children's Society, available at https://foodpovertyinquiry. files.wordpress.com/2014/12/food-poverty-feeding-britain-final.pdf

Atkinson, W. (2013). Class habitus and perception of the future: Recession, employment insecurity and temporality. *British Journal of Sociology*, 64(4): 643–661.

Atkinson, W. (2015). *Class*. Cambridge: Polity Press.

Atkinson, W., Roberts, S., & Savage, M. (2012). *Class Inequality in Austerity Britain: Power Difference and Suffering*. Basingstoke: Palgrave Macmillan.

Belfield, C., Cribb, J., Hood, A., & Joyce, R. (2014). *Living Standards, Poverty and Inequality in the UK: 2014*. London: IFS.

Cappellini, B., Parsons, E., & Harman, V. (2015). 'Right taste, wrong place': Local food cultures, (dis)identification and the formation of classed identity. *Sociology*, doi:10.1177/0038038515593033

Chatzitheochari, S., & Arber, S. (2012). Class, gender and time poverty: A time-use analysis of British workers' free time resources. *The British Journal of Sociology*, 63(3): 451–471.

Collier, R. (2013). Rethinking men and masculinities in the contemporary legal profession: The example of fatherhood, transnational business masculinities and work-life balance in large law firms. *Nevada Law Journal*, 13(2): 101–130.

Crompton, R., & Lyonette, C. (2008). Mothers' employment, work-life conflict, careers and class. In J. Scott, S. Dex & H. Joshi (eds) *Women and Employment: Changing Lives and New Challenges*: 213–233. Cheltenham: Edward Elgar Publishing.

Devine, F. (2004). *Class Practices: How Parents Help Their Children Get Good Jobs*. Cambridge: Cambridge University Press.

Dex, S., & Bond, S. (2005). Measuring work–life balance and its covariates. *Work, Employment and Society*, 19(3): 627–637.

Dorling, D. (2015). *Injustice: Why Social Inequality Still Persists*. Bristol: Policy Press.

Eby, L.T., Casper, W.J., Lockwood, A., Bordeaux, C., & Brinley, A. (2005). Work and family research in IO/OB: Content analysis and review of the literature (1980–2002). *Journal of Vocational Behavior*, 66(1): 124–197.

Fagan, C., Lyonette, C., Smith, M., & Saldaña-Tejeda, A. (2012). *The Influence of Working Time Arrangements on Work-life Integration or 'Balance': A Review of the International Evidence*. Conditions of Work and Employment Series No. 34, International Labour Organisation, Geneva, available at http://www.ilo.org/travail/whatwedo/publications/WCMS_187306/lang—en/index.htm

Fagan, C., McDowell, L., Perrons, D., Ray, K., & Ward, K. (2008). Class differences in mothers' work schedules and assessments of their 'work–life balance' in dual-earner couples in Britain. In J. Scott, S. Dex & H. Joshi (eds) *Women and Employment: Changing Lives and New Challenges*: 199–212. Cheltenham: Edward Elgar Publishing.

Fox, E., Pascall, G., & Warren, T. (2009). Work-family policies, participation and practices: Fathers and childcare in Europe. *Community, Work and Family*, 12(3): 313–326.

Friedan, B. (1963/2010). *The Feminine Mystique*. Harmondsworth: Penguin.

Goode, J. (2009). For love or money? Couples' negotiations of credit and debt in low-income families in the UK. *Benefits*, 17: 213–224.

Hacker, J.S., Rehm, P., & Schlesinger, M. (2013). The insecure American: Economic experiences, financial worries, and policy attitudes. *Politics*, 11(1): 23–49.

Hall, S.M. (2016). Everyday family experiences of the financial crisis: Getting by in the recent economic recession. *Journal of Economic Geography*, 16(2): 305–330.

Hutson, S., & Jenkins, R. (1989). *Taking the Strain*. Milton Keynes: Open University Press.

Lawler, S. (2005). Disgusted subjects: The making of middle class identities. *The Sociological Review*, 53(3): 429–446.

Lewis, S., Gambles, R., & Rapoport, R. (2007). The constraints of a 'work-life balance' approach: An international perspective. *International Journal of Human Resource Management*, 18(3): 360–373.

Marshall, G., Swift, A., & Roberts, S. (1998). *Against the Odds?: Social Class and Social Justice in Industrial Societies*. Oxford University Press.

McFall, S.L. (ed). (2012). *Understanding Society—UK Household Longitudinal Study: Wave 1–2, 2009–2011, User Manual*. Colchester: University of Essex.

Mescher, S., Benschop, Y., & Doorewaard, H. (2010). Representations of work–life balance support. *Human Relations*, 63(1): 21–39.

Özbilgin, M.F., Beauregard, T.A., Tatli, A., & Bell, M.P. (2011). Work-life, diversity and intersectionality: A critical review and research agenda. *International Journal of Management Reviews*, 13(2): 177–198.

Paton, K. (2014). *Gentrification: A Working-Class Perspective*. London: Ashgate.

Piketty, T. (2014). *Capital in the Twenty-First Century*. Harvard University Press.

Purdam, K., Garrat, E.A., & Esmail, A. (2015). Hungry? Food insecurity, social stigma and embarrassment in the UK. *Sociology*, Published online before print August 11, 2015, doi:10.1177/0038038515594092

Ransome, P. (2007). Conceptualizing boundaries between 'life' and 'work'. *International Journal of Human Resource Management*, 18(3): 374–386.

Reay, D. (2005). Doing the dirty work of social class? Mothers' work in support of their children's schooling. In L. Pettinger, J. Parry, R. Taylor & M. Glucksmann (eds) *A New Sociology of Work*: 104–116. London: Wiley-Blackwell.

Savage, M. (2015). *Social Class in the 21st Century*. London: Penguin Books.

Sayer, A. (2005). *The Moral Significance of Class*. Cambridge: Polity.

Shildrick, T., MacDonald, R., Webster, C., & Garthwaite, K. (2012). *Poverty and Insecurity: Life in Low-pay, No-pay Britain*. Bristol: Policy Press.

Skeggs, B. (1997). *Formations of Class and Gender*. London: Sage.

Skeggs, B., & Loveday, V. (2012). Struggles for value: Value practices, injustice, judgment, affect and the idea of class. *The British Journal of Sociology*, 6(3): 473–489.

Southerton, D. (2002). Boundaries of 'us' and 'them': Class, mobility and identification in a new town. *Sociology*, 36(1): 171–193.

Standing, G. (2011). *The Precariat: The New Dangerous Class*. London: Bloomsbury.

Tyler, I. (2015). Classificatory struggles: Class, culture and inequality in neoliberal times. *The Sociological Review*, 63(2): 493–511.

Vaitilingam, R. (2009). *Recession in Britain: Findings from Economic and Social Research*. Swindon: ESRC.

Vogler, C.M. (1994). Money in the household. In M. Anderson, F. Bechhofer & J. Gershuny (eds) *The Social and Political Economy of the Household*: 225–262. Oxford: Oxford University Press.

Warren, T. (2003). Class- and gender-based working time? Time poverty and the division of domestic labour. *Sociology*, 37(4): 733–752.

Warren, T. (2015). Work-time underemployment and financial hardship: Class inequalities and recession in the UK. *Work, Employment and Society*, 29(2): 191–212.

Warren, T., & Lyonette, C. (2015). The quality of part-time work in Britain. In F. Green, A. Felstead & D. Gallie (eds) *Unequal Britain at Work: The Evolution and Distribution of Intrinsic Job Quality in Britain*: 62–82. Oxford: Oxford University Press.

Warren, T., Pascall, G., & Fox, E. (2009). Innovative social policies for gender equality from Europe: Implications for the work-life reconciliation of low waged women in England. *Gender, Work and Organization*, 16(1): 126–150.

Warren, T., Pascall, G., & Fox, E. (2010). Gender equality in time: Paid and unpaid work in the UK. *Feminist Economics*, 16(3): 193–219.

8 Self-Employment in Times of Economic Crisis
Work–Life Challenges

Laura Den Dulk, Anne Annink and Bram Peper

This chapter focuses on the experiences of self-employed workers following the 2008 financial crisis. It is important to consider the work–life experiences of the self-employed not only because their experiences can differ from those of employees but also because conflicts and tensions between life domains can influence workers' health and well-being and the duration of self-employment (Williams, 2004; OECD, 2011). Research on work–life balance (WLB) concentrates on employees employed by large organizations (Den Dulk and Peper, 2009), although there are exceptions (see, for example, Prottas and Thompson, 2006; Nordermark et al., 2012; Johansson Sevà and Öun, 2015). It is unlikely that research findings from employed workers can be generalized to the self-employed. Their work situation differs in many respects from that of employees: they tend to work longer and more irregular hours, have more flexibility and autonomy (control over when, where and how they work) and report more job insecurity and lower levels of social support than employed workers (Taris et al., 2008; Tuttle and Garr, 2009). Unlike employees, the self-employed are not always covered by the social security system in their country (Annink et al., 2016b) and in most countries they do not have full access to public work–life policies that aim to support the ability to combine work and personal/family life (Annink et al., 2015). Although research indicates that self-employed workers may experience difficulties combining life domains, they remain an under-researched group of workers and it is not yet clear what kind of work–life support is most helpful for them (Annink et al., 2015).

Difficult economic times makes it even more important to look into this group of workers, since the economic crisis has been stressful for many self-employed people. Orders and incomes have declined as clients cut back on external suppliers, consultants and contractors (De Veer and Francke, 2009). Some workers are forced into self-employment because they lack alternatives (Eurobarometer, 2009; Tuttle and Garr, 2009; Kelley et al., 2011). These so-called involuntary or necessity-driven self-employed typically work as subcontractors to one or limited number of employers, making them vulnerable to the unpredictability of the market place. At the same time, the European Union considers self-employment crucial for economic prosperity. The question addressed in this chapter is: What are the implications of self-employment for WLB in difficult economic times? A focus on the self-employed is worthwhile, as this is a growing category of workers whose WLB can also be affected by the economic context, although the processes can be different from those of employees.

Below we first outline the trends in self-employment since the economic crisis. Secondly, we discuss research and theoretical arguments about self-employment and WLB. After that, we present data from a recent qualitative interview study in Spain and the Netherlands among solo self-employed independent professionals, illustrating WLB experiences of an under-researched but growing group of self-employed workers in times of recession and beyond (Leighton and Brown, 2013). Finally, we make some concluding remarks and discuss the policy implications with respect to self-employment.

Self-Employment in Europe during the Financial Crisis and beyond

Within the work–family literature it is increasingly recognized that WLB experiences need to be understood within multiple, intersecting layers of context, including the workplace context and the wider societal context, such as economic conditions, national policies and norms and expectations with respect to work–family issues (Lewis et al., 2009; Ollier-Malaterre et al., 2013). The general economic downturn that followed the financial crisis of 2008 is likely to intersect with cultural norms, policies and practices in shaping WLB experiences of the self-employed. Within academic and policy debates, the financial crisis and its consequences are still widely discussed. These debates often promote entrepreneurship as a strategy for recovery and sustainable economic growth, and European and national programmes are devoted to supporting self-employment. In June 2010, the EU Directive on self-employed workers and assisting spouses came into force, aiming to improve social protection for the self-employed by establishing a right to maternity leave for the first time. Since 2010, 40% of the rise in jobs in Europe can be attributed to self-employment (Hatfield, 2015). Countries differ, however, with respect to the percentage of self-employed in the labour force and whether their numbers are growing or declining (Holthuis and Pratt, 2010; Pedersini and Coletto, 2010).

Figure 8.1 shows the trends in self-employment between 2004 and 2014 in various European countries. Traditionally, the extent of self-employment is much higher in Eastern European countries such as Poland and Estonia and in Southern European countries such as Spain. This is due to the kind of work, mainly traditional agricultural work, as well as low-paid service-based work. There is also substantial informal self-employment in these regions (Hatfield, 2015). Luber and Leicht (2000) point to the 'North–South Slope', where the relative importance of self-employment in the economy is

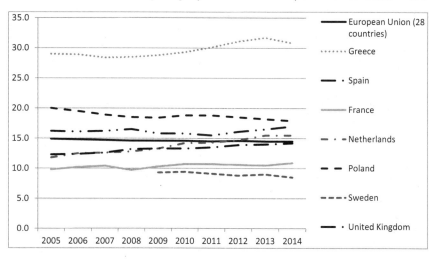

Figure 8.1 Trends in self-employment across EU countries, 2005–2014
Source: Eurostat Labour Market Database (Eurostat, 2014)

low for the Northern European countries and high for the Southern European countries. Self-employment is less attractive in Northern European countries like Sweden or Norway because of the higher level of social security (Erikson et al., 1987) and less available because of the lower amount of informal work. In many countries, the number of self-employed is stagnating or declining since the economic crisis hit Europe. Notable exceptions are the Netherlands and the United Kingdom, which both show a steady progress in the proportion of self-employed (see Figure 8.1). An increase in self-employment in difficult economic times can be seen as a sign of entrepreneurial spirit and/or as a rise of necessity-driven self-employment. The EU defines the self-employed as 'all persons pursuing a gainful activity for their own account, under the conditions laid down by national law' (European Parliament, 2010: 3). New forms of self-employment are emerging, referred to as precarious or necessity driven self-employment—whereby people are pushed into self-employment because of a lack of alternatives in the labour market (Eurobarometer, 2009; Kelley et al., 2011). In Europe, 28% of the newly self-employed reported that they were forced into self-employment (Eurobarometer, 2009). On the other hand, research shows a growing group of 'independent professionals', also referred to as freelancers or portfolio workers, that represent the highly skilled, qualified self-employed who work for themselves in the service sector but who do not employ others (Leighton and Brown, 2013). Nowadays, self-employment covers a wide range of different contexts: entrepreneurs with employees, craft workers, traders and farmers (who often work with family members), traditional independent professionals such as doctors and lawyers, skilled solo self-employed workers or freelancers in unregulated occupations like the independent professionals, and self-employed workers in unskilled occupations (Pedersini and Coletto, 2010). Researchers have only recently started to investigate the emerging and growing group of independent professionals in relation to outcomes like work–life experiences (Clinton et al., 2006; Wood and Michaelides, 2015). Before turning to the WLB experiences of this specific group of self-employed, we will discuss two competing arguments in the literature on self-employment and WLB.

Self-Employment and WLB

Within the work–family field, the Job Demands–Resources (JD–R) model is often used to explain the relation between self-employment and WLB (Taris et al., 2008; Glavin and Schieman, 2012; Annink et al., 2015; Johansson Sevà and Öun, 2015; Wood and Michaelides, 2015). The JD–R model focuses on specific work characteristics, demands and resources that either require effort or are a source of support for WLB (Voydanoff, 2005; Bakker and Demerouti, 2007). Current research makes a distinction between challenge and hindrance demands (Schaufeli and Taris, 2013; Wood and Michaelides, 2015). This is an important addition since demands are not always experienced as negative, which makes the distinction between demands and resources less clear-cut. Challenge demands do involve physiological and psychological costs but are experienced as positive, unlike hindrance demands, because of the potential gains they may entail. For instance, the responsibility for the survival of the business can be experienced as a challenge leading to high work engagement and positive feelings like enthusiasm. In contrast, the insecurity of having not enough work might be a source of anxiety and as such be experienced as a hindrance work demand (Wood and Michaelides, 2015).

Based on the JD–R model, two competing arguments are present in the literature with respect to the interdependencies between work and family/personal life of the self-employed (Glavin and Schieman, 2012; Johansson Sevà and Öun, 2015). Firstly, there are scholars who argue that the self-employed experience more difficulties combining work and family/personal life than employees because they face more demands, like longer working hours and a higher level of job insecurity, and have lower levels of on-the-job social support (Taris et al., 2008; Tuttle and Garr, 2009). These work characteristics are all known for their negative impact on people's work–life balance. They create tensions and stress and increase the likelihood of work–family conflict (Parasuraman and Simmers, 2001; Prottas and Thompson, 2006). In difficult economic times, work demands, such as working hours and insecurity, are likely to increase as orders and incomes are declining (De Veer and Francke, 2009). Insecurity about the amount of work available can diminish the ability to turn work down, which increases the workload. In addition, the self-employed may experience financial constraints or expect financial problems in the (near) future as orders decline. These feelings of economic hardship create stress and tensions and are negatively related to overall well-being (Annink et al., 2016a).

Secondly, there are scholars who argue that people appreciate self-employment because it offers resources like autonomy and flexibility, which increase the ability to combine paid work and personal/family life (e.g. Prottas and Thompson, 2006; Sullivan and Meek, 2012). Within the work–family literature, autonomy, that is control over when, where and how work is done, is seen as an important resource in balancing work and family life, along with social support (Voydanoff, 2005; Valcour, 2007). In general, the self-employed also report having more work and time/spatial autonomy than employed workers (Taris et al., 2008; Tuttle and Garr, 2009). Autonomy is highly valued among the self-employed. Being your own boss is in fact an important reason to become self-employed and being able to achieve a better WLB an important factor for many. The latter is in particular true for women (Milkie and Peltola, 1999; Kirkwood and Tootell, 2008; Myrie and Daly, 2009). Unlike employees, the self-employed do not need to deal with unsupportive line managers and workplace cultures that make it more difficult to manage the work–life interface. Workplace culture—norms, values and assumptions about how work is done in the organization—is often predicated on an image of the ideal worker as someone who works full-time, is fully available to work all year and who does not allow non-work commitments to interfere with work. Such time and career demands embedded in the organizational culture form a barrier to achieve a satisfactory work–life balance (Lewis et al., 2009; Den Dulk et al., 2016).

Despite the fact that the self-employed are their own boss and do not have to deal with a unsupportive workplace culture, research findings tend to confirm the first argument by showing higher levels of work–family conflict among the self-employed compared to workers employed by organizations (Parasuraman and Simmers, 2001; Nordenmark et al., 2012; Johansson Sevà and Öun, 2015; Annink et al., 2016a). The empirical evidence appears to suggest that autonomy is not always able to offset work demands such as long working hours and insecurity that comes along with being your own boss. Research comparing self-employed workers with employees with those without employees suggests that the self-employed with employees are particularly at risk of experiencing work–family conflict (Prottas and Thompson, 2006; Bunk et al., 2012; Johansson Sevà and Öun, 2015). Female independent self-employed who work for themselves and do not employ others seem to be better able to benefit from their relatively high level of autonomy. They work shorter working hours and report the least work–family conflict (Johansson Sevà and Öun, 2015).

Prottas and Thompson (2006) argued that being self-employed is a double-edged sword: the greater pressure of being responsible for one's own business success detracts from the advantages of having autonomy over when, where and the number of hours worked. A qualitative study among female self-employed in the Netherlands working in different sectors of the economy indicated that the actual degree of autonomy self-employed persons experience and whether they are able to gear this towards realising a satisfactory WLB depends on work characteristics, like the nature of the work, the prevailing work time regime and clients' expectations (Annink and Den Dulk, 2012). Moreover, Clinton et al. (2006) show how high levels of uncertainty about the demand for work can affect the amount of autonomy that is experienced. Being uncertain about whether there will be enough work in the near future, the portfolio workers in their study felt less in control over the types of jobs they take on. This may in particular occur in sectors that are hit hard by an economic crisis.

Few studies, however, address the heterogeneity in work contexts among the self-employed (Prottas and Thompson, 2006; Craig et al., 2012; Johansson Sevà and Öun, 2015). Freelancers, subcontractors and small business owners have different working conditions, which are likely to have different work–family implications. For instance, the self-employed with employees have more responsibilities than do solo self-employed, but they may also have more opportunities to work flexibly because they can delegate tasks (Craig et al., 2012). In addition, self-employed persons who work alone lack the support of co-workers or business partners and depend on social support from their family or wider social and professional network. Social support can buffer the influence of work and household demands, generally found to be negatively related to WLB satisfaction (Scherer and Steiber, 2007; Valcour, 2007; Den Dulk et al., 2011).

The various types of self-employed workers are then likely to differ in their resources and demands, depending on their sector and whether or not they depend predominantly on one client, work from home, have employees, or are the main family breadwinner. Moreover, resources and demands are influenced by social, cultural and economic contexts, and may therefore differ between institutional contexts. Work–life supportive policies are assumed to contribute to WLB, although Annink et al. (2016a) found that public work–life policies have no significant effect on the WLB of self-employed workers. Based on research showing that work tends to conflict more with family life than vice versa (Frone, 2003), it might be that support for the self-employed individual's business work or making it easier for them to do business is more effective than support directed at their family or personal lives. Support needs may vary across diverse work and family cultural contexts. Both Spain and the Netherlands are examples of the conservative corporatist welfare state regime in which the family plays an important role in relation to work–family issues (Esping-Andersen, 1990, 1999). In particular, in Spain the traditional family is expected to take care of the welfare of relatives. In the next section, findings are presented from a qualitative study of WLB experiences of independent professionals in two national contexts, Spain and the Netherlands. Although other types of self-employed workers may face different demands and resources, findings based on this specific group may shed some light on how demands and resources are linked to the work and national context. So far, the JD–R model has been mainly applied on individual job characteristics and to a lesser extent on the role of the wider context, when considering self-employment and WLB experiences (Annink et al., 2016a).

The Case of Work–Life Balance of Spanish and Dutch Independent Professionals in Difficult Economic Times

In 2015, an interview study was conducted among 33 independent professionals in Spain and the Netherlands to explore their WLB experiences. We focus on this group because the highly skilled solo independent professionals are the fastest growing group in the European labour market (Leighton and Brown, 2013). They differ from other groups such as necessity-driven self-employed whose decisions are a direct result of the economic crisis. The independent professionals in our study indicated that they became self-employed out of opportunity and the autonomy of becoming their own boss made managing their WLB particularly salient to them. Independent professionals work for themselves, do not employ others and are engaged in service activities. They offer their skills, know-how and work in a range of different organizations (Rapelli, 2012), reflecting the changing nature of work and employment relations (Leighton and Brown, 2013). They experience different work demands and resources than employees employed by the large organizations that are normally studied within the work–family literature. The selected independent professionals in our interview study were all engaged in professional, scientific and technical activities (NACE code M), and this is the sector with the highest percentage of independent professionals (25%) in Europe (Leighton and Brown, 2013). As a result, their activities were limited to management, consultancy, technology, public relations, communication, architecture, design, photography and translation.

In each country, the owners of several office blocks in which self-employed workers share a work location in a major city (Rotterdam and Valencia) were approached to invite independent professionals to participate in the research. Next, the interviewees were asked to forward the invitation to other independent professionals working from home. An advantage of this snowballing method is that it allowed us to ensure variation in the sample, for example, in location of the workplace, duration of being self-employed, occupation, gender and child care responsibilities. The final sample consists of 16 participants working in the Netherlands and 17 in Spain. Data were collected through audio-taped interviews, lasting approximately one hour. The interviews covered four topics: 1) WLB at the time of research, 2) capabilities and restrictions to achieve their ideal work–life situation, 3) social support for WLB and 4) public support for WLB. The interviews were conducted in 2015, and interviewees talked about their experiences of self-employment from the 2008 recession (or later if they became self-employed more recently) to the current time. Before presenting our main findings, we outline the different institutional and social cultural contexts.

Both the Netherlands and Spain were hit by the financial crisis, although the nature of the recession differed between the two national contexts. In Spain, the unemployment rose very quickly towards 30% between 2008 and 2013 (http://www.tradingeconomics.com/). In Spain it was mainly younger employees who were laid off. In the Netherlands, the effect on unemployment was visible, but far less than in Spain: in 2013 the unemployment rate in the Netherlands was 6.7% compared to 26.1% in Spain (Eurostat, 2014). In the year before this research was carried out, both economies were slowly recovering from the crisis. In the last few years, the Netherlands has been characterized by a growing number of self-employed. The growth of independent professionals in particular grew rapidly, by 93% in the period 2004–2013 (Leighton and Brown, 2013). The Spanish percentages of self-employment (17.9%) and own account self-employment (11.9%) are comparable to the Dutch: 16,1% versus 11,5% (Eurostat, 2014).

The relatively high unemployment rate is Spain might be the reason for a higher proportion of necessity-driven self-employed in Spain, 30% versus 16% in the Netherlands (GEM, 2015). Starting a business, registering properties, getting credits and paying taxes, for example, is easier in the Netherlands than in Spain (DoingBusiness, 2014). The tax rates as a percentage of profit are also lower in the Netherlands (39%) than in Spain (58.2%) (Leighton and Brown, 2013).

Regarding work–life support, Dutch self-employed mothers are relatively better off; they receive an 80-day maternity leave with a maximum of the minimum wage (1,486 euros a month). Leaves are financed by contributions and taxes. Spanish self-employed mothers receive 42 days of maternity leave at a flat rate (532.51 euros a month). Here, insurance is compulsory. The Dutch self-employed fathers do not receive paternity leave, and parental leave is unavailable for the self-employed in both the Netherlands and Spain (Annink et al., 2015). In Spain, public funding for childcare for children under three years of age has decreased during the last few years (Ibid.). In the Netherlands, childcare support depends on the level of income and hours worked, which might imply that the self-employed need to return part of the support when work was less than expected (Yerkes and Den Dulk, 2015). Analysis of the interview data generated a number of themes relating to self-employed workers' experiences of demands and resources and of WLB, which we now outline.

Experiences of Financial Hardship, Growing Demands and Insecurity

Financial demands can be substantial for the self-employed particularly in difficult economic times. Financial hardship has been defined as a subjective perception of financial constraints or expectations of financial problems in the future (see Schieman and Young, 2011). For the self-employed, these constraints and expectations reflect developments in the sector, financial reserves, personal network contacts and current jobs. The case study shows that subjective perceptions of financial hardship are influenced not only by the financial situation, but also by the context in which it is experienced. The Spanish independent professionals in our study, for instance, reported fewer feelings of financial hardship than the Dutch participants, because they had lower expenses and more financial support from their parents.

> *Why should I live alone? I have a good relation with my parents. They try not to ask me about my private life. I am good with my family. I don't have the money to live alone. I don't pay for a room, not for food, no stress. I am fortunate to receive support of my family. I don't need to live alone in this moment.*
>
> (ES16, Spanish student service provider, male, aged 31)

This illustrates that resources and demands are also affected by contexts outside work, such as the family. All independent professionals in our study experienced an increase in demands, however. Three (increasing) major demands and their effects on work–life balance in difficult economic times were identified: higher work-load, insecurity about income and insecurity about the continuity of the business.

Spanish participants mentioned that some customers did not pay them; as a result, they had to work more hours for the same amount of money, resulting in higher workloads. In Spain, payment rates for independent professionals are lower than in the Netherlands and this difference has increased in the past few years as the economic crisis decreased rates in Spain. The Spanish independent professionals in this sample who recently graduated and started their business noted a pessimistic attitude regarding the labour market among their peers. The general message that they received from the media and their contacts was that there would be few opportunities for them after graduation. Some perceived starting their own business as an alternative to unpaid internships, which offered them no security. The recently graduated self-employed argued that they kept their own business going in order to stay motivated. The more experienced self-employed workers in this sample often had a larger network and clients for a longer period of time, which increased their stability. They often had a partner with an income or family investments from which they receive money. Overall, those without children or a mortgage were less stressed about their financial situation compared to those with a family and larger financial obligations.

Both the Spanish and Dutch independent professionals report that they feel vulnerable in times of financial austerity because companies cut external assignments and extra services first. Especially those without a financial buffer felt stressed because of income insecurities. It is not only income, however, that causes insecurity, worries and stress. In the Netherlands, independent professionals felt especially insecure about the continuity of their work, not knowing how much work there will be in the future. Those who did not have strong marketing and business skills, which are needed to make their job more profitable, felt particularly vulnerable. Not all respondents see themselves as business managers, but rather would call themselves freelancers. Freelancers thought that business and management skills would help them to make their business more profitable, although they were not very interested in learning these. A lack of continuity in assignments, however, undermines security and regularity in working hours, which causes stress regardless of the independent professional's current income, financial buffer or marketing skills:

> *I find it very difficult not having an idea how it will be next week. I feel like we must be able to live the life we are living now. But I have no continuity in work. When I get more work, I don't have these kind of worries.*
> (ES14, Spanish video editor, male, 48, one child)

> *My income depends on what I'm doing. If I have a financial setback, I feel like I have to do something, otherwise I cannot pay my rent. It's difficult, because I can't do anything, really. Now I still can just live and eat. So it's all fear for the future.*
> (NL4, Dutch text writer, female, 33)

Decreasing Autonomy

An attraction of self- employment may be the possibility of greater autonomy, which could impact on WLB. The importance of autonomy is illustrated by the following quote:

> *I want to be able to do what I like each day. I want to be able to realize all ideas I come up with. But I have more ideas than I can realize, so I need the discipline to reflect on what makes sense. On the one hand I need to think out of the box, on the other hand I need to focus a lot.*
> (NL11, Dutch online community manager, female, 54, two children)

This quote suggests that autonomy is not only an end in itself, but also a precondition for the successful execution of their work. An increase in working hours and insecurity due to the financial crisis, however, often resulted in less control over time, space, contents of the work and relationships.

> *If my sales are low, I am the only one to do something about it. It means that I have to go out, focus on marketing, something I don't really like. I have side jobs for income, they determine my deadlines and priorities*

too. They limit my flexibility, I would prefer to work fulltime on my own ideas, to be creative.

(NL10, Dutch product designer, male, 25)

The importance of autonomy differed between Dutch and Spanish independent professionals, however. In the work domain, job autonomy was restricted by lower incomes. Most independent professionals in the sample were unable to invest in their business to let it grow in the near future. They were more likely to do everything themselves, instead of outsourcing tasks. Because of this, they worked long hours and felt they were busy with small tasks and could not focus on long-term growth and expansion of the business. The financial situation made them feel they are "stuck". Because their income is directly related to their investments and efforts, many self-employed equate time with income:

I have to do a little bit more, faster, better . . . I don't feel calm enough to take a day off on Sundays. Until I earn enough money, I cannot take time off. I have to work every day.

(NL3, Dutch illustrator, male, 45, two children)

Despite earning less money, all participants reported that they preferred to be self-employed rather than searching for a job as an employee. They sometimes considered applying for a job, searched for vacancies and then decided to stay self-employed in the end, rather than taking on irregular and low-paid jobs. This was in particular true for the Spanish independent professionals. Emotionally, participants suffered from feelings of guilt about being unemployed and for having to be reliant on their parents, partner or the government. Financial insecurity makes some of them doubt themselves:

Maybe it is my fault. I don't want to live with the pressure and the stress, but I do. I am hoping one day there will be a balance. But it is very difficult, I don't know how I can try to be less stressed. I am always saying it's the work, but maybe it is my fault. I don't know how to change.

(ES14, Spanish video editor, male, 48, one child)

The self-employed men were more likely to feel pressured to earn a reasonable income, especially if they were the main breadwinner. The mothers in this sample, both in Spain and the Netherlands, were more likely than men to prioritize their family life over work and to report experiencing stress resulting from having to simultaneously meet the role demands of being a mother, a housekeeper, a wife, a friend and a businesswoman. This is consistent with Hobson's (2014) suggestion that women traditionally may lack a notion of their own WLB, because their identities are so tied to the household needs of others.

For the self-employed without a family, the financial situation might be a reason to stay with their parents or to move back in with them. This limited their sense of being in control of their lives, for instance their relationships or ability to start a family, especially in Spain:

> *In the ideal situation, I would have liked to spend more time with my girlfriend. But I need to work more hours now, and my girlfriend is working too . . . I would like to live together with her, but I stay at my parents because of the economic situation. My girlfriend moved abroad for work, then she came back, unemployed.*
> (ES16, Spanish student service provider, male, 31, no children)

The value of autonomy as a resource for WLB differs across the two countries. In the Netherlands, it is more valued and more common for young people to live on their own, for example. Within the Dutch individualistic culture, living on your own is part of education and learning to be independent. However, the average moving-out age of 22.4 years is rising because of increasing unemployment and use of temporary contracts. Also the duration of scholarships, unemployment benefits and the supply of rental housing influenced the financial opportunities and timing for young independent professionals to move out (*cf* Stoeldraijer, 2014). The single Spanish independent professionals often lived in their parents' home, even when they were over 30. Moving out is considered to be a waste of money and children are 'by tradition' taken good care of by their mothers, especially boys (Hooper, 2006). Even if they do not live at home, their mother may still take care of them, as illustrated by this account:

> *For me, my mother is like a partner. She is giving me the money for the business and we have discussions about that. I call her three times a week. I start by telling my personal things, than work work work and I finish with something that I did.*
> (ES3, Spanish student service provider, male, 31, no children)

This example illustrates how in conservative welfare regimes in Southern Europe, where familism is a predominant characteristic of family relations and of social policies, individuals have a preference for tightly knit frameworks. Relatives are expected to look after each other in exchange for loyalty. In Spain, more than in the Netherlands, the family is the unit with primary responsibility for the welfare of individuals. Family obligations and mutual help extends beyond the nuclear family, including grandparents, grandchildren and sometimes siblings or other relatives (Den Dulk, 2001). In the Netherlands, more emphasis is put on individual responsibility and public policies. Although recent reforms of the Dutch welfare state are putting more pressure on citizens to extend informal care to people outside their immediate family (Yerkes and Den Dulk, 2015). The Spanish independent professionals who are financially supported by their parents and welcomed back home nevertheless feel obliged to reciprocate by helping family members and attending family events on weekends. The Spanish independent professionals are also less likely to live far away from their family, while Dutch participants prefer not to accept financial support from relatives, relieving them from any social obligation or expectations.

Our case confirms that autonomy and flexibility are not always able to offset work demands. Especially in times of economic downturn, increasing demands tend to decrease autonomy (see also Clinton et al., 2006). This made it more difficult to achieve WLB. In addition, participants noted that stress related to financial insecurity had a direct effect on their relationships with their partner and children at home. For example, some independent professionals could become moody and snappy or withdraw themselves from their family life, for example by locking themselves up in their office. Financial insecurity also created worries among the partners and parents of the independent professionals, as is illustrated by a Spanish engineer talking about his partner:

She is much more thinking about it [my work] than me. We talk about our financial situation a lot. She is always asking how it goes, financially. And wondering what we should do if I don't earn enough . . . She cannot work now, because she is dedicating herself to our baby.

(ES3, Spanish architect, male, 29, one child)

Overall, financial hardship increases job demands such as work intensity and feelings of insecurity among this group of independent professionals in both countries. Moreover, financial hardship and related insecurities diminish the feeling of being in control over their lives. Nevertheless, participants also saw positive outcomes from financial austerity for WLB. For instance, due to the effects of the crisis on the housing market, it became cheaper to rent an office at an external location. The independent professionals mentioned an external office as the solution to separating work from other life domains and to expanding their social network. Some realized that they were lucky having a job, rather than being unemployed. Financial hardship and related insecurities and stress made them reflect on why they want to be independent, their focus and their strong and weak points.

The stronger effects of the financial crisis in Spain did not always result in more financial hardship compared to the Dutch independent professionals in our study. This was related to the social support offered by family members among the Spanish independent professionals. However, tight family relations and receiving support could also decrease autonomy and create dependency on others (*cf* Albert and Couture, 2013). The findings indicate that the resources and demands approach needs to move beyond the work or job contexts and needs to consider how the family context generates demands and resources. In particular, the Spanish case illustrates how family support may form an important resource that helps independent professionals to deal with increasing demands in times of austerity. Experiences differed also according to age and gender. Despite having more resources, older independent professionals in both countries were most worried about income, as they often had caring responsibilities for their family. Male breadwinners especially experienced these gender role expectations as pressuring. The recently graduated independent professionals were most worried about their future career, but did experience less financial stress, as they were often supported by their parents. In Spain, it is common for young professionals to live with their parents in order to save money. In the Netherlands, young professionals were most worried about the continuity of their business and often felt pressured to consider applying for a salaried job to guarantee an income.

Conclusion

The self-employed are a diverse group of workers, who are often subsumed in one category. They are an important and growing category of workers. Differences in work contexts mean that the nature and role of job demands and resources differ between the self-employed and employees and amongst types of self-employed. For instance, the nature of the social support the self-employed draw upon differs from that of employees, as they often work alone and do not have access to support from co-workers or the wider organizational context. They depend more on social support from family members and their social network (Annink et al., 2016a). The findings from our study of independent professionals indicate that the nature and degree of social support from family members differ across national contexts, shaped by their social values and practices.

European policy makers increasingly acknowledge the importance of work–life state support for self-employed workers. The European Commission has recently proposed the Entrepreneurship 2020 Action Plan, which suggests making social benefits for the self-employed comparable to those for employees. However, the self-employed might have different needs than employees. For example, they may benefit more from leave policies that allow flexibility in their use over time, as for many solo self-employed, taking leave is difficult to combine with keeping the business going. On the other hand, high-quality childcare, which can be used in a flexible way, would allow the self-employed to better combine and alternate childcare duties with running a business. Instead of putting the self-employed into the same system as employees, it might be better to develop a system that fits their flexible working patterns (Annink et al., 2015; Yerkes and Den Dulk, 2015). It is important how policies are structured and formulated, since this will affect their utilization and whether they are indeed supportive of the WLB of the self-employed. For instance, in the Netherlands, childcare support for the self-employed currently depends on the level of income and hours worked, which makes it risky for the self-employed to use it since they need to return part of the support if they have less work than expected (Yerkes and Den Dulk, 2015).

In addition, European policy makers and national governments could pay attention to a social safety net that also includes the self-employed. Research suggests that the availability of unemployment allowances for the self-employed results in less feelings of financial hardship and is able to buffer the relationship between financial hardship and well-being. People may feel more secure knowing that they can rely on unemployment benefits if their business earnings should prove insufficient (Annink et al., 2016b). This is crucial for the social justice dimension of the triple WLB agenda.

Other chapters in this book consider the triple agenda for supporting employees, employers and social justice during difficult economic times. The case is somewhat different when discussing the self-employed. The dual agenda is clear, as the well-being of workers and the business are interdependent. However, in the absence of an employer, national social policy and supports are even more crucial to the social justice agenda for this group of workers. The comparative study reported here suggests that, while there are common policy and support needs across contexts, the national context also makes a difference. It may be that support for individual self-employed workers is more necessary in the Netherlands where stress levels in uncertain times may be higher than in Spain. On the other hand, the ramifications for families supporting self-employed members through difficult times is a topic that requires research attention. Supports for families may be even more important in the Spanish cultural context.

Further research is particularly required into the role of families in supporting self-employed members and more generally about different forms of self-employment in different contexts on WLB. Priority might be given to the involuntary or necessity-driven self-employed who are pushed into self-employment because of a lack of alternatives in the labour market (Eurobarometer, 2009; Kelley et al., 2011). Such understanding is vital for the development of public policy that addresses the WLB and well-being of the self-employed.

References

Albert, M.N. and Couture, M.M. (2013). *The Support to an Entrepreneur. SAGE Open*, 3(2), doi:10.1177/2158244013492779

Annink, A., & Den Dulk, L. (2012). Autonomy: The panacea for self-employed women's work-life balance? *Community, Work and Family*, 15(4): 383–402.

Annink, A., Den Dulk, L., & Steijn, B. (2015). Work-family state support for the self-employed across Europe. *Journal of Entrepreneurship and Public Policy*, 4(2): 187–208.

Annink, A., Den Dulk, L., & Steijn, B. (2016a). Work–family conflict among employees and the self-employed across Europe. *Social Indicators Research*, 126(2): 1–23.

Annink, A., Gorgievski, M., & Den Dulk, L. (2016b). Financial hardship and well-being: A cross-national comparison among the European self-employed. *European Journal of Work and Organizational Psychology*. doi:10.1080/13594 32X.2016.1150263

Bakker, A.B., & Demerouti, E. (2007). The Job Demands-Resources model: State of the art. *Journal of Managerial Psychology*, 22(3): 309–328.

Bunk, J.A., Dugan, A.G., D'Agostino, A.L., & Barnes Farrel, J.L. (2012). Understanding work-to-family conflict among self-employed workers: Utilising a cognitive appraisal framework. *The Journal of Entrepreneurship*, 21(2): 223–251.

Clinton, M., Totterdell, P., & Wood, S. (2006). A grounded theory of portfolio working. Experiencing the smallest of small businesses. *International Small Business Journal*, 24(2): 179–203.

Craig, L., Powell, A., & Cortes, N. (2012). Self-employment, work-family time and gender division of labour. *Employment and Society*, 26(5): 716–734.

De Veer, A.J.E., & Francke, A.L. (2009). Werken als zelfstandige, of toch maar niet? *Tijdschrift voor Verpleegkundigen*, 7(8): 34–35.

Den Dulk, L. (2001). *Work-Family Arrangements in Organizations: A Cross-National Study in the Netherlands, Italy, the United Kingdom and Sweden.* Amsterdam: Rozenberg Publishers.

Den Dulk, L., Bäck-Wiklund, M., Lewis, S., & Redai, D. (2011). Quality of life and work in a changing Europe: A theoretical framework. In: M. Bäck-Wiklund, T. van der Lippe, L. Den Dulk & A. van Doorne-Huiskes (eds) *Quality of Life and Work in Europe: Theory, Practice and Policy*: 17–31. Hampshire and New York: Palgrave Macmillan.

Den Dulk, L., & Peper, A. (2009). *Managing Work-life Policies in the European Workplace: Explorations for Future Research.* Working Papers on the Reconciliation of Work and Welfare in Europe. RECWOWE Publication, Dissemination and Dialogue Centre, Edinburgh.

Den Dulk, L., Peper, A., Kanjuo-Mrčela, A., & Ignjatović, M. (2016). Supervisory support in Slovenian and Dutch organizations: A contextualizing approach. *Community, Work and Family*, 19(2): 193–212.

DoingBusiness. (2014). *Economy Rankings*, available at http://www.doingbusiness. org/rankings

Erikson, R., Hansen, E.J., Ringen, S., & Uusitalo, H. (1987). *The Scandinavian Model: Welfare States and Welfare Research.* London: M.E. Sharpe.

Esping-Andersen, G. (1990). *The Three Worlds of Capitalism.* Polity Press: Cambridge.

Esping-Andersen, G. (1999). *Social Foundations of Postindustrial Economies.* Oxford and New York: Oxford University Press.

Eurobarometer. (2009). *Entrepreneurship in the EU and Beyond.* Flash Eurobarometer 283. The Gallup Organization, available at http://ec.europa.eu/public_opinion/ flash/fl_283_en.pdf

European Parliament. (2010). Directive 2010/41 EU of the European parliament and the council. *Official Journal of the European Union*, available at http://eur-lex. europa.eu/LexUriServ/LexUriServ.do?uri¼OJ:L:2010:180:0001:0006:EN:PDF

Eurostat. (2014). *Eurostat Labour Market Database*, available at http://ec.europa. eu/eurostat/data/database.

Frone, M.R. (2003). Work–family balance. In J.C. Quick & L.E. Tetrick (eds) *Handbook of Occupational Health Psychology*: 143–162. Washington, DC: American Psychological Association.

GEM. (2015). *Global Entrepreneurship Monitor—Adult Population Survey Measures*, available at http://gemconsortium.org/data/key-indicators

Glavin, P., & Schieman, S. (2012). Work–family role blurring and work–family conflict: The moderating influence of job resources and job demands. *Work and Occupations*, 39(1): 71–98.

Hatfield, I. (2015). *Self-Employment in Europe*. London: Institute for Public Policy Research.

Hobson, B. (2014). *Worklife Balance: The Agency and Capabilities Gap*. Oxford: Oxford University Press.

Holthuis, E., & Pratt, S. (2010). *European Employment Observatory Review: Self-Employment in Europe*. Luxembourg: Publications Office of the European Union.

Hooper, J. (2006). *The New Spaniards*. London: Penguin Books.

Johansson Sevà, I., & Öun, I. (2015). Self-employment as a strategy for dealing with the competing demands of work and family? The importance of family/life style motives. *Gender, Work and Organizations*, 22(3): 256–272.

Kelley, D.J., Singer, S., & Herrington, M.D. (2011). *The Global Entrepreneurship Monitor*. 2011 Global Report, available at http://www.gemconsortium.org/

Kirkwood, J., & Tootell, B. (2008). Is entrepreneurship the answer to achieving work–family balance? *Journal of Management and Organization*, 14(3): 285–302.

Leighton, P., & Brown, D. (2013). *Future Working: The Rise of Europe's Independent Professionals (Ipros)*. London: EFIP.

Lewis, S., Brannen, J., & Nilsen, A. (eds). (2009). *Work, Families and Organisations in Transition. European Perspectives*. Bristol: Policy Press.

Luber, S., & Leicht, R. (2000). Growing self-employment in Western Europe: An effect of modernization? *International Review of Sociology*, 10(1): 101–123.

Milkie, M., & Peltola, P. (1999). Playing all the roles: Gender and the work-family balancing act. *Journal of Marriage and the Family*, 61(2): 476–490.

Myrie, J., & Daly, K. (2009). The use of boundaries by self-employed, home-based workers to manage work and family: A qualitative study in Canada. *Journal of Family and Economic Issues*, 30(4): 386–398.

Nordenmark, M., Vinberg, S., & Strandh, M. (2012). Job control and demands, work-life balance and wellbeing among self-employed men and women in Europe. *Vulnerable Groups and Inclusion*, available at http://dx.doi.org/10.3402/vgi.v3i0.18896

Ollier-Malaterre, A., Valcour, M., Den Dulk, L., & Kossek, E.E. (2013). Theorizing national context to develop comparative work-life research: A review and research agenda. *European Management Journal*, 31(5): 433–447.

Organization for Economic Co-operation and Development. (2011). *Chapter 1: Families Are Changing*. Doing Better for Families, available at https://www.oecd.org/els/soc/47701118.pdf

Parasuraman, S., & Simmers, C.A. (2001). Type of employment, work–family conflict and well-being: A comparative study. *Journal of Organizational Behavior*, 22(5): 551–568.

Pedersini, R., & Coletto, D. (2010). *Self-Employed Workers: Industrial Relations and Working Conditions*. Dublin: European Foundation for the Improvement of Living and Working Conditions.

Prottas, D.J., & Thompson, C.A. (2006). Stress, satisfaction, and the work-family interface: A comparison of self-employed business owners, independents, and organizational employees. *Journal of Occupational Health Psychology*, 11(4): 366–378.

Rapelli, S. (2012). *European I-Pros: A Study*. Professional Contractors Group (PCG), UK, available at https://www.ipse.co.uk/sites/default/files/documents/research/efip_report_english-v1.pdf

Schaufeli, W., & Taris, T. (2013). Het Job Demands-Resources model: Overzicht en kritische beschouwing. *Gedrag & Organisatie*, 26(2): 182–204.

Scherer, S., & Steiber, N. (2007). Work and family in conflict? The impact of work demands on family life in six European countries. In D. Gallie (ed) *Employment Systems and the Quality of Working Life*: 137–178. Oxford: Oxford University Press.

Schieman, S., & Young, M. (2011). Economic hardship and family-to-work conflict: The importance of gender and work conditions. *Journal of Family and Economic Issues*, 32(1): 46–61.

Stoeldraijer, L. (2014). *Jongeren Blijven Langer Thuis Wonen: Bevolkingstrends 2014*. The Hague: Centraal Bureau voor de Statistiek.

Sullivan, D.M., & Meek, B.R. (2012). Gender and entrepreneurship: A review and process model. *Journal of Managerial Psychology*, 27(5): 428–458.

Taris, T.W., Geurts, S.A.E., Kompier, M.A.J., Lagerveld, S., & Blonk, R.W.B. (2008). My love, my life, my everything: Work-home interaction among self-employed. In K. Naswall (ed) *The Individual in the Changing Working Life*: 147–168. Cambridge: Cambridge University Press, available at http://dx.doi.org/10.1016/j.jbusvent.2008.01.007

Tuttle, R., & Garr, M. (2009). Self-employment, work-family fit and mental health among female workers. *Journal of Family and Economic Issues*, 30(3): 282–292.

Valcour, M. (2007). Work-based resources as moderators of the relationship between work hours and satisfaction with work-family balance. *Journal of Applied Psychology*, 92(6): 1512–1523.

Voydanoff, P. (2005). Toward a conceptualization of perceived work-family fit and balance: A demands and resources approach. *Journal of Marriage and Family*, 67(4): 822–836.

Williams, D.R. (2004). Effects of childcare activities on the duration of self-employment in Europe. *Entrepreneurship Theory and Practice*, 28(5): 467–485.

Wood, S., & Michaelides, G. (2015). Challenge and hindrance stressors and wellbeing-based work–nonwork interference: A diary study of portfolio workers. *Human Relations*, 69(1): 111–138.

Yerkes, M., & Den Dulk, L. (2015). Arbeid-en-zorgbeleid in de participatiesamenleving. Een vergroting van de mogelijkheden? *Tijdschrift voor Arbeidsvraagstukken*, 31(4): 510–528.

The Physical Workplace
and Work–Life Balance
Perspectives from Practice

Ziona Strelitz

Introduction: Place, Technology and Work–Life Balance— a Triangle in Flux

Despite the growth in remote working, the physical workplace is still a normative setting. Millions of people go to a defined place of work every day, and with their multiple life strands to coordinate, their workplace is directly relevant to workers' work–life balance (WLB). The physical workplace also converges with the interests of HR personnel, as custodians of productivity and workers' welfare. But as physical space, the workplace is closely allied to property development, and whilst this sector has latterly developed a view that property is about people, it is a business sector that shapes the physical settings of other economic activities, but with an impetus and timescales of its own.

Although the initiation of property projects relates to prevailing economic cycles, the built environment comprises costly, relatively stable, infrastructure that outlasts the alternating conditions of boom and recession. Thus, whilst its drivers relate to mainstream social currents, the core of the physical workplace—its buildings—evolve somewhat independently of, and with a time-lag relative to, wider economic shifts. Nevertheless, employers have agency in shaping the physical workplace, and whilst they are typically driven by cost and organisational objectives, their strategies have an impact on the well-being and WLB of their employees.

There has been a significant trend for big employers to consolidate operations that were formerly accommodated in different buildings and locations in larger, unified, more modern premises. This offers the benefits of cost-effective workspace and bolstered corporate image, whilst also generating the economies of scale to provide facilities like restaurants and gyms that are perceived as conducive to employees' interests. Although austerity adds momentum to the cost savings that can be achieved by rationalising work premises on these lines, the trend was pre-existing, with extensive realisation in recent decades across both the private and public sectors.

Countering the trend to workplace consolidation in single buildings or clusters, technology has enabled organisations and individuals to operate in spatially distributed modes. The scope for many operations to continue functioning without individuals being physically present—connoted in the now ubiquitous term 'New Ways of Working'—is central to contemporary workplace concepts and designs. As this typically involves desk-sharing rather than specific desks allocated to individual workers—a template for providing the same or more from less, austerity gives it added resonance with employers (for more on new ways of working, see Lyonette et al. in Chapter 4).

This chapter considers the implications for workers. Drawing on my knowledge of workplace provision through involvement in teams delivering workplaces, through judging workplace awards over many years, and from systematic research with people in their workplace, it questions the relevance of consolidated workplaces with enhanced amenities for employees' WLB. It also underlines the scope for spatially distributed third-place work settings to support both productive work and work-life integration.

The sections that follow address, first, the interface between WLB and the physical workplace, as this has evolved in policy and practice, and as influenced by location and technology—forces that are independent of economic cycles, but accentuated by austerity. The next section discusses drivers and trends in workplace provision, focusing on the effects of magnetic urban centres and the consolidation of multiple workplaces in single buildings or campuses—both of which increase the distance to where workers live. These are then contrasted with workers' realities, including the frequent challenge of long journeys to work, and people's common desire to work away from home in a collective place. The penultimate section considers evidence on aspects of the physical workplaces that matter for workers' WLB, compared with more marginal provisions. The conclusion addresses strategies for workplace provision that can better align physical workplaces with workers' as well as employers' needs. This focuses on smaller-scale, simpler, more flexible workplaces, and more spatially distributed work in third places—neither corporate workspace nor workers' homes, which also align with social justice objectives by making workspace accessible to more people.

WLB and Workplace: Recent History

The history of the modern workplace is one of work separated from the domestic realm—spatially and culturally. When WLB emerged in organisational and policy attention, the physical workplace was largely absent from consideration. The foci centred rather on legislation and employment strategies for flexible working and time-management, mostly related to maternity and women's continued employment thereafter (Strelitz, Edwards and Ben-Galim, 2005). Breaking ground in 2005, research examined what a family-friendly office might be (Strelitz and Edwards, 2006). This widened the question away from workers with young children, reshaping it to include all workers and their range of involvements. The study identified the physical provision that employers had made for work-life as focused on workplace facilities, like nurseries (relatively uncommon) and cafés, as well as free-standing amenities like table tennis and pool tables. These were viewed as sufficiently distinctive to gain industry attention, even though provisions like company dining rooms, canteens and sports grounds had been familiar in the post-war decades into the 1980s.

Whilst the new facilities became icons of workplace change, other, more fundamental, shifts occurred, with scant recognition of their impact on employees. A potent influence was financial deregulation in the late 1980s. Enlarging organisations' geographic scope of operation, it prompted physical corporate mobility. This in turn highlighted the comparative labour and premises costs of conducting business in different locations and presented lower-cost work environments like business parks as alternatives. Thus new locales were promoted for the quality of workplace accommodation they offered at competitive cost, with relative blindness to the implications of their locations and scale for employees' WLB.

Developments in IT enabled more footloose activity, further promoting the potential for new work locations. IT also heralded changes in work processes: new work modes and operational platforms, flatter structures and shorter lines of authority. Early e-business led in catalysing change in the culture, design and visual presentation of the workplace, projecting work as fun. Bright colour and striking graphics replaced traditional, staid décor. New interior settings emerged, with 'imaginariums', 'chill out zones', 'think pods' and suchlike, complementing the previously familiar rows of desks, corridors of offices and conventional meeting rooms.

This new way of framing work appealed to the cadre of interior designers, project sponsors and facilities managers who construct and run physical workplaces. It enlivened their work, and distinguished it for peer recognition and affirmation: the more novel the settings they delivered, the likelier they were to gain media attention. This shift in the nature of the physical workplace was evident in submissions for national workplace awards over the decade 1995–2005. The new style could also succeed as 'cheap and cheerful', eclipsing low-cost installations without losing impact. This was exemplified in call centres, the emergent workplace type where colourful finishes and fantasy theming featured prominently to motivate employees who worked in prescriptive, intense operational environments, with short breaks for respite (Strelitz, 1999a).

Call centres are the case in point of the IT revolution, bringing together innovation in work locations, stylistic representations of work, new work processes and associated innovations in employment. Whilst their emergence provoked considerable criticism as stressful places to work (Strelitz, 1999b; Khalid et al., 2013), their positive scope to widen participation in economic activity through new opportunities to combine paid work with other involvements—in family life, as performers, as students, etc.—has been less acknowledged (Jenkins and Delbridge, 2014).

Call centres also demonstrate the complex changing interface between work process, physical place and employment opportunity. First, off-shoring call centres to cheaper labour markets reduced employment opportunities in higher-cost locations like the UK. Next, the maturation of web-based processes facilitated a notable shift from both telephony-based and residual face-to-face customer engagement, reducing the requirement for call centre work. Then, with the resourcing profile changing again through the portion of transactions that customers could undertake directly online, and in response to pressure from local clients to engage with agents who shared their cultural context, remaining call centre employment began to revert to the national home market. The call centre example conveys the evolution of contemporary employment for both employers and employees. As well as changes in employment opportunities for individuals, the dynamic scenario involves shifting connections of work to workplace, and of workplace to geographic place.

IT has been hugely transformative of both work processes and locations, as well as employee experience. Unlike previous cohorts, whose contact with non-work life was circumscribed when they were at work, the wide dissemination of personal communication devices like mobile and smart phones has ensured much freer access (Deloitte, 2015). This affords reach beyond the workplace, even where employers restrict personal use of the organisation's web infrastructure. Whilst this permeability of work and non-work involvements may be greater the higher the employees' status, across the spectrum of employment, workers' IT enables them to manage other aspects of life whilst they are at work. This enhances employees' autonomy and influences the operation of the contemporary workplace towards engagement in place of control. The associated perceived need to enlist employee interest pre-dates, and has continued through, the recession. In particular, the 2008 economic crisis did not diminish the impetus to court those workers who remained especially prized in the 'war for talent'.

Drivers and Trends in Contemporary Workplace Provision

Thus, the physical workplace emerged as a tool to attract employees, and the trend continues. For example, a conference in 2015, entitled *Workplace: retaining London's talent*, examined *"how London is creating workplaces which compete globally in this hyper competitive market."* The agenda was defined as follows: *"In this current climate, cities are having to work harder to attract and retain fresh talent. Companies are increasingly recognising the importance of the workplace in attracting the most talented and innovative workers"* (New London Architecture, 2015).

The path-breakers in deploying the physical workplace as a lever of staff attraction were financially well-resourced employers who echoed the former provision of company dining rooms and sports grounds in contemporary ways. Foremost among these was BA Waterside, British Airways' much-heralded headquarter complex near Heathrow, in 1999. With its running track, hairdresser, beauty salon, supermarket, bank, restaurants, cafés and facilities for outdoor barbeques, this set a new bar for employee amenities at the workplace (Ross, 2012). Other employers followed with their conspicuous employee provisions. Notable award-winning workplaces that contributed to this trend were Enron in London, with a lavishly equipped gym and well-stocked 'pit stops' on every floor, offering pricey energy drinks free for employee consumption (Barrow, 2012); Goldman Sachs with its climbing wall (The Economist, 2005); and Clifford Chance with its high-level swimming pool overlooking Canary Wharf (British Council for Offices, 2015). The company's website (Clifford Chance, 2016) describes the purpose of the *"20 x 8 metre swimming pool which, like the gym, features floor-to-ceiling windows with views out over Canary Wharf"* as amongst *"the additional things we offer, designed to enhance the well-being of everyone here, which really make our office stand out."* Notwithstanding a focus on individual well-being that has developed as a wider agenda in the decade since the building's construction, industry comment on the pool, and the company's advertisement for free swimming lessons in social media, imputes its significance as differentiating the employer (Connelly, 2015).

Expensive as such facilities may seem, the rationale for their provision is predicated on a cost-benefit model that has become widely embedded in the community of workplace suppliers. The ratio 1:5:200 (or variants thereof) refers, left to right, to the capital cost of delivering a new workplace over a twenty-five year accounting frame, next the cost of running the building and its utilities over the same period, with the big figure on the right referring to staff costs—as core to the activity inside. Hence the concept that property is—ultimately—about people and, based on this, the argument proposes that facilities which play a part in attracting, motivating and retaining workers represent a small fraction of total workplace costs, whilst poising the organisation for significant added value in productivity. This ratio and its reasoning have been influential in positioning employee amenities at the workplace not as 'frills', but as purposeful business strategy. Critique by academic specialists in construction economics (Hughes et al., 2004; Ive, 2006) has done little to detract from the ratio's continued use.

Seeking to differentiate office developments and enhance their appeal to tenants, the real estate sector has reinforced the trend to expand facilities at the workplace. Epitomised by the innovative design and branding of the Chiswick Park office development as *Enjoy-work* (Chiswick Park, 2015), developers have extended the concept of the workplace to include not just buildings, but also landscape, plazas, water features and curated programmes of lunchtime events. The intention is to enhance these properties' appeal with facilities that complement people's work experience. Many UK businesses that could not, or choose not to, compete at the level described have introduced other provisions for employees—from theatre-style restaurants to low-cost items like pinball machines, table tennis tables, basketball hoops and televisions.

From a social justice perspective, a relevant question is what such provisions represent to workless people, who not only lack access to economic activity, but also to the wider resources that these workplaces offer. This issue is more relevant in a period of austerity, with contraction in public spending reducing the availability of public facilities like library services and adult education. The issue also concerns workers like contract cleaners, whose entitlement to use such settings is limited by their role. Acknowledging that some organisations do open up their facilities to community use, and that further scope for this is relevant to the triple social agenda, this chapter focuses on the core rationale, scope and effects of providing such workplace amenities for employees' use.

Irrespective of the actual effects of workplace amenities on employees' WLB, economic agglomeration is a powerful factor pressurising workers' lives. Centralisation impacts in two notable ways. One is the clustering effect of business in urban centres, which, combined with housing costs and the associated residential movement away from central areas, increases the distance between homes and workplaces. With the massive physical scale of conurbations, this results in long commutes. In the particular case of Greater London's magnetic pull, the average travel to work distance for its 4.5 million workplace population (ONS, 2011a) was 17.8 km in 2011. This increases to 25.4 km for the 8% who work in the City of London (ONS, 2011b), where few people both live and work—indeed, just 0.09% of London's population reside there (ONS, 2015b). There is also heavy congestion in and around towns and cities (TomTom International, 2015).

The second effect—through organisations' internal agglomeration— relates more directly to amenities at the workplace. The common trend for large organisations to consolidate operations from multiple sites in a single building or campus has strong attractions from a property perspective. These include: a rationalised estate, usually with superior buildings and facilities that enhance corporate profile, and efficiencies in servicing the organisation's accommodation. Consolidation also brings previously disparate business streams and a wider pool of workers together, offering potential for additional value through cross-fertilisation and functional synergies.

However, no single site that involves the merging of what were previously geographically dispersed buildings can be as close to where all employees live. Although the location of any combined new workplace may be closer to home for some, with a newly integrated workforce, such change invariably also involves 'losers' who face increased travel. Unimposing, even tired, as local or branch offices might have been, and comparatively inefficient as standalone premises, as a network of local workplaces their spatial spread is likely to be closer to more workers' homes. With moves to large-scale premises, some employees must either move home or undertake longer journeys to work. In both cases there are associated impacts for workers and their immediate circle. Longer commutes have additional specific effects. As well as the extra time and energy spent on travel, research has identified anxiety about unpredictable travel conditions—intensified by distance, more complex journeys, and concern about meeting responsibilities at both ends of the trip in a timely way (ZZA, successive workplace studies, unpublished).

This section has described a new array of workplace facilities that employers provide to help attract staff and promote productivity. While large workplace consolidations typically generate the economies of scale to afford these, they also increase the distance between home and work for many employees. Against the backdrop of these journeys and extreme commuting to urban centres, the next section considers the realities of workers' lives in negotiating long journeys to work and coordinating their varied responsibilities.

Workers' Realities

The challenges posed by large workplaces accentuate separate demographic and fiscal pressures on workers, which austerity further intensifies. Expansion in higher education (HESA, 2015), student debt (Salter, 2014) and limited job prospects extend youth inactivity (ONS, 2015a) and promote youth dependency (ONS, 2012, Watt, 2014). High housing costs prolong young people's reliance on their parents, to help procure independent housing or for protracted accommodation in the parental home (ONS, 2014b, 2015b,c). Both in turn increase pressure on employees who are parents. In parallel, workers' own later parenthood will have reduced the age gap with their parents (ONS, 2014a). At the same time, extended life spans and growth of the older population increase the responsibilities for elder care that impinge on working children, a burden exacerbated by the pension and wider fiscal crisis. Thus, the economically active 'sandwich generation' is subject to increased dependency from both ends of the age spectrum, whilst factors such as the need to commit to mortgage payments influence its members' need to be economically active for longer, increasing their breadth and mix of responsibilities.

Delivered by developers, estate agents, architects, interior designers and contractors, workplaces typically result as property projects, while the HR function tends to be less involved in strategic premises decisions. People, in contrast, live joined-up lives that involve multiple physical settings. Home, workplace, nursery, school, hospital, gym, cinema, supermarket, doctor, dentist are just a few of the places of engagement that form the context of workers' routine lives—irrespective of both employment level and gender. The report, *Liveable lives* (Strelitz, 2010), identifies common employee predicaments arising from disconnections between physical workplaces and the realities that workers experience. Drawing on interview data, it presents composite case studies of work-life tensions that employees encounter in reconciling their work and other life domains, arising from distance between home and work, and ambivalence about physical presence at work. Both these conditions relate in part to employers' quest for efficiency that austerity further promotes.

The most familiar of the cases from this research is the predicament of the mother, recently returned to work from maternity leave, experiencing the daily stress of getting to work in the morning after taking her child to nursery, and reaching nursery again in time for the evening cut-off, whilst dealing with both typical delays in leaving the workplace and travel contingencies. Less recognised is the father who has arranged to work 'home-based' two days per week, whilst his partner has a similar arrangement with her employer on two other days. Dispensing with paid childcare on these days, the couple minimises costs, but the father finds that caring for a pre-school child reduces his ability to work effectively, to an extent that exceeds his comfort zone. Next in life cycle stage is the manager bidding for promotion to director level, but deeply concerned that her biological clock is ticking. Her challenge is the long commute on a crowded train after a full day in the office, arriving home too tired to cook or converse, let alone try to conceive. Another worker has managed to support her elderly father in remaining at home by going in to see him at lunchtime. However, since her office has merged with another across town, the added distance makes it infeasible for her both to sustain this and experience her working day as sufficiently coherent and productive.

Though equivalent scope is far from universal in the working population, these individuals have considerable discretion to work at home, and the technology to facilitate it. Nevertheless, they feel a strong impetus to be at their workplace. What is common to their predicaments, and others described in the report, is tension at the nexus of home and work.

A follow-up study with people who both can choose where they work and are digitally equipped to work away from a fixed workplace (Strelitz, 2011) focuses on the reasons for working in 'third places'—a setting other than a formal workplace or home. Based on an online global sample of 17,800 business owners and senior managers from over 60 countries, and a face-to-face sample of 86 individuals working in third places in Greater London, New York/New Jersey, Greater Paris, Hong Kong and Mumbai, the findings identify a suite of reasons drawing people to a collective place that they use for work. The report's title, *Why place still matters in the digital age* (Strelitz, 2011), references these pulls to a place for work—for the sociability it offers, the structure it affords and the satisfaction people experience from effective engagement with work when they work there—all distinct from 'presenteeism' to signify commitment.

Alongside the multiple pulls to work in collective places, the report also identifies pushes from home. With many competitive activities that side-track people from work activity, home is reported as distracting. In addition to family interaction and domestic tasks that pose well-recognised diversions, interviewees cite interruptions from neighbours, constant trips to the fridge and the allure of hobbies and pets. They frequently say that they can focus on their work only when they are away from home. Associating different physical settings with different roles, the interviewees use specific places to distinguish their respective activities, and to shield their work, family life and downtime from interruption. Such regulation is at the heart of the balance the interviewees seek. The irony is that with the potential that IT has unleashed to 'work wherever you are', workers now use specific physical places to optimise both their work and other involvements.

The common work-life conflicts described, at different phases of the life course, arise from significant distance between home and work, coupled with workers' widespread draw to work away from home in a place that they designate for work. The next section considers evidence on workplace provisions, in terms of what is most relevant, and more marginal, to workers' WLB.

The Physical Workplace: What Really Matters to Workers

Learning from workers who can choose where they work is instructive in indicating likely wider preferences. Although the online respondents to the research described above were enlisted without knowledge of where they work, 52% reported working in a 'business centre or lounge', and 48% in 'informal spaces' for any or all of the time (Strelitz, 2011). For most of the face-to-face sample (72%), the coffee shop, library or business centre where they were interviewed was their most frequent place of work, with home the second most frequent (for 45%). For both sets of respondents, the primary benefit of working in such a setting is 'convenient location', which the qualitative interview data characterises as being 'close to home'. The findings identify the advantages as making life easier, by reducing travel time and dovetailing more easily with home life. Other benefits include less pressure and more control, with interviewees reporting improved peace of mind since working in easy reach of home and family, and being buffered from home and family when they work. The findings support the hypothesis that convenient location—a fundamental aspect of the physical workplace—is key to productive work, easier work-family interface, and WLB.

Aside from convenient location, other aspects of their physical workplace also influence employees' WLB. Whereas providers propose distinctive facilities and amenities as relevant, the basics of workplace accommodation are assumed as givens. Research with building users shows some rationale to this, as elements like thermal, lighting and acoustic comfort have the effect of 'hygiene' factors—they are taken for granted when they function well, and typically enlist comment only when they impact as irritants. However, focused research on positive as well as negative experience of the workplace shows that interior comfort can promote workers' sense of well-being and quality of life. In a recent study of employees' experience of a new building (ZZA, 2015), most interviewees reported their workspace as enhancing their well-being (75%), with the rest saying it makes no difference (25%). The following comments illustrate perceived linked effects:

> *The building itself and the surroundings have a positive effect on my working day. I have a better journey to work, come to a bright space, have a happy team, and it's easy to circulate. It's 1000 times better, and has a very positive effect on me mentally. I smile! It promotes a shift in culture. Plus I walk up and down stairs thirty times a day. I feel healthier and happier with my team.*

Interviewees were less affirmative on the effect of facilities on their well-being (57% 'positive'; 39% 'makes no difference'), and those facilities that were specifically cited involved intrinsic workplace resources like the WCs, canteen and breakout space, rather than 'extras'. Furthermore, some interviewees referenced qualitative features like a calming colour and views to outside as beneficial for well-being, rather than facilities per se. Employees' awareness of good environmental conditions is not always as pronounced as in this very well designed workplace. Spatial quality—how space feels—is more nebulous than tangible facilities, but as an inherent attribute, its positive effect endures through the building's life, as does the missed potential when it is absent (Strelitz, 2008).

Relative to the pre-eminence of workplace location, and the lasting influence of spatial quality, how relevant are the new wave of workplace amenities described? Do large, consolidated workplaces with more luxurious provision have greater sustained appeal to employees and support for WLB? Do they counterbalance the negative aspects of a big centralised workplace? A parallel, if less spoken, agenda for providing ancillary facilities at workplaces is to reduce the time that employees may spend elsewhere, leaving more time for the employer.

In contrast, a consistent finding in ZZA's workplace studies is employees' desire to leave the building when they have a break, to step away from the employment environment, undertake practical errands, have a walk or run, meet friends who are not part of the organisation, identify as someone other than a worker in their organisation, pop into an exhibition, or buy a sandwich of their choice from the outlet they prefer on a given day. This is about recharge, autonomy and individuals' sense of self. It situates workers outside the spatial and social zone where a manager or colleague can 'just' check what time the next meeting is scheduled, how soon the target is likely to be achieved, or when the report they are awaiting will be complete. And whilst some workers value having an in-house gym to use before, after—or even during—work hours, many have other commitments at the start of the day, and/or after work, and many like to undertake elective activities like exercise closer to home and with people other than co-workers. These perspectives challenge a key proposition of large workplace scale, of which high-end amenities are a correlate.

Another provider argument for large-scale workplaces is the theoretical promise that more people and functional sectors in a single physical place position the organisation for fertile encounters between employees, spawning new platforms for value. However, empirical data indicates that those with whom workers typically sit during breaks or at lunchtime are members of their team, or friends in the organisation. My research on the role of workplace design in fostering social capital suggests that even in environments that are well-resourced with facilities like coffee shops and outdoor seating areas, relatively few people forge new connections with workers who are not direct colleagues. Where it exists, the workplace cycle store is a notable exception, as a facility that brings together people who share an interest in or passion for cycling.

In general, the findings cited are from studies in new workplaces that typically reflect the trajectory of employers' moves to bigger, newer workplaces with more facilities in the building and/or on site. In 2011, I led a study on workplace transformation that involved the reverse situation (Strelitz, 2012b). A large company had located one of its businesses in a bespoke new building designed by a well-recognised architect. Commended in a national workplace awards scheme, this comprised 1,650 workstations in high-quality accommodation, plus a gym, shop, beauty salon and even a music room, in addition to a large staff restaurant and extensive breakout space (British Council for Offices, 2004). Within eight years, the business had vacated the building, moving its employees to a network of existing buildings that the company had long operated as technical facilities, but where technological change had made space available. The research covered staff experience in one of these centres, a far smaller and simpler workplace than the building they had moved from, with little by way of facilities other than a small rest area and outdoor picnic table. The interviewees recognised the physical differences between their previous and current accommodation, but on key measures, most employees evaluated the new workplace positively or as making no difference. These include: 'Improves the scope for the work you do on an individual basis', 'Improves the scope for team work' and 'Feel comfortable and "at home" when you come to this workspace'.

An important factor in accounting for this apparent anomaly was the choice on vacating the disbanded building for employees to work in the company workplace closest to where they lived. The second factor was reduced physical scale. Working in a much smaller building simplified entry and egress. Now people not only had a shorter journey to work, but could just enter and ascend one flight of stairs, rather than negotiate a significant entrance lobby with associated turnstiles, multiple flights of stairs and long floor plates. Interviewees valued this relative ease when they arrived at and left the workplace, and when they went out for quick breaks or fresh air during the working day. The third influential factor was the sense of community in the smaller workplace, with people feeling that they knew those who worked around them, whereas the large building—accommodating teams that lacked both spatial contiguity and substantive work connections—had felt anonymous. The contrast was epitomised by the comment that: *"Now we're no longer rattling around in the Marie Celeste."*

On an index of luxury, the first and second workplaces were chalk and cheese, but with the plainer accommodation being functionally and environmentally fit for purpose, its compactness, simplicity and sense of community prevailed. The study has been valuable in generating evidence on what matters to employees, against the assumptions of workplace providers. With high-end facilities often integral to large physical scale and the strains it induces, these are not clear-cut as assets that contribute to employees' WLB. Indeed, no employee is obliged to use such facilities, but all must engage with the related set of conditions associated with their provision.

This section has considered aspects of the physical workplace that research shows as mattering to workers' WLB—location, spatial, quality, environmental comfort and physical scale, versus non-core facilities that are relatively marginal. The chapter concludes with a focus on strategies for workplace provision that can better align physical workplaces with workers' (and employers') needs, focusing on smaller-scale, simpler, more flexible workplaces and more spatially distributed work in 'third places', which also contributes to social justice by making workspace accessible to more people.

Conclusions: Spatially Distributed Working and the Triple Agenda

In considering aspects of the physical workplace that impinge on employees' WLB, the chapter identifies location as the most relevant factor. A workplace is generally convenient when it enables work close to, but away from, home; conversely, where workplaces involve challenging distance between work and home, they induce strain. Given the demographic and fiscal pressures on workers to absorb more of the care responsibilities that fall on them from both ends of the generational spectrum, austerity accentuates the relevance of locally accessible workspace.

At the same time, technological and cultural changes in modes of work have generated new, practical scope for people to work more sustainably, closer to home. 'Company towns' are now long bygone, and the realities of contemporary life involve far wider residential dispersal than employers can match in workplace provision. However, the rise of third places—where employees can work in conveniently located, collective, supported settings, at least for some of their work, can serve organisations' as well as workers' objectives. Employees benefit by conserving time and energy through reduced travel, sustaining concentration and motivation by working in a work milieu, and supporting their quality of life and WLB through being able to return home without significant delays. Third places are also a neutral or low-cost way for employers to offer dispersed physical workspace with wide spatial reach.

Incorporating employee use of such space as part of their organisations' workplace strategies can help employers to align the quantity of their corporate accommodation with realistic requirements. Strategies to reduce corporate real estate can release capital and reduce revenue costs, gains that are especially useful to employers—hence to employment continuity—in recession. This typically involves savings on core space, by reducing the ratio of work positions that are dedicated to individuals. The practice has already been widely adopted in response to industry recognition that the utilisation of individually allocated desks is commonly around 40%, given the effects of employees' holidays, illness, and work in meeting rooms, conferences and client sites on space use. The study on workplace transformation discussed cites examples of significant space reduction by both a large UK company and local authority (Strelitz, 2012b).

The research on third places described indicates that third-place working was a norm already in 2011. Since then, the great and visible expansion in 'co-work venues', 'hubs' and similar settings, which expressly provide for agile work in the company of others, demonstrates that this mode is even more widespread now. Fuelled in part by their characteristic social mix, as well as convenient location (Strelitz, 2012a), third-place workplaces are becoming more embedded as available options (Greater London Authority, 2015).

The chapter's focus on interior comfort and spatial quality indicates the positive effect on employees when these conditions are present, contributing to individuals' mood and experience. Workplaces that offer these benefits arise from productive decisions about building scale, volume, proportion, light and air, taken early in the course of design. Given typical building life, and the fact that such decisions relate to thoughtfulness more than cost, basic design that benefits employees is independent of austerity. However, well-designed buildings that incorporate simple systems like operable windows that users can control are also more flexible and easier to adapt over time. This advantages employers and employees alike, in all economic conditions, but particularly when organisations revise their workplace accommodation in economically stringent times.

In considering workplace facilities that are conceived to attract and motivate employees, the chapter concludes—contrary to workplace provider thinking—that provisions unrelated to core work functions lack strong relevance for employees, especially when part of a large centralised workplace, almost invariably at a distance from where many live. This is well expressed in the following assessment by an employee in an investment bank (*Quora*, 2014): the plus points include: "*Fantastic on-site facilities*"; the shorter list of minus points: "*Long hours. You may have to forgo the 'life' part of the*

'WLB' sometimes!" This employee's summation focuses on factors that are substantive to work—ambition, inspiring colleagues, leading edge content and learning, rather than the physical workplace itself, even though this is richly resourced with facilities. To the extent that austerity may drive further workplace consolidation that generates the budget for more facilities on site, this will diverge from employees' needs: increased distance challenges WLB and workplace facilities that cater to elective activities are essentially tangential.

In terms of social justice, any discussion of the issues of both employees and employers must be distinguished from the situation of 'workless' people. Having paid work and access to a workplace—even one that is less than ideally located, resourced or designed—positions workers' challenges with their physical workplace as problems of relative privilege. Usefully, technology's enablement of spatially remote access to work enlarges opportunities for economic participation, as does the advent of third-place working. The dissemination of personal devices and the increase in third places—many in municipal spaces with open access where people can work free of charge, also promote scope for those whom austerity has edged out of employment to be economically active, further contributing to society's triple agenda. The current impetus to expand the provision of third-place work settings in outer as well as central areas—with many also offering on-site services to support people in economic activity, opens a wider field to research the effectiveness of spatially distributed workplaces in promoting productive enterprise and WLB.

References

Barrow, B. (2012). For sale: Glittering remnants of enron. [Online] *The Telegraph*, available at http://www.telegraph.co.uk/news/uknews/1385757/For-sale-glittering-remnants-of-Enron.html

British Council for Offices. (2004). *BCO Awards—2004 Corporate Workplace Award*, available at http://www.bco.org.uk/Awards/Winners/2004/Corporate-Workplace2004.aspx

British Council for Offices. (2015). *2015 Awards Winners*. [Online], available at http://www.bco.org.uk/Awards/Winners/2015/Award-Winners-2015.aspx

Chiswick Park. (2015). *Chiswick Park Enjoy-work*. [Online], available at http://www.enjoy-work.com

Clifford Chance. (2016). *Our Canary Wharf office*, available at http://www.clifford-chance.com/careers/experienced_lawyers/u_k/our_canary_wharfoffice.html

Connelly, T. (2015). *Surely Future Magic Circle Lawyers Aren't Sufficiently Superficial to be Swayed by the Promise of a Free Swim*, available at http://www.legalcheek.com/2015/09/surely-future-magic-circle-lawyers-arent-sufficiently-superficial-to-be-swayed-by-the-promise-of-a-free-swim/

Deloitte. (2015). *Mobile Consumer 2015: The UK Cut Game of Phones*. [Online] London: Deloitte, available at http://www.deloitte.co.uk/mobileuk/assets/pdf/Deloitte-Mobile-Consumer-2015.pdf

The Economist. (2005). *Up the Wall*, available at http://www.economist.com/node/3909004

Greater London Authority. (2015). *London Open Workspaces*, available at https://www.london.gov.uk/priorities/business-economy/for-business/business-support/london-workspaces

Higher Education Statistics Agency. (2015). *General Student Numbers*, available at https://www.hesa.ac.uk/free-statistics

Hughes, W., Ancell, D., Gruneberg, S., & Hirst, L. (2004). Exposing the myth of the 1:5:200 ratio relating initial cost, maintenance and staffing costs of office buildings. In Khosrowshahi, F. (ed), *Proceedings 20th Annual ARCOM Conference*, 1–3 September 2004: 373–381. Association of Researchers in Construction Management, Edinburgh, UK.

Ive, G. (2006). Re-examining the costs and value ratios of owning and occupying buildings. *Building Research & Information*, 34(3): 230–245.

Jenkins, S., & Delbridge, R. (2014). In pursuit of happiness: A sociological examination of employee identifications amongst a 'happy' call-centre workforce. *Organization*, 21(6): 867–887.

Khalid, A., Sarfaraz, A., Ahmed, S., & Malik, F. (2013). Prevalence of stress among call center employees. *Pakistan Journal of Social and Clinical Psychology*, 11(2): 58–62.

New London Architecture. (2015). *Workplace: Retaining London's Talent*, available at http://www.newlondonarchitecture.org/programme/events/2015/september-2015/workplace-retaining-londons-talent

Office for National Statistics (ONS). (2011a). *Population (workplace population)*, available at http://www.nomisweb.co.uk/census/2011/wp101ew

Office for National Statistics (ONS). (2011b). *Distance Travelled to Work (workplace population)*, available at http://www.nomisweb.co.uk/census/2011/wp702ew

Office for National Statistics (ONS). (2012). *Recent Graduates Now More Likely to Work in Lower Skilled Jobs*, available at http://www.ons.gov.uk/ons/rel/mro/news-release/recent-graduates-now-more-likely-to-work-in-lower-skilled-jobs/recentgraduates0312.html

Office for National Statistics (ONS). (2014a). *Live Births in England and Wales by Characteristics of Mother 1, 2013*. London: Crown Copyright, available at http://www.ons.gov.uk/ons/rel/vsob1/characteristics-of-Mother-1—england-and-wales/2013/rtd-cm1.xl

Office for National Statistics (ONS). (2014b). *Young Adults Living with Parents, 2013*. [Online] London: Crown Copyright, available at http://www.ons.gov.uk/ons/rel/family-demography/young-adults-living-with-parents/2013/sty-young-adults.html

Office for National Statistics (ONS). (2015a). *Educational Status, Economic Activity & Inactivity of Young People*. [Online] London: Crown Copyright, available at http://www.ons.gov.uk/ons/rel/lms/labour-market-statistics/april-2015/table-a06.xls

Office for National Statistics (ONS). (2015b). *Estimated Resident Population Mid-year by Single Year of Age*, available at https://files.datapress.com/london/dataset/office-national-statistics-ons-population-estimates-borough/2015–09–28T13:02:40/population-estimates-single-year-age.xls

Office for National Statistics (ONS). (2015c). *Statistical Bulletin: Families and Households, 2014*. London: Crown Copyright, available at http://www.ons.gov.uk/ons/dcp171778_393133.pdf

Quora. (2014). *What Is It Like to Work at Goldman Sachs?* available at https://www.quora.com/What-is-it-like-to-work-at-Goldman-Sachs

Ross, P. (2012). *British Airways Building by Niels Torp in Heathrow, UK.* The Architectural Review. 24th July, available at www.architectural-review.com/buildings/british-airways-building-by-niels-torp-in-heathrow-uk/8633352.article

Salter, J. (2014). *The Borrowers.* Demos, available at http://www.demos.co.uk/files/TheBorrowers_REPORT.pdf

Strelitz, Z. (1999a). Calling for better design. *Architect's Journal*, 209(25): 56–59.

Strelitz, Z. (1999b). Letter: Call-centre stress. *The Independent.* 6th November, available at http://www.independent.co.uk/arts-entertainment/letter-call-centre-stress-1128638.html

Strelitz, Z. (2008). *Buildings that Feel Good.* London: RIBA Publishing.

Strelitz, Z. (2010). *Liveable Lives.* Chertsey, Surrey: Regus Management Limited.

Strelitz, Z. (2011). *Why Place Still Matters in the Digital Age: Third Place Working in Easy Reach of Home.* Chertsey, Surrey: Regus Management Limited.

Strelitz, Z. (2012a). *Energy, People, Place: Sustainable Urban Paradigm.* Hexham, Northumberland: SHP in association with Northumbria University.

Strelitz, Z. (2012b). *Improved Productivity at Lower Cost: Evidence from Research on Workplace Transformation.* London: ZZA Responsive Environments ©, Telereal Trillium.

Strelitz, Z., & Edwards, M. (2006). *Getting It Together: The Work-life Agenda and Offices.* London: British Council for Offices.

Strelitz, Z., Edwards, M., & Ben-Galim, D. (2005). *Family-friendly Offices: The Policy, Practice and Legislative Context.* London: British Council for Offices.

TomTom International. (2015). *TomTom Traffic Index: Measuring Congestion Worldwide.* [Online], available at http://www.tomtom.com/en_gb/trafficindex/#/list

Watt, N. (2014). Youngsters bear debt burden as older generation avoids squeeze, poll shows. *The Guardian.* 10th February 2014, available at http://www.theguardian.com/money/2014/feb/10/young-carry-debt-burden-older-generation-avoid-poll

ZZA (2015). Lloyd's Register's GTC at Boldrewood: Post Occupancy Evaluation, Report to Grimshaw Architects, Confidential, ZZA Responsive User Environments, June 2015

10 Revisiting the Dual Agenda

Why Companies Miss the Point If They Retract Flexible Work Arrangements during Bad Times

Hyosun Kim, Lotte Bailyn and Deborah M. Kolb

In February 2013, Marissa Mayer, Yahoo's newly appointed CEO, stopped its working from home policy and asked all employees to be in the office starting the following June. The reason given:

> To become that absolute best place to work, communication and collaboration will be important, so we need to be working side-by-side. That is why it is critical that we are all PRESENT in our offices. Some of the best decisions and insights come from hallway and cafeteria discussions, meeting new people, and impromptu team meetings. Speed and quality are often sacrificed when we work from home. We need to be one Yahoo!, and that starts with physically being together.
>
> (Swisher, 2013)

Shortly thereafter, Hubert Joly, the new CEO of Best Buy, ended its Results Only Work Environment (ROWE) program, which had allowed work groups to set their own schedules to accomplish their work. Again, a spokesman explained:

> Bottom line, it's "all hands on deck" at Best Buy and that means having employees in the office as much as possible to collaborate and connect on ways to improve our business.
>
> (Bhasin, 2013)

This was despite research from the University of Minnesota that showed that Results Only Work Environment groups had significantly decreased labor turnover and provided better health and well-being for employees (Moen et al., 2011).

What are we to make of this? It seems that when bad times hit, managers may revert to outdated assumptions about what is required for productive work. What are these assumptions? First is the belief that by being together all the time there will be more creativity and innovation. Good ideas can come from interactions, but creativity also requires times away from work and down time (Amabile et al., 1996). And productive work entails both interaction and individual contributions. Even Marissa Mayer, in her keynote on April 18, 2013 to the Great Place to Work conference—a group of human resources professionals—conceded that "people are more productive when they're alone" (Tkaczyk, 2013).

It would seem, rather, that underlying such statements about working practices, is an employer or manager need for control over employees, which strengthens in difficult times. It is noticeable, however, that as companies demand presence during the "normal" work day, at the same time they encourage continuing to work away from the office during off times. Indeed, as Mayer was demanding everyone be in the office, she also provided everyone with a smart phone, signaling that when employees are home during off times, they can be available (Lavey-Heaton, 2014). This distinction between not allowing work from home during official office time but encouraging it in off times was identified as a form of control by Perin (1991) some time ago.

That managerial control is behind much of this insistence on facetime at work is echoed also by Joly of Best Buy who goes beyond advocating the need for being together for innovation to take place. He also objects to ROWE because it is "based on the premise that the right leadership style is always delegation."

> It [ROWE] operated on the assumption that if an employee's objectives were agreed to, the manager should always delegate to the employee how those objectives were met.
>
> (Bhasin, 2013)

One wonders why not. It does not make sense unless the manager feels a need for control over what the employee does to meet the agreed upon goals (cf. Bailyn, 1985). It also seems out of keeping with changes that are taking place in other U.S. organizations. Zappos, for example, has joined a group of other organizations—including Washington state government—in trying what is called holacracy:

> Holacracy is based on a term and concept coined by anti-totalitarian political writer Arthur Koestler. Its central tenets include individual autonomy and self-governance. In a holacracy, employees aren't told how to work. Instead, they belong to voluntary groups called "circles," or peers who help vet new ideas or problems. Everyone has equal say, and employees are evaluated and rewarded by peers, instead of by a boss.
>
> (Noguchi, 2015)

However, the most basic assumption—relevant to this chapter—is not even articulated; it is hidden in the societal belief that the economic and domestic domains are completely separate. Despite years of feminist analysis (e.g.

Ferguson, 1985; Ferree, 1990; Martin, 1990; Fletcher, 2001), organizations still act as if they can organize and structure their work arrangements for employees that have no other interests or responsibilities than to their paid employment (Kanter, 1977)—that is, for traditional men. This assumption is still so taken for granted, so beneath the surface, that its consequences can only be inferred from practices that with a keener eye through a gender lens are clearly seen to be dysfunctional for both employees, particularly women, and the organizations for which they work. Indeed, some of the gains made by feminists in highlighting gender issues at work may have been lost since the financial crisis. For example, the gender agenda and focus on reconciling employment and family life, once recognized as key to policy for promoting women's activation in the European labor market are no longer at the fore-front of discussions in the European Commission (Guerrina, 2015; Walby, 2015). So a gender lens on organizations is even more important than ever.

Our action research projects in organizations have dealt with interventions geared to challenging gendered assumptions about ideal workers and the separation of economic and domestic spheres. The goal of these projects is to raise awareness of the consequence of these outdated and gendered assumptions and to create work changes that lead to better, mutually beneficial, outcomes. In the next section, we describe what we mean by the Dual Agenda, which underpins these action research projects, and provide some specific examples from our work. This is followed by a fuller description of our method. Finally, we consider some strengths and limitations of the action research method and the implications of moving from a dual to a triple agenda in future research,

The Dual Agenda

The concept of the Dual Agenda emerged from a series of action research projects, mostly supported by the Ford Foundation, in the 1990s and beyond. The goal was the social justice objective of gender equity in the workplace. The participation of women in the workforce had greatly increased, but they were still behind their male equivalents on all counts: job prospects, promotion to senior positions and pay and benefits. While many progressive companies had established policies designed to help employees with family obligations (Galinsky et al., 1991; Bond et al., 2005), these policies are based on an individualized model that locates the problem in the individual woman and accommodates her needs. What is necessary, instead, is to focus on the obstacles in the workplace, which is typically not designed for people with external interests and responsibilities (Ely and Meyerson, 2000a, b; DeVault, 2014).

Moreover, so-called family-friendly policies are superimposed on all the work practices and cultural expectations that had evolved when the workforce was more homogeneous and the work itself less complex. They represent individual accommodations for a particular problem group (almost always women, primarily mothers) who seem unable to meet the expectations of an ideal worker. As such, these practices actually reinforce an inequitable status quo (Bailyn, 2006). It was clear, therefore, that in order to meet the social justice goal of gender equity; solutions have to be more systemic; they have to bridge the separation between employees' work and their family and other personal interests and responsibilities. Only in that way can a situation that disadvantages women be alleviated.

Initially, the goal of the action research projects was to identify and try out changes in the way work was accomplished that would help employees integrate their work with their personal lives (and thus enhance gender equity), without hindering the effectiveness of the work. The biggest finding of that original work was that these changes both help employees *and* the effectiveness of the work. This happens because the outdated gendered assumptions that make lives difficult for employees turn out also to be inefficient and ineffective for the more technical, global and knowledge-based work of today. And so the Dual Agenda was born. It refers both to an approach to diagnosis—using a gender lens and bringing work and family together by taking employees' needs and work needs jointly into account—and an outcome of intervention: helping both gender equity and work effectiveness (Fletcher and Bailyn, 2005; Kolb, 2014).

We now describe some of these projects and the lessons learned from them as well as their implications for gender equity.

Telecommuting Helps the Work

The first insight we had into how changes in practices could help the work was in the financial reporting group of a large bank. Employees were in a continuously frantic state trying to keep up with the demands made on them to produce the reports that the board and senior executives needed— a situation particularly hard on the women. Their supervisor, moreover, desperately needed a template to keep track of all the parts of these reports, but there was never enough time to build it. These workers asked repeatedly for a day or so at home to catch up on their work without the chaos of the office. Management refused. Only when a team of action researchers came in and analyzed the situation jointly from the employees' as well as the bank's point of view did management agree to an experiment. It was agreed that those who wanted to do so could take two days a week at home; management even set them up with the necessary equipment. They could not connect directly to the office LAN (Local Area Network) but were able through another route to access the material they needed. The results were soon evident. The employees were much less frantic—which was noticed by their colleagues. Also, with more control over their time and without a long commute, they were able to attend family events and still get all their work done. And now they had the time and the motivation to develop the template the supervisor had always wanted, so coordination was greatly improved. It worked so well that even the supervisor began to take one day a week at home. This was a clear Dual Agenda outcome: both worker and work benefitted. And when the office LAN went down for a few days and the only people who could get any work done were the ones who were at home—the experiment became institutionalized (Rayman et al., 1999).

Collective, not Individual Flexible Work Arrangements

The second insight concerned the way that flexible work arrangements are implemented. Typically an individual asks for one form of flexible arrangement and the manager supports it or not. Management discretion is considered crucial. We learned differently from a project in the Customer Service Division of a large corporation. The corporation had very progressive work–family policies—job sharing, four-day work weeks, flexible start and end times—but they were rarely used. Although workers, particularly women, made requests, they were more often than not turned down by supervisors who feared loss of control. As a result, people stopped asking, which only confirmed management's belief that flexible work arrangements were not necessary. Absenteeism, not surprisingly, was high. The Dual Agenda diagnosis showed that the individual accommodation approach they had been using was having negative consequences for both workers and work. The head of the division was then willing to try an experiment: anybody who wanted to take advantage of an alternative arrangement could do so, as long as the work got done. A number of things happened. First, almost everyone wanted a different schedule, including men, single people and non-parents. Second, it was no longer possible for supervisors to negotiate changes on an individual basis. The work group had to manage their schedules collectively. And the results? Employees found it much easier to integrate work with their personal lives, which helped everyone, but was particularly useful for women with small children. The organization also benefitted: absenteeism went down 30% and customer service improved—a Dual Agenda outcome. What is critical is for the work group to control its own arrangements. Flexible work arrangements have to be recognized as important for getting the work done; if seen only as individual accommodations neither the work nor the worker will benefit (Bailyn et al., 1997; Bailyn, 2011). Such a collective approach, by allowing all constituents to take advantage of flexible working arrangements, creates a new work norm that allows all employees—not just women with childcare needs—to successfully integrate their work and family without being stigmatized as less committed to work. As women are likely to be the main beneficiaries of normalizing flexible working, this has the potential to advance gender equity.

Removing the Bias from Evaluation Procedures

In a scientific organization, we found that it is not only changes in flexibility in the time and place of work that can affect the Dual Agenda of gender equity and work effectiveness; equally important are formal and informal evaluation procedures. In this organization, where employees had advanced degrees in science, women were being recruited but not advancing, typical of many science, engineering and technology organizations (Herman and Lewis, 2012). When researchers were asked to help with this problem they found a culture where it was not seen as appropriate to ask for a promotion or to express any desire to move up in the organization. The taken-for-granted assumption was that leadership will find you: all that matters is the work you do. We know, of course, that such assumptions systematically work against women, or anyone different from the dominant employee (Castilla and Benard, 2010), so it was important to find out how this process of "finding" leaders actually worked. As it turned out, top management would establish brainstorming sessions and would pick for promotion those who excelled in them. But who was invited to these meetings? Anyone that top management, all men, could think of. And, not surprisingly, that seemed to be primarily men. When we pointed out this dynamic, and how it worked against their honest desire to promote more women into leadership positions, they were amazed and changed their procedures. They then introduced into their decision making a devil's advocate, charged to ensure that no particular group is left out of the invitations (Fletcher et al., 2009). Women were then better represented in these critical meetings.

Changing the Narrative of Time

Sometimes change is not immediately obvious. This was the case with a global organization of research scientists, one of our action research projects. Similar to the science organization just discussed, the impetus was a concern, held by the Director and some female staff, that women were underrepresented at the professional and managerial levels and that the work environment was experienced as inhospitable to women. The research found that time was a significant problem in this organization. People felt overwhelmed by their workloads. A shift in organization priorities and the demands of collaboration across divisions and the need to work more closely with scientists and policy makers in the field, meant that meetings and other types of professional interactions were encroaching on much of the work day. The organization operated in continual crisis mode and the researchers were forced to work on their own research in off hours—a clear problem for women with families and the quality of work they could produce, which impacted on perceptions of their competence. We presented our diagnosis in a series of roundtables, and one significant experiment came out of these sessions—it was called the 'quiet time' experiment—three mornings a week people could close their door and not be interrupted. The goal was to protect time for the research scientists to do their independent work during normal hours.

The quiet time experiment did not work as planned, but it had symbolic significance because it communicated that the organization accepted responsibility for some of the time pressures employees experienced. This led, we discovered when we returned a year later, to a new narrative of time. Previously, the belief was that the ways in which people used their time were an individual choice. A new narrative replaced it in which time was seen as a systemic issue that had to be dealt with by the organization. It helped all the research scientists, regardless of gender, and it enabled the organization to expand its collaborations and have a greater impact on the populations it was supposed to serve, again a Dual Agenda outcome (Kolb and Merrill-Sands, 1999).

Changing Work-Related Norms

Just as in the case of a new narrative of time which slowly emerged, changes in work practices can eventually feed back to changes in basic understandings and norms. A government supported action research experiment in South Korea illustrates how this works. In two parts of a mid-sized hospital, a nursing ward and a rehabilitation centre, successful interventions were introduced in the structure of work shifts. On a nursing ward, which was suffering from high attrition—especially of nurses after maternity leave—the Dual Agenda team convinced the hospital to introduce a new short day shift (from 8 AM to 2 PM) for nurses with the most pressing work–family needs. The nurses in the short day shift assisted doctors during rounds, helped patient discharge, took care of bedding and other support work, which allowed night shift nurses to focus on handoff. As a result, overtime for night shift nurses was significantly reduced. Moreover, nurses found the newly created short day shift to suit their increased family responsibility and almost all of them returned after their maternity leave. The reduction in overtime and turnover costs of skilled nurses made up, to an extent, for the investment in the extra shift (Kang et al., 2014), which made these interventions feasible even in difficult economic times.

In the rehabilitation centre, which didn't require 24-hour coverage, the change was from a universal schedule with everyone involved in all tasks to staggered shifts with different work assignments for each. As a result, employee satisfaction increased and patients received better care. Because these Dual Agenda outcomes came from an interactive process, they resulted also in changes in work-related norms: by expanding the definition of "real work" to include all necessary tasks, not only the most valued ones; by increasing the understanding that performance does not suffer when time flexibility is introduced; and by accepting and seeing the value of employee participation in decision making (Kang et al., 2014).

In all of these cases, management was open to the diagnosis achieved through systematically bringing employees' needs together with business needs, and looking at work through a Dual Agenda and gender lens (more on the methods used below). But this is not always the case. The deep-seated belief in the gendered separation of the domestic and economic spheres can lead to denial of such a diagnosis and to the perpetuation of dysfunctional management processes.

Resistance Is Part of the Process

In a professional services firm where there was concern that women employees were leaving the company before reaching partner status, management firmly believed that women were leaving for family reasons. As Dual Agenda researchers, however, we came to a different conclusion. Not only were men leaving proportionately as frequently as women, but for neither was family the key issue. Rather, it was the way the company managed its client contracts that resulted in tremendous stress and overwork. For management, getting a client was more important than being realistic about planning and staffing. That meant that schedules were always tight and in a crisis mode, which created great personal stress for the consultants involved. No wonder turnover was so high, for both men and women, and costly to the company. Further, when people left the firm they were resentful, which meant that if they moved to client companies they did not recommend this firm to their new employer. The issue was not the family concerns of women, but the toxic environment created by dysfunctional management processes. In the end, the firm's leaders resisted the analysis and failed to support an experimental intervention. The Dual Agenda diagnosis challenged their framing of the problem as solely about women and family, which blinded them to the ways that their work processes exacerbated long hours and unpredictability for both their male and female employees. If it were not for these blinders, the organization might have seen and addressed work problems that hurt their employees and cost the company dearly (Padavic and Ely, 2013; Kolb, 2014).

Summary of Learning from Dual Agenda Projects

We seem to be in a period of cultural lag (Ogburn, 1957; Brinkman and Brinkman, 1997) where both workers and work have changed, but the culture, norms and practices of the workplace lag behind. Particularly in difficult economic times, organizations seem to revert to a culture of control, even as the changing world requires a much more adaptive and flexible culture (Kang et al., 2014. These projects have shown us that flexible work arrangements are indeed important, but are underutilized unless they are managed collectively within a team. And we see how changes to work that help workers in the end also help the work. We need to change assumptions, norms and narratives about time, about competence and commitment, about gender roles and about the structure of work and the definition of "real work"—the particular tasks that are most valued. Only then will we make progress toward real gender equity in the workplace.

In the process of doing these action research projects, we developed a method—an approach that allowed us to surface those gendered assumptions, and the practices associated with them, that made life difficult for employees, had a differentially negative impact on women as compared to men and turned out also to be dysfunctional for the work (Rapoport et al., 2002; Bailyn, 2011). We call the method Collaborative Interactive Action Research (CIAR).

Collaborative Interactive Action Research (CIAR)

Access for a CIAR project usually is motivated from the company's point of view by a concern that they are losing women or that women are not moving up in the organization. The first step, typically, is to establish a liaison committee at the organization for the researchers to work with. This is the beginning of a collaborative interaction where researchers have expertise on gender dynamics and organizational change and organizational partners have expertise on their organization's structures and culture—what Fletcher (1998, 2001) has called *fluid expertise*. No successful Dual Agenda outcome can be achieved without this interactive collaboration from the beginning.

Jointly a site is chosen. Usually it is a site with some problems, which makes sense from the company's point of view; perhaps the problem can be helped, but presumably no great harm can be done. From the researchers' point of view it is important that the site has a workforce consisting of both men and women in various family situations. Depending on the size of the site, either all or a sample of employees is chosen for interviews.

These interviews consist of details about the person's work as well as his or her family and personal life. From the beginning, we link the two domains very explicitly, asking, in essence, what it is about work that makes employees' lives difficult. We also ask about the organization: who gets promoted; how is success defined; what is expected around time and presence; any differential issues for different groups of employees. Contrary to some interviewing techniques, we view these interviews as a setting for what we have called micro-interventions. For example, a male employee tells us about his successful career. He also tells us that his wife has stayed at home and raised the children. At this point we might ask: do you think you could have had the same success in your career if your wife had also followed a demanding career? The goal of these micro-interventions is to bring to the fore the key intersection between what goes on at work and what happens in the family and in life outside of work. How counterintuitive this is was made obvious when people would often say to us, "why are you asking us about our work—aren't you the work–family people?"—i.e. dealing with policies for

174 Hyosun Kim, Lotte Bailyn and Deborah M. Kolb

those who need them and staying quite divorced from anything having to do with work itself. It is against this separation of the personal and work domains with its negative consequences for women workers, and toward an explicit linking that these micro-interventions are directed.

On the basis of an initial sense of what's going on, we then have group meetings with employees who were interviewed as well as those who were not. The purpose of these meetings is to allow people to understand that the personal issues they face in dealing with their work are not only their individual concerns but are shared widely and typically stem from systemic sources. And discussion often brings up key organizational issues that create some of these problems. Again, these sessions are seen as micro-interventions, where the researches try to make explicit the systemic nature of these links.

These interviews and the group meetings comprise the data for the Dual Agenda analysis. Normally it is the researchers who do the analysis, though in back and forth contact with the liaison committee. The goal here is to identify underlying, typically gendered assumptions and the practices flowing from them that guide the way the work is done and how success in that work is defined. Though we identify the value of these practices for the work, the key of the analysis is to show the unintended consequences of gendered workplace assumptions for work–personal life integration and gender equity, on the one hand, and for the effectiveness of the work, on the other. Because both the workforce and the work are changing and because these ways of working have typically been around a long time and are rarely questioned, they very often have unintentional negative consequences for the effectiveness of the work itself, as well as for employees' lives.

The key moment comes when this analysis is fed back to management and the entire group. The feedback consists of three to four assumptions and the practices that comprise them; the functions that they seem to have fulfilled; the unintended negative consequences for the work; and the unintended negative consequences for gender equity and work–personal life integration. Often this analysis is eye-opening; the conclusions resonate with people. The ensuing discussion further emphasizes the universality of the issues— i.e. these are not just a few people's problems but they affect everyone, and they have a systemic source. Sometimes this feedback session is followed by group meetings where employees discuss what practices could be changed to both ease their lives and make the work more effective. And some of these groups then discuss ways to make these changes. But the main emphasis is on the group designated for the key intervention, which then meets with the researchers to plan it. The action part of CIAR is designed completely collaboratively.

Typically the intervention is planned as an experiment or pilot for a limited amount of time, with key metrics identified both on the personal and the work side. It is also critical to keep both sides of the Dual Agenda on the table throughout the experimental period. We have had the experience of the personal side (personal needs) dominating and the work demands being ignored (Bailyn et al., 2007) as well as the work side taking over while ignoring the personal consequences (Kolb and Meyerson, 1999; Ely and Meyerson, 2000). Both situations preclude successful outcomes. Successful CIAR projects require continuous monitoring by researchers or insiders attuned to the needs of the Dual Agenda. And this takes time, resources and a commitment to change, which can be daunting in difficult economic times but has long-term pay-offs.

Modification to the CIAR Process

A promising revision of these guidelines occurred in the Korean projects. There, because of the researchers' limited time and resources, many more aspects of the process were taken over by organizational members: they carried out the interviews and participated actively in the analysis and produced successful Dual Agenda results. The researchers, though still important, acted more as advisers.

It should be noted that the hospital in which these projects occurred had a strong orientation toward organizational learning, long before these projects came along. Further, there were two previous attempts to design a Dual Agenda intervention which did not work, but which nonetheless increased the understanding of the process and contributed to the success of the project. Importantly, gender played a different role in this case since it involved an all-female workforce. The ability to modify and adapt CIAR and to incorporate it into existing organizational processes to make it less time consuming and costly demonstrates a way that the Dual Agenda approach can have wider exposure (Kang et al., 2014).

Discussion

These projects show how many areas of change become available when management is open to challenging its existing beliefs and is willing to experiment, and when decisions are made and ideas emerge from all those involved. In this process women can act as canaries in the mine—indicating the presence of toxicity in the environment (Kolb, 2014). The approach, therefore, contributes to both gender equity and work effectiveness.

The essence of the method is to think of employees' problems not as things that need to be fixed, but as opportunities to rethink the organizational processes that are causing these problems in the first place (Bailyn, 1993; Meyerson and Fletcher, 2000). The key finding of our work has been that this rethinking process helps all employees, not only those with problems, and also makes the work itself more effective. Gender equity and work effectiveness can go together; employees' personal needs can constructively be brought together with business needs. We suggest that this more extensive and inclusive win–win thinking is particularly helpful during more difficult times.

Though the Dual Agenda approach to workplace change sounds reasonable, it is not easy to accomplish. The culture of hierarchy and control that has been embedded in business organizations for so long is not easy to unbend. As an effort at cultural change, dual agenda projects aim to change not only the cultural artifacts but also the underlying assumptions regarding gender and work and family (Schein, 1992). Since cultural assumptions are very hard to surface, the CIAR method was developed as a way to challenge assumptions through experimentation. But, as discussed above, though there have been examples of success where changes have been sustained, there also have been failures from which we can learn.

The problem is that these changes may not last long as organizations operate in a world where the traditional assumptions about employee control are still a dominant logic. Hence even when an alternative—based on a more flexible and participative logic—is shown to be successful, as in some of these Dual Agenda projects, the old culture can reassert itself. The danger is that this may happen particularly in periods of economic crisis, which is counterproductive. In fact, sustaining practices that help both the worker and the organization (the Dual Agenda) can be particularly valuable during difficult financial times (for an example see Lyonette et al. in Chapter 4).

Finally, a number of questions remain that have to do with social justice. Does the dual agenda with its emphasis on helping both employees and the work mean that gender equity and providing for workers' family and personal needs have no value in and of themselves? Does it let businesses off the hook in terms of providing for the well-being of their employees independent of its effect on the business? Does it take away the pressure for businesses to be more than profit-oriented and be responsible also for their social impact? Lyonette and colleagues (see Chapter 4), in their analysis of UK public sector austerity cuts, have identified a change in how "work–life balance" policies are being used. In this context, rather than curtailing existing flexibilities organizations seem to be promoting and developing them in order to save costs. For example, employees can work from home to save money on buildings; or have reduced hours so they can be paid less. This turn away from a more social justice emphasis to a purely economic one may, however, be masked if it is presented within a discourse of employee well-being and mutual benefits (i.e. the Dual Agenda), which is one area of concern.

Another problem relating to social justice concerns the populations that Dual Agenda projects have dealt with. They tend to engage primarily professional and white-collar groups that have much more flexibility in resources, or companies that are privileged in this way. We need to know more about service workers and other low-income workers whose main concern is with making ends meet. For low-income workers, reduction in hours is not the answer. What is at stake here is the predictability and stability of hours. Workers need to know their schedules and be able to count on a regular income. In the U.S., this issue is beginning to get attention. The *Schedules that Work Act,* which has recently been introduced in Congress, would alleviate some of the worst practices. So the particular issues may be different, but the approach of legitimating personal needs and using that lens to rethink work procedures should still be valid. It is important to analyze the needs of this part of the workforce more closely to ensure that suggested changes will benefit them as well (Lautsch and Scully, 2007).

This book addresses a triple agenda which includes wider social justice. Our emphasis on gender equity is actually an example of trying to assure social justice—fairness in the workplace. Nevertheless, if the goal is to ensure that businesses think of the social implications of their procedures, then the emphasis on how changing practices can help their business goals may not be sufficient to further this goal. Nor does the Dual Agenda take into account other aspects of social justice: fairness of roles in the family, reduction of gender stereotypes and other aspects of social inequities. Future research could consider ways of meeting a wider agenda of equity for all at work; effectiveness of work; and social justice at work, at home and in the community.

Conclusion

In times of austerity, there is a tendency to revert to rigid routines, to command and control and to think of flexibilities as luxuries that one can no longer afford. But flexibilities are not luxuries. Dealt with correctly, they are the necessary means to a more adaptable as well as equitable workplace—exactly what is needed in bad economic times. We have presented and illustrated a way of thinking and a means of proceeding that could help. Although we realize these are not simple best practices, but rather a process of change, they may be more important than ever as economic conditions evolve and as work becomes ever more complex and the workforce more diverse.

References

Amabile, T.M., Conti, R., Coon, H., Lazenby, J., & Herron, M. (1996). Assessing the work environment for creativity. *Academy of Management Journal*, 39(5): 1154–1184.

Bailyn, L. (1985). Autonomy in the industrial R&D lab. *Human Resource Management*, 24(2): 129–146.

Bailyn, L. (1993). *Breaking the Mold: Women, Men, and Time in the New Corporate World*. New York: Free Press.

Bailyn, L. (2006). *Breaking the Mold: Redesigning Work for Productive and Satisfying Lives*. Ithaca, NY: Cornell University Press.

Bailyn, L. (2011). Redesigning work for gender equity and work–personal life integration. *Community, Work & Family*, 14(1): 97–112.

Bailyn, L., Collins, R., & Song, Y. (2007). Self-scheduling for hospital nurses: An attempt and its difficulties. *Journal of Nursing Management*, 15(1): 72–77.

Bailyn, L., Fletcher, J.K., & Kolb, D. (1997). Unexpected connections: Considering employees' personal lives can revitalize your business. *Sloan Management Review*, Summer: 11–19.

Bhasin, K. (2013). *Best Buy CEO: Here's Why I killed the 'Results Only Work Environment'*, available at http://www.businessinsider.com/best-buy-ceo-rowe-2013-3

Bond, J.T., Galinsky, E., Kim, S.S., & Brownfield, E. (2005). *National Study of Employers*. New York: Families and Work Institute.

Brinkman, R.L., & Brinkman, J.E. (1997). Cultural lag: Conception and theory. *International Journal of Social Economics*, 24(6): 609–627.

Castilla, E.J., & Benard, S. (2010). The paradox of meritocracy in organizations. *Administrative Science Quarterly*, 55(4): 543–676.

DeVault, M.L. (2014). Mapping invisible work: Conceptual tools for social justice projects. *Sociological forum*, 29(4): 775–790.

Ely, R.J., & Meyerson, D.E. (2000a). Theories of gender in organizations: A new approach to organizational analysis and change. *Research in Organizational Behavior*, 22: 103–151.

Ely, R.J., & Meyerson, D.E. (2000b). Advancing gender equity in organizations: The challenge and importance of maintaining a gender narrative. *Organization*, 7(4): 589–608.

Ferguson, K.E. (1985). *The Feminist Case Against Bureaucracy*. Philadelphia: Temple University Press.

Ferree, M.M. (1990). Beyond separate spheres: Feminism and family research. *Journal of Marriage and Family*, 52(4): 866–884.

Fletcher, J.K. (1998). Relational practice: A feminist reconstruction of work. *Journal of Management Inquiry*, 7(2): 163–186.

Fletcher, J.K. (2001). *Disappearing Acts: Gender, Power, and Relational Practice at Work*. Cambridge, MA: MIT Press.

Fletcher, J.K., & Bailyn, L. (2005). The equity imperative: Redesigning work for work-family integration. In E. Kossek & S. Lambert (eds) *Work and Life Integration: Cultural and Individual Perspectives*: 171–189. Mahwah, NJ: Erlbaum.

Fletcher, J. K., Bailyn, L., & Blake-Beard, S. (2009). *Critical management studies at work: Negotiating tensions between theory and practice*. Cheltenham, UK: Edward Elgar.

Galinsky, E., Friedman, D.E., & Hernandez, C.A. (1991). *The Corporate Reference Guide to Work-Family Programs*. New York: Families and Work Institute.

Guerrina, R. (2015). Socio-economic challenges to work-life balance at times of crisis. *Journal of Social Welfare and Family Law*, 37(3): 368–377.

Herman, C. & Lewis, S. (2012) Entitled to a sustainable career? Motherhood in science, engineering and technology. *Journal of Social Issues* 68(4): 767–789.

Kang, H., Kang, H., Ku, J., & Kim, H. (2014). Dual Agenda: A critical requirement in flexible work arrangements. *Korea Academy of Management*, 22(3): 63–98.

Kanter, R.M. (1977). *Work and Family in the United States*. New York: Russell Sage Foundation.

Kolb, D.M. (2014). *Getting Women In and Up: Lessons from a Dual Agenda Approach to Change*. Presented at the Korean Academy of Management Forum on work-family balance and organizational innovation, Mimeo. Boston: Center for Gender in Organizations, Simmons College School of Management.

Kolb, D.M., & Merrill-Sands, D. (1999). Waiting for outcomes: Anchoring a dual agenda for change to cultural assumptions. *Women in Management Review*, 14(5): 194–203.

Kolb, D.M., & Meyerson, D.E. (1999). Keeping gender in the plot: A case study of The Body Shop. In A. Rao, R. Stuart, & D. Kelleher (eds) *Gender at Work: Organizational Change for Equality*: 129–154. West Hartford, CT: Kumarian Press.

Lautsch, B.A., & Scully, M.A. (2007). Restructuring time: Implications of work-hours reductions for the working class. *Human Relations*, 60(5): 719–743.

Lavey-Heaton, M. (2014). Working from home: How Yahoo, Best Buy and HP are making moves. *The Guardian*, available at http://www.theguardian.com/sustainablebusiness/working-from-home-yahoo-best-buy-hp-moves

Martin, J. (1990). Deconstructing organizational taboos: The suppression of gender conflict in organizations. *Organization Science*, 1(4): 339–359.

Meyerson, D.E., & Fletcher, J.K. (2000). A modest manifesto for shattering the glass ceiling. *Harvard Business Review*, 78(1): 126–136.

Moen, P., Kelly, E.L., Tranby, E., & Huang, Q. (2011). Changing work, changing health: Can real work-time flexibility promote health behaviors and well-being? *Journal of Health and Social Behavior*, 52(4): 404–429.

Noguchi, Y. (2015). *Zappos: A Workplace Where No One and Everyone Is the Boss*, available at http://www.npr.org/2015/07/21/421148128/zappos-a-workplace-where-no-one-and-everyone-is-the-boss

Ogburn, W.F. (1957). Cultural lag as theory. *Sociology and Social Research*, 41: 167–174.

Padavic, I., & Ely, R.J. (2013). *The Work-Family Narrative as a Social Defense: Challenging Conventional Wisdom*. Boston MA: Harvard Business School.

Perin, C. (1991). The moral fabric of the office: Panopticon discourse and schedule flexibilities. In P.S. Tolbert, & S.R. Barley (eds) *Research in the Sociology of Organizations 8*: 241–268. Greenwich, CT: JAI Press.

Rapoport, R., Bailyn, L., Fletcher, J., & Pruitt, B. (2002). *Beyond work-family balance: Advancing gender equity and workplace performance*. New York: Jossey-Bass.

Rayman, P., Bailyn, L., Dickert, J., Carré, F., Harvey, M., Krim, R., & Read, R. (1999). Designing organizational solutions to integrate work and life. *Women in Management Review*, 14(5): 164–177.

Schein, E.H. (1992). *Organizational Culture and Leadership* (2nd Ed.). San Francisco: Jossey-Bass.

Swisher, K. (2013). *'Physically Together': Here's the Internal Yahoo No-Work-from-Home Memo for Remote Workers and Maybe More*, available at http://allthingsd.com/20130222/physically-together-heres-the-internal-yahoo-no-work-from-home-memo-which-extends-beyond-remote-workers/

Tkaczyk, C. (2013). *Marissa Mayer Breaks Her Silence on Yahoo's Telecommuting Policy*, available at http://fortune.com/2013/04/19/marissa-mayer-breaks-her-silence-on-yahoos-telecommuting-policy

Walby, S. (2015). Crisis. Cambridge: Policy Press.

11 Towards a Triple Agenda for Work–Life Balance beyond Recession and Austerity

Deirdre Anderson, Jonathan Swan and Suzan Lewis

This book has explored some impacts of recession and austerity on organisational working practices and workers' experiences of work–life balance (WLB). We have considered whether social justice, insofar as it was ever implied in the WLB agenda, gets lost in turbulent economic times or whether the three prongs of the triple agenda may be reconcilable. Below we begin by summarising the key issues that have been addressed in earlier chapters. We then present short case studies of three organisations to illustrate some of the strategies used in adjusting the organisational approach to flexibility and WLB during, but not necessarily because of, the recession and austerity. We discuss implications for employees, employers and social justice and conclude with some thoughts about working towards a triple agenda beyond the recession.

We have seen that research on trends in the provision of flexible work arrangements since the 2008 recession generates mixed findings, with some practices declining and others increasing. There does appear to be greater use of remote working in a number of contexts. On one level, it seems that traditional working practices and expectations of rigid working hours in a central workplace may be giving way to increased flexibility. This could have the potential to provide more opportunities for some workers to vary where and when they work in order to integrate work with personal lives, although it appears to be more of a cost-cutting exercise than one driven by employee needs or even notions of mutual benefit (see Stokes and Wood, Chapter 3; Lyonette et al., Chapter 4; Strelitz, Chapter 9). On the other hand, a strong theme throughout the book is of employers seeking to do more with less. Work intensification and the blurring of work/non-work boundaries by technology, job insecurity and pressure at work, deteriorating employment conditions including casualisation associated with, or exacerbated by, recession and austerity, can all have negative repercussions for workers' experiences of WLB, particularly their ability to work and care and to sustain health and well-being (see Kinman and McDowall, Chapter 2).

Moreover, even when options for working less or more flexibly are available, employees are often reluctant to use them in times of recession or austerity due to heightened job insecurity, wider earnings inequalities and increased financial pressures on households, especially when traditional ideal worker assumptions persist (see Fagan and Vermeylen, Chapter 1).

Most research on WLB focuses on middle class, relatively privileged, knowledge workers employed in large organisations. This book has pointed to the importance of also understanding how difficult economic times have had an impact on working-class lives (see Warren, Chapter 6), on the self-employed (see Den Dulk et al., Chapter 8), and especially on women combining precarious low-paid work with unpaid care-giving (see Fagan and Vermeylen, Chapter 1; Busby and James, Chapter 5). In such circumstances, it is not just the time squeeze but real financial hardship that is the problem. Another important theme in the book is the disproportionate impact of austerity on women as workers and carers and on gender equity (see Busby and James, Chapter 5; Kim et al., Chapter 10). Women are affected not only by changes in their workplaces and employment protection, but also by cuts to public services on which working carers, predominantly women, depend.

The challenge of the triple agenda is to find ways of organising work to meet the needs of diverse employees at all levels of organisation and to sustain effective workplaces in socially just ways. Trade unions and collective bargaining can play a key role in campaigning for gender equity and for WLB support for all workers, although processes and outcomes vary across national institutional contexts (see Milner, Chapter 6). The ability of unions to influence policy-makers and to introduce or enforce employee rights in the workplace has been adversely affected by changes since the 2008 recession. There have been some successes whereby collective bargaining in some large companies has been able to develop a progressive WLB agenda which has also influenced the development of legal rights. Nevertheless, significant sections of the workforce, particularly the most vulnerable, remain exposed to negative effects of the post-2008 crisis.

Researchers can also make a difference to workers' experiences of WLB, particularly those taking an action research approach. There are examples in this book of innovations to meet a dual agenda of supporting workers' WLB and workplace effectiveness from the US and Korea (Kim et al., Chapter 10). Importantly, these are not quick fixes but the outcomes of a collaborative action research approach which engages work teams and researchers in methods of change and rethinking organisational processes. The approach, therefore, contributes to both gender equity and work effectiveness. Some examples of how small workplace innovations can work in the recession and austerity in the UK are discussed below in this chapter. However, employers are more accustomed to speaking of mutual benefit or a dual agenda than a triple agenda that also takes account of social justice. Moreover, workplace practices are only part of the broader picture of the impact of economic downturn and austerity. The wider social policy and regulatory frameworks and safety nets for vulnerable workers are crucial to the wider social justice element of the triple agenda.

Case Studies

Below, we provide examples of organisations that have continued to address issues of workplace effectiveness and support for employees' WLB despite challenges presented by economic difficulties in recent years. We also explore the organisational understanding of, and approach to, social justice. We conducted interviews with a representative from each of three organisations: a British small business (ManufCo), a company in the utilities sector (UtilCo) and a UK government department (GovDept). The interviews began with a question about the organisational approach to workplace flexibility in general and any innovations during recent challenging economic times. We asked about employee responses to changes in working patterns, whether of time or place, and explored perceptions of any impact on business and delivery of services or products. We were also particularly interested in exploring the triple agenda of workplace effectiveness, employee work–life benefits and social justice. It is interesting to note that, although the interviewees were keen to discuss the mutual benefits of various initiatives to employer and employee, none of them raised the issue of wider social justice until specifically asked about it. They then discussed their own understanding of social justice and how the organisation engaged with this, highlighting some interesting initiatives. Several themes emerged from the interviews: retention and talent management, values-led approach to people management, focus on output rather than presenteeism, use of technology in supporting work away from the office and the importance of trust and respect.

ManufCo

ManufCo is a thriving manufacturing small business in the Midlands employing between 50 and 60 people in mainly semi-skilled production roles. This case thus addresses the call, in other parts of the book, to extend discussion of WLB practices beyond the focus on the relatively privileged to include more working-class workers. The CEO explained that there is a great emphasis within the organisation on its 'Commitment to Employees', a stated aim of *"achieving the best match between meeting the needs and aspirations of employees and running an efficient customer-focused business"*. He is an enthusiastic supporter of the dual agenda which had emerged from the organisation facing difficulties over 15 years ago; multi-skilling of staff was the approach taken to ensure survival of the business. As he pointed out, *"We start with the business need, but work towards the best solution for everyone. We don't package it as work–life balance but as a win-win scenario."*

The company did have to make changes to their ways of working when the recession hit in 2008 because their order intake reduced by 30% for about a year. This resulted in redundancy for five members of the workforce and further changes for the remainder for a period of 12 months. Contracts of employment did not allow for a temporary reduction in the working week and management consulted with all employees explaining the need to reduce costs further. Management preference was to reduce the working week (and pay) by 10% rather than the alternative of another five redundancies. Employees were asked to vote, agreeing that the majority vote would apply to all employees. The result was that out of 45 attendees, 43 voted for the reduction in working week option, which involved a compressed working week of Monday to Thursday for production workers and a long weekend (Friday to Monday inclusive) on a rota basis for office staff. Three of the people who were made redundant have subsequently re-joined the company.

Jobs were also redesigned. Multi-skilling enables the production workers to have greater variety of work through job rotation and a points system links the number of machines/processes they are competent to run to an increase in pay and a higher grade. There are a minimum of three people in the factory trained for any operation and a similar situation with regard to office duties.

Flexible working is described as the way to meet the ever-increasing needs of customers and workers at the same time. The CEO commented that *"rather than trying to find reasons for not doing things, we say, how do we make it work?"* This attitude means that staff are encouraged to discuss any possible change to their working patterns with colleagues to explore how the team can collaborate to accommodate the individual, overcoming any potential objections and then approaching management with a solution rather than a problem. The focus is on meeting individual needs and such conversations take place when people join as well as when personal circumstances change.

Several examples were given to illustrate the positive working relationships and the variation in requests as well as the willingness to make short-term changes on a trial basis. For instance, one young woman was a trained beautician/hairdresser and the opportunity arose for her to work part-time in a hair salon, which necessitated reducing her hours at ManufCo. A trial period of three months was agreed upon, during which she decided that she preferred working in the factory and keeping the beauty therapy/hairdressing as a hobby/sideline. She asked if she could return to full-time work and, as the trial period applies to both employer and employee, this was agreed. One new starter travelled by bus and so start and finish times were agreed in relation to the bus timetable. Another example was of a man in his 50s who worked in the warehouse and was a lover of fine art. He was delighted to have the opportunity to study for a degree in Fine Art on a part-time basis of one day per week. For the duration of his degree, his employment contract at ManufCo was a mix of a compressed work week and annualised hours (working longer weeks during university vacations). Other requests have related to caring responsibilities of either children or elderly relatives. The CEO explained that it is important to know your staff so that they feel able to approach management with their requests. The reason behind the request is not relevant in seeking a solution that works for the individual, her or his colleagues and the business.

Although there was an explicit focus on the dual agenda, it is clear that a sense of fairness and positive relationships with all employees are of paramount importance, and this has a positive effect. When solutions are mutually beneficial, staff are less likely to worry about situations outside of work and so can focus more when in work. Social justice for this organisation relates to listening to their staff and ensuring that they feel valued, encouraging collaboration and recognising that they are likely to be more productive and innovative as a consequence, hence supporting the triple agenda argument.

UtilCo

UtilCo is in the Utilities industry and employs over three thousand people within the UK. Prior to the 2008 recession, the organisation had already begun looking for more efficient and effective ways of working that would both deliver better productivity and provide the opportunity for costs savings. The organisation, according to the Diversity and Inclusion HR consultant, was focussed on becoming more effective by moving away from a presence-based towards an output-based way of working, enabling employees to work from different and more remote locations. This involved a significant mindset shift for line managers, who had to adopt a high trust way of working, managing employees working in different physical locations.

Like many organisations, in order to facilitate this move to an output-based way of working, the organisation has, post-recession, introduced 'agile working', using developments in technology to achieve its objectives of higher productivity. Savings have been made through the use of new and more efficient ways of working such as digital meetings, which minimise travel costs, and also through the use of local hubs and reducing real estate costs of centrally based offices. An emphasis on technology met some scepticism about the benefits, and employees fitting an older demographic profile in the workforce who were not used to or comfortable with technology were not initially receptive. However, the organisation took a collaborative approach to the usability design of technology, helping employees buy into tools that they had helped co-design, and the HR consultant described technology as "*a big game changer*". In addition to becoming a location-neutral employer, there have been tangible business benefits from the spread of technology, including improvements in customer relationship management and enhanced service delivery. The interviewee emphasised that individual choice is the determining factor in whether an employee works remotely. Although technology has made it easier for employees to work away from the office or at home, they are not required to do so.

The organisation has developed the idea that employees can control their own working time, with an emphasis on employees finding the right work–life fit for themselves. While there is a 'core hours' framework within which employees may establish a working pattern that suits them, customers increasingly expect 24/7 service, and so good work scheduling is key. '*Working patterns are clearly set out so that boundaries can be set between work and home*', reports the HR consultant. This important caveat minimises the risk of spillover from, for example, being digitally connected to the office. In addition, there are formal reviews of working practices that aim to identify any practices that impede work and life balance. WLB is supported through monitoring of workplace metrics, such as the career progression of female part-time workers. The ambition for the organisation is described as '*to push flex into specific roles, then into all roles.*'

The organisation has, through its internal and external activities, incorporated the third element of the 'Triple Agenda' of social justice. The Diversity and Inclusion work they undertake has the goal of making them a rounded employer, and they want to ensure that they have an inclusive and representative workforce in terms of both protected characteristics and also of society more generally. This means that UtilCo takes steps to recruit widely to encourage a large range of potential employees to consider them as employers. Perhaps most relevant to the topic of this book, the organisation also takes its wider role in the economy seriously, and makes efforts, for example, to recruit employees, where possible, who have been made redundant. They describe this as trying to absorb some of the employment consequences of austerity.

GovDept

GovDept is a UK ministerial department employing over 70 thousand people. WLB is often discussed in terms of flexible working patterns which have been available for a number of years. The recent initiative of using existing departmental buildings in varying locations as local office hubs has emerged as part of a more strategic view looking at how staff work. This has been driven in part by the need to reduce the carbon footprint and real estate occupation in London. Staff retention, particularly of women continuing in employment after their return from maternity leave, was another issue.

The review of working practices is linked to wider initiatives focusing on smarter working across other governmental departments and would probably have taken place anyway, but the recession provided an added impetus for moving forward with the sale of buildings in London. Consultation with staff indicated that some do not want to work at home, perhaps because they have young children or simply due to a lack of suitable space to allocate as a workstation. This preference was acknowledged and the following alternative option to homeworking was developed. This government department has many buildings which are essential to the wider provision of services, but are not necessarily fully occupied at all times, so the aim was to improve the utilisation of those buildings. Existing office spaces were therefore identified as local hubs and a booking system introduced to allow visiting staff the certainty of a desk. The emphasis is on equipping staff with a laptop and a phone and a range of collaborative technology tools is available and encouraged to maintain relationships and teamwork. People can therefore work from home, go into their main office, or a local hub, thereby facilitating employee choice. Some staff prefer to work in a designated office space surrounded by colleagues; others may need to use facilities such as printers that they do not have at home. An important factor here was the recognition that staff may wish to avoid a long commute and so the local hubs tend to be in surrounding areas rather than Central London, thus enabling reduction of office space in the city.

From an organisational perspective, wider networking occurs. For instance; staff meet colleagues who they may not have met in the course of their work at their own office base: *"It's opened people's eyes to other working conditions. They may have worked on projects in HQ and never seen the day to day activities in the local areas. So it gives a broader perspective about the reality of our work"*.

The interviewee suggested that for this organisation, social justice relates to the consequence of retaining talent, facilitating employment for people who may have other demands or challenges which mean that working traditional hours would be prohibitive. Men and women can more easily attend to caring responsibilities while continuing to work at levels commensurate with their abilities and experience. Those with disabilities are able to avoid a long commute and work in a local hub, and for some, this may be a crucial factor in maintaining their employment. As well as the individual benefits from reduced travel costs, the Department is tracking the time and carbon footprint saved by staff working in the hubs, and also trying to assess the spending within the local community on lunches and coffees, an important aspect during the recession.

From Dual to Triple Agenda

From these case studies of very different organisations, it is interesting to identify some overlapping themes relating to the three elements of the triple agenda. A broad approach to placing people at the centre of the success of business was reported in all three case studies. Specific reference was made to retention and talent management of skilled and experienced staff and the need to address individual needs in order to achieve organisational effectiveness—the win/win solution referred to by the CEO of ManufCo. Interestingly, he was referring to a different type of employee than those usually intended in such discussions; semi-skilled production workers who may not be targeted in a "war for talent" but nevertheless are valued for the contribution they make to the organisation and the investment made in their training. Collaboration with and among staff was described as an integral part of any change initiatives in ManufCo, as in the cases discussed by Kim et al. (Chapter 10).

All interviewees also talked about enabling staff to attend to their caring responsibilities while maintaining a paid work role. They linked this to the values of the organisational approach to people management in general and flexibility in particular and talked of "going beyond the legislation". Within this values-led approach, trust and respect were seen as underpinning a good relationship between employer and employee and demonstrate a concern for employee well-being as discussed in Chapter 2 (Kinman and McDowall). Trust was also linked strongly to performance management with a shift from a presence-based to an output-based way of working in all the organisations.

Technology was presented as an enabler of flexibility. For ManufCo, multi-skilling of staff on machinery enabled variety of work as well as maintaining work flows, essential to the successful running of the business. In the two larger organisations, technology facilitates working away from the main offices, leading to the sale of unnecessary office space (GovDept) and the ability to have staff living across a wider geographical area (UtilCo and GovDept). The sale of buildings may have facilitated remote working at home and in local hubs, the third places referred to by Strelitz (Chapter 9), but the longer-term impact is yet to be experienced and may have unanticipated consequences.

The interviewees talked enthusiastically about the mutual benefits to the individual and the employer, but discussed social justice only when prompted, suggesting that this is not (yet) part of organisational discourses. However, all three then demonstrated an understanding of some ways in which their organisation addresses this third aspect of the triple agenda, leading us to question why people are more reticent to overtly express the issue of social justice and perhaps address fairness issues more explicitly. Evidence from a recent annual benchmark of employer WLB and flexible working policy and practice (Working Families, 2015) shows that although participating employers are implementing policies to ensure equality of access to, and fairness in the availability of WLB opportunities for employees, and are responsive to their employees' needs, they do not see these activities through the lens of social justice. When asked if "Flexible working is a means of addressing structural social inequalities", only a third of respondents in 2015 agreed. The benchmark shows that these employers are vigilant in their activities around diversity and equality and link these with flexible working practices in some instances. However, social justice tends not yet to be considered by employers in a coherent way. Large organisations with an HR function, in particular, approach this through the diversity and equality lens, but this tends to be quite narrow and looks at the diversity strands (some of which, like gender, are only partially addressed) rather than more fundamental workplace changes.

The benchmark results suggest that the organisational view of WLB and flexible working remains in a silo, with responsibility primarily resting with Human Resources and Diversity departments. Despite senior support and an overall organisation-wide vision or values statement for flexibility, the formation and deployment of policy remains with HR. Indeed, in the two large organisations discussed above it was the senior HR or diversity specialists who were spokespeople on WLB. This focus on delivery from a single specialist area of the organisation may make it more difficult to clearly see the links between day-to-day activities and a social justice agenda. Thus, for organisations to develop greater awareness of social justice, and indeed to understand how their existing activities are already addressing the triple agenda of win–win–win objectives, it will be important for WLB to move out of the narrow HR silo and become organisation-wide. The very terminology of WLB may, however, be a barrier to this. It is noticeable that the CEO of ManufCo spoke of collaborative solutions and innovations that are the best for everyone and deliberately does not package these as work–life initiatives.

Beyond Recession and Austerity: Implications for the Future Triple Agenda

The initial formulation of the dual agenda (Kim et al., Chapter 10) demonstrated that changes in the nature of work that challenge outdated gendered assumptions and help employees to integrate their work with their personal lives (and thus enhance gender equity), benefit both employees and workplace effectiveness. The term dual agenda is now widely used in relation to win–win outcomes, although associated initiatives do not always result in challenging deep seated assumptions about ideal workers or workplace practices. The triple agenda model proposes that organisations can develop practices that support employees' WLB and contribute to wider social justice in terms of, for example, enhancing gender equity, social mobility and inclusiveness, enabling workers to fulfil care responsibilities and addressing the WLB needs of the vulnerable and low skilled as well as those traditionally referred to as "talent", while at the same time enhancing or at least not harming workplace effectiveness. The cases discussed in this chapter, as well as some referred to in other chapters, suggest that some employers are already beginning to work towards this approach by, for example, collaborating with workers about how to meet organisational and employee WLB needs in ways that are perceived to be fair, or by taking steps to ameliorate the impacts of recession and austerity by recruitment strategies that target those who have lost jobs. Nevertheless, even many highly progressive employers seem to be uncomfortable with discussing social justice in relation to workplace practices. They tentatively discuss their existing practices in social justice terms and realise that they can contribute in this way, but perhaps because initiatives have to be justified in terms of the "business case", especially in challenging economic times, the possibility of meeting not one but two other agendas is rarely articulated. This is important because language determines how we think. If social justice cannot be explicitly articulated in WLB debates, this limits possibilities for creative thinking.

Similarly, while corporate social responsibility is widely accepted, connections with WLB are more rarely made. Therefore, we argue that now is the time to start "changing the conversation", that is, to broaden the ways in which employee WLB is talked about.

Having said this, we do not intend to imply that employers should or could be solely responsible for WLB and well-being, or for enabling care-giving, in difficult economic times or in other contexts. The capability of workers across the social spectrum to work and care for themselves and others depends not only on employee practices but also on the social, political and regulatory environments within which organisations operate. For example, without appropriate regulation, the legality of practices, such as zero-hours contracts, perpetuates social injustice. Fagan and Vermeylen (Chapter 1) describe the intensifications of the pre-existing expansion of precarious forms of employment and job insecurity in some countries since the recession, facilitated by legal reforms. Fixed-term contracts, agency work, zero-hours contracts, fragile types of self-employment and undeclared casual work have expanded in poorly regulated sectors; such arrangements may suit a minority of workers with access to other resources but not those low-paid workers who rely on a regular income. Busby and James (Chapter 5) note that austerity measures in the UK have disproportionately disadvantaged and reduced protection for the large numbers of women workers who combine low-paid, precarious work with high levels of care-giving for children and others, while cuts to public services risk upsetting the finely tuned arrangements on which those who provide care alongside paid work depend. Fagan and Vermylen (Chapter 1) discuss national policy measures to support the reconciliation of paid work and family as social investments which deliver benefits for the triple agenda of employee well-being and quality of life, workplace productivity and social justice, including gender equality and individual and family well-being. A social investments perspective on WLB has important implications for both government and employer policies and practices.

In conclusion, we argue that debates about WLB require reframing with a greater emphasis on social justice as well as workplace effectiveness, addressing the interface of social policy and workplace practices. We are mindful of the need to engage with business leaders in developing this conversation. It may be argued that there is a danger that a greater emphasis on social justice may lead to a loss of support in many businesses, but we doubt that many employers would actually argue that fairness and social justice are bad for business. As the CEO of ManufCo said:

> *I don't have a problem with talking about a triple agenda rather than a dual agenda and agree that social justice or social responsibility is important. Most companies understand the concept of corporate social responsibility and I would prefer to talk about reaching solutions which meet the needs of the business (and customers) and employees/potential employees in a socially responsible way.*

However, it is important to ensure that policy makers and businesses accept the triple agenda as being good for all. When business is faced by crisis or challenge, flexibility becomes more important, supported by multi-skilling. Therefore, it is important to convince business leaders that employee motivation is key to surviving austerity. It is also crucial that employees perceive flexibility to be fair and to take account of their needs. This requires a collaborative approach illustrated by organisations such as Working Families, which works with employers and policy makers, promoting flexible workplace cultures and advocating for working families and working carers. Sarah Jackson, CEO of Working Families, the UK's leading work–life balance organisation, which works with employers and individuals to find workplace practices which enable a better balance between responsibilities at work and home, commented that flexibility is not always perceived as mutually beneficial and points to the deeper changes that are needed:

> *Online parent forums are hugely cynical about flexible working and agility. "It's about employers forcing more out of less"; "it's about loss of control". The challenge is to rethink and redesign work. The way we work today is bad for our health and wellbeing, bad for our relationships, bad for our children and bad for our performance at work. A 24/7 consumer culture can bring disastrous consequences for family and societal wellbeing. We have the tools—now we have to start asking the really difficult questions about the purpose of work and what we really mean by work–life balance. Asking the questions and proposing the answers will take courage and imagination—but it's about work, rest and play. Our bodies, our minds, and our spirits are designed for those to be in balance.*

An important role for future academic research is to expand the WLB research agenda to provide evidence of the feasibility and outcomes of the triple agenda. Meanwhile, the cases discussed above and issues covered in the preceding chapters show that there have been some potentially positive developments in relation to WLB even in difficult economic times, but that they are often double edged. Inevitably, there remain many obstacles and challenges to more fundamental changes in workplace assumptions and practices. Nevertheless, it will be important to keep social justice on the agenda and learn lessons about how to protect individual WLB and well-being, sustain organisations and ensure social justice in the event of future economic crises.

Reference

Working Families. (2015). *Top Employers: Changing the Way We Live and Work: Benchmark Report 2015.* London: Working Families, available at http://www.workingfamilies.org.uk/wp-content/uploads/2015/09/WF_A4_16pp-Top-Employers-Benchmark_2015_FINAL_PR_03.pdf

Index

absenteeism 24, 30, 31, 93
Advisory, Conciliation and Arbitration
  Society (ACAS) 83–4
agency work and workers 4, 96, 189
agile working 161, 184, 190
anti-discrimination laws 79
anxiety 24, 27
assumptions: gendered xvii, 98, 167,
  168, 173–4, 188; workplace 174,
  190
austerity: and boundary management
  25–7; business decisions during 75;
  definitions xv, xvii; effect on flexible
  work options 46–7; effect on service
  delivery 72–4; effects of 189; factors
  related to 24; flexibility during 177;
  impact on women 80; impact on
  worker/carers 86–9; and new ways
  of working 68–9; in the United
  Kingdom 63; and the work-life
  balance 35–6, 56
Austria, short-time working in 5
autonomy: and self-employment 135–6,
  140–4; job 5, 10, 58, 63, 96, 131,
  135–7, 140–4, 152, 158; working-
  time 10; in the workplace 166

BA Waterside 153
BAe Systems Submarines 104
Ballarin, Jérôme 102
Barcelona Summit 3
bedroom tax 121
Behavioural Risk Factor Surveillance
  System 25
Belgium 12, 14–15
Best Buy 165, 166
boundaries: blurring of 180;
  management of 25–7, 33
Britain 120, 122–8; see also United
  Kingdom

British Airways 153
British Household Panel Survey 117
built environment 149
Bulgaria 2, 3, 12
burnout 27
Businesses' Charter for Working
  Parents 102

call centres 151–2
career tracks, gendered 100
care for children see childcare
care for older adults see elder care
care-giving responsibilities 187, 188;
  social benefits of 87–9; unpaid
  78–81; see also childcare; elder care
care provision, informal 85–8
care workers 88
casual work and workers 30, 189
casualisation 96; see also precarious
  work
Catalonia 15
Chartered Institute for Personnel and
  Development 24, 65
childcare 2–3, 45, 52–3, 120, 156, 183;
  allowances for 93, 98–100, 104–5;
  EU targets for 12–13; in France 94,
  98–100; policy debate in the UK 98;
  vouchers for 52
Children and Family Act (UK) 81;
Chiswick Park 153
class inequities 112–13, 116
Clifford Chance 153
collaboration 75, 170, 186, 190;
  interactive 173–5
Collaborative Interactive Action
  Research (CIAR) 173–5;
  implementation of 175–7;
  modifications to 175
collective bargaining 93, 98, 100;
  decentralisation of 100; in France

101–6; in the UK 100, 104–6; on work-life balance 102–5
commutes 154–5, 156
competency frameworks 36
compressed hours 46, 51, 60, 63
compressed working week 183
conflict: strain-based 26; time-based 26; work-life 26, 58–9; work-nonwork 58, 60; work-to-home 35
conservation of resources model 29
Cooperative Banking Group 104
core hours 185; *see also* working time arrangements
co-rumination 27, 28, 29
Croatia 12
Cyprus 2

Denmark 12, 26
Department for Business, Innovation and Skills (BIS) 82
depression 24, 27
digital crowdsource platforms 4
discrimination: pregnancy and maternity-related 82, 88–9; workplace 80
Diversity and Inclusion work 184–5
domestic and economic spheres, gendered separation of 26, 167, 172
Dual Agenda 167–8; analysis 173–5; changing work-related norms 171–2; collective flexible work arrangements 169; and the narrative of time 170–1; removing bias from evaluations 170; resistance as part of the process 172; summary of learning from projects 172–3; and telecommuting 168–9
dual employed couples: hours of weekly labour market work 119; in financial hardship 124–6

earnings inequalities 180
economic hardship *see* financial hardship
economic inequalities 3–4
economic insecurity 127
elder care 29, 86, 114, 155, 183; leave for 52–3
emergencies, time off for 46, 52
emotional support 35
employees: well-being of 25; use of WLB practices by 57–8

employment *see* job insecurity; work arrangements; working time arrangements
employment law *see* labour law
Employment Appeal Tribunal (EAT) 84
employment inequalities 2–4, 11, 16
employment law, deregulation of 80
employment rate 3
employment relations institutions 100–2
Employment Rights Act (ERA) 82
Employment Strategy (European Union) 3
employment tribunal fees 84
e-nomads 9
Enron 153
Entrepreneurship 2020 Action Plan 144
Equal Treatment Directive 82
Equality Act (UK) 80–1, 89
Equality and Human Rights Commission (EHRC) 82
Estonia 12, 15, 132
European Court of Justice 104
European Labour Force Survey 4, 5
European Quality of Life Survey 3–4
European Union: Employment Strategy 3; self-employment in 132–4, 144–5
European Working Conditions Survey (EWCS) 6, 24
evaluations, removing bias from 170
expertise, fluid 173

family friendly provisions 45–6, 48–9, 52–4, 79
family leave *see* maternity leave; parental leave; paternity leave
feminism, second wave 86
financial hardship: dual employed couples reporting 125–6; effects on health 23, 28–9; men reporting 123; and self-employment 138–40; in United Kingdom 122–4; women reporting 123; *see also* poverty
financial security, and work-life balance 119–22
Finland 13, 14; *see also* Nordic countries
fixed-term contracts 4, 189
flexibility 177, 187, 190
Flexible Working Act (Netherlands) 14
flexible working arrangements (FWAs) 31–4, 46, 50–2, 63–4, 150, 180, 183–8, 190; in Britain 64–6;

collective approach to 169; effect of austerity on 46–7; impact on employees 47, 58-9, 70–2; impact on line managers and service delivery 72–4; in the public sector 64–5; qualitative study 66–7; traditional 67–8; use of 57–8
flexitime/flexible working time 9, 10, 31, 51, 58, 63, 93, 184–5; *see also* working time arrangements
fluid expertise 173
Ford Foundation 167
France: childcare in 12; childcare support in 13; collective bargaining in 101–6; employment relations institutions in 101–2; gender equality in 101–2; investment in childcare in 94; labour changes in 84–5; labour legislation in 98–100; reconciliation measures in 12; short-time working in 5; trade unions and work-life balance in 94–5, 97–106; working-time regulations in 15
France Télévisions 104
freelancers 133, 140

gender agenda 167
gender differences, in household division of work 9–10
gender equality 101–2; action plans 11; in caregiving 79, 86, 89; and flexible working arrangements 74–5; in France 98, 103, 104; *see also* assumptions, gendered; career tracks, gendered; domestic and economic spheres, gendered separation of; gender equity; gender inequality; implications, gendered; pay gaps, gendered; roles, gendered
Gender Equality Bonus (Sweden) 13–14
gender equity 167–8, 177; and the CIAR process 175; and the dual agenda 188; in evaluations 170; *see also* gender equality
gender gap 10; in France 94; in unemployment and employment 2–3
gender inequality 45; *see also* class inequality; gender equality
Génisson law 101, 102, 103
Germany 5, 13, 14, 15
globalisation 65
Goldman Sachs 153
GovDept 182, 185–6, 187

Great Place to Work conference 166
Greece 2, 12, 13, 14, 26
Guy, Gillian 84

health: effects of economic hardship on 23, 28–9; and work-life conflict 26–7
holacracy 166
homeworking *see* working from home
hot desking 69, 70, 74
House of Commons Library 86
human capital 46
Hungary 14, 15

ICT *see* information communication technology
ill health 24
implications, gendered 81
income inequalities 17
income insecurity, and self-employment 139–40
independent professionals: Dutch 137–9, 141–4; Spanish 137–9, 141–3
inequalities: earnings 180; economic 2–3; employment 2–4, 11, 16; gender 45
information communication technology (ICT) 8–9, 31
information technology (IT): and the freedom of location 157–60; and the workplace 151
information technology (IT) infrastructure 68, 79, 74
information technology (IT) systems, 64
insecurity, objective vs. subjective 27; *see also* job insecurity
Institute of Fiscal Studies 86
instrumental support 35
intersectionality 80
Ireland, unemployment in 2
IT *see* information technology
Italy: flexible working in 14; paternity leave in 14; reconciliation measures in 12; unemployment in 2

job analysis 68
job demands 134–5, 138–40, 143–4; Resources (JD–R) model 28, 134, 137
job insecurity 4, 17, 23, 24, 27–8, 36, 74, 180, 189; in France 95; and self-employment 131, 134
job loss 75; *see also* unemployment
job redesign 68

job sharing 31, 46, 51, 57, 60, 63
jobs *see* work arrangements; working time arrangements
Joly, Hubert 165, 166

Koestler, Arthur 166
Korea: dual agenda in 181; modified CIAR projects in 175

labour law 78–82, 87; changes in xviii; and flexible working arrangements 65; labour legislation 45; labour legislation in France 98–100; reform of 98, 103
Latvia 2, 3, 12
leave entitlements and options 13–14, 31; *see also* maternity leave; parental leave; paternity leave
legal advice 82–3
line managers, and flexible working arrangements 72–5
Lisbon Summit 3
Lithuania 2, 3
Liveable Lives 155–6
Lloyds 104
lobbying, by trade unions 97
local hubs 186
London 152–3
low-income households 1; childcare for 12–13; and the Dual Agenda 176–7; and work-life balance 121–2; *see also* working class

Malta 15
managers 10; attitudes and perceptions of, 49, 54–6, 59, 67–8, 74
manual workers 10; *see also* working class
ManufCo 182–4, 186–7, 189
Maternity Action 83, 85
Maternity and Parental Leave regulations 81
maternity leave 13, 14, 15, 17, 81–5, 58, 132, 138, 156, 171, 185; discrimination related to 82, 88–9
Maternity Leave Directive 15
maternity rights 79
May, Theresa 80
Mayer, Marissa 165, 166
men: hours of weekly labour market work 118; parental leave for 120–1; reporting financial hardship 123; self-employed 141; taking family leave 33–4; as typical workers 167; use of flexible working arrangements by 57; working 156
micro-interventions 173–4
middle-class workers 181; work-life balance in 112, 114, 117, 124–5
mobile working 74
mommy track 33
multi-skilling 190
multi-tasking 34
mutual benefits agenda 69, 74

National Survey of the Changing Workforce (US) 30, 32
neo-liberalism 87
Netherlands: cuts to parental leave in 14; flexible working in 14; independent professionals in 137–9, 141–4; reconciliation measures in 12; self-employment in 133; welfare state in 136; working-time regulations in 15
networking 186
New Public Management (NPM) 65, 72
New Ways of Working 150
non-standard work arrangements 29–31; *see also* precarious work
Nordic countries: gender equity in 3; low work-life conflict in 26; reconciliation measures in 12; state help for care responsibilities in 45; working-time regulations in 15
norms, work-related 171–3
Norway 26, 133; *see also* Nordic countries
Nursery Act (Poland) 12

organisations: cost-cutting measures in 68–9; gendered 96
organizational support 34–5
overtime 5, 10, 24, 50, 94, 98, 104, 171

paid work/unpaid care equation 78–81
parental leave 33, 45–6, 81, 93, 120; in France 98, 99, 104; *see also* maternity leave; paternity leave
parenting styles, and economic pressure 29
parents, reliance on 155
part-time employment 1, 5, 9, 10, 31, 79, 103, 117; in France 94; in UK 95
paternity leave 45, 120–1; in UK 104

pay gaps, gendered 88
Poland 12, 13, 132
Portugal 2, 15
poverty 4, 113, 121; *see also* financial hardship
pregnancy 81–5; discrimination related to 82, 88–9
Pregnant Workers Directive 82
presenteeism 30, 71, 72
professional workers 10; *see also* independent professionals
psychosomatic complaints 27
public sector, transformation of 65–6; debt 46

quality of working life 102
'quiet time' experiment 170–1

Recast Directive 82
recession: and class inequity 113; effect on work-life conflict 58–9; effects of 1–4, 16–17, 56; employee's recessionary experience 50, 57–8; and employment inequalities 2–4; and flexible work options 46–7; impacts of, 36–7, 49–50; and self-employment 132; *see also* economic crisis
reconciliation policies 11–12; care services 12–13; leave entitlements 13–14; length of working hours 15–16; rights to flexible working arrangements 14–15
reduced hours 31, 51, 60, 63, 74, 117
remote working 32, 68, 74, 149, 184; negative aspects of 75–6
resource-drain theory 25
restructured hours 31
Results Only Work Environment (ROWE) 165, 166
right to request flexible working 10–11, 31–3, 65, 97, 103
retirement schemes 5
risk factors, psychological 24
role modelling 35
roles, gendered 117
Romania 15
rumination, effect on health 26

sandwich generation 155
Sarkozy, Nicolas 98–9
Schedules that Work Act 176–7
self-employment 4, 189; advantages and disadvantages of, 135–6; and

economic crisis 131–2; in European Union 132–4, 144–5; and financial hardship 138–40; and income insecurity 139–40; involuntary 131; and work-life balance 131–2, 134–7, 144–5; *see also* independent professionals
service delivery, and flexible working arrangements 72–5
Shared Parental Leave (UK) 14
short day shift 171
short-time working 5–6
Skills and Employment Survey 24
Slovakia 2
Slovenia 12
small business owners 136
social isolation and withdrawal 27, 32
social justice 11, 16, 64, 65, 76, 93, 112, 113, 128, 145, 150, 154, 160, 162, 167, 168, 176–7, 180–2, 184–90
social support, and WLB 136
South Korea 171–2
Spain: childcare in 12; cuts to childcare services in 13; flexible working in 15; independent professionals in 137–8, 141–3; reconciliation measures in 12; self-employment in 132; unemployment in 2; welfare state in 136; work-life conflict in 26
staggered shifts 171
statutory maternity pay (SMP) 81
stress, work-related 24
subcontractors 136
Survey of Employers 72
Sweden 12, 13, 133; *see also* Nordic countries

tax incentives 87
technology: and flexibility 187; and remote working 184; and the physical workplace 149–50; role of 34–5
telecommuting 168–9
telework 9
temporary work 30–1
term-time working 46, 51
Thales 103
time: flexible 9, 10, 31, 51, 58, 63, 93, 184–5; management of 150; narrative of 170–1; *see also* working time arrangements
trade unions: and employment relations institutions and practices 100–2;

impact of crisis on 96; increased
female membership 96–7; policy
environment and the role of the state
97–100; and work-life balance 93–4
Trades Union Congress (TUC) 95, 97–8
triple agenda xv–xvii, 11, 16–17, 65,
75, 93, 102, 112, 129, 154, 162,177,
180–182, 184-190; and spatially
distributed working 160–2; and
work-life balance 180–1

UK *see* United Kingdom
UK Labour Force Survey 23
Understanding Society 117
unemployment 2–3, 27, 95
unfair dismissal 80
Unifi union 104
Unite the Union 104
United Kingdom: budget cuts in 63;
childcare services in 13; childcare
support in 13; collective bargaining
in 100, 104–6; drop in GDP 23;
effect of recession in 58–61;
employment relations institutions
in 100; financial hardship in 122–4;
flexible work opportunities in 14,
63–76; gender equity in 79–89; help
for care responsibilities in 45; job
insecurity in 27–8; labour changes in
85–6; modern workplaces in 152–3;
parental leave in 14; paternity leave
in 104; presenteeism in 30; self-
employment in 133; trade unions and
work-life balance in 94, 95–6, 97–8,
100, 104–6; welfare reform in 28;
WLB policy in 97–8, 100; worker
well-being in 23–4 ; working-time
regulations in 15; work-life balance
practices in 46–56
United States 46, 181
US *see* United States
UtilCo 182, 184–5, 187

virtual teams 73, 75
Vitamin model 30

wage freezes 47
welfare reform 1, 28
welfare regimes, and work-life conflict
26
welfare/work mix 79–80
well-being: effects of austerity on
23–5, 36, 80, 86–9, 189; decrease

in 25; effect of facilities on 158;
employment rate in France 94; and
flexible working arrangements 75;
impact of work on 23
women: as caregivers 78–81, 85–9;
economic impact on 1; impact of
austerity measures on 80, 86–9,
189; informal care provision and
employment 85–8; hours of weekly
labour market work 118; job
insecurity among 4; job loss by 2;
as part-time workers 95; pregnancy
and maternity leave 81–5; reporting
financial hardship 123; responsible
for elder care 28–9, 54; self-employed
141; as trade union members 96–7;
transition to parenthood 45; as
unpaid workers 10; use of flexible
working arrangements by 57; and
WLB in France 95; working 156;
working-class 121, 181; work-life
needs of 167–8; *see also* maternity
leave
Women's Budget Group 86, 87
work arrangements: casual 4, 30, 189;
fixed 8; job sharing 31, 46, 51, 57,
60, 63; mobile working 74; non-
standard or precarious 6–8, 23, 27,
29–31; remote working 32, 68, 74,
149, 184; negative aspects of 75–6;
staggered shifts 171; subcontracting
136; telecommuting 168–9; telework
9; temporary work 30–1; term-time
working 46, 51; zero-hours contracts
4, 31, 96, 121, 189; *see also* flexible
working arrangements (FWAs); self-
employment; working from home
work-family agenda 45; *see also* work-
life balance
work inequalities 2–4, 11, 16
working class: and financial hardship
122–8; needs of 181; prejudice
against 115–16; work-life balance in
112–1, 114–16; *see also* low-income
households
Working Families 190; Sarah Jackson
190
working from home 46, 51, 57–8, 60,
63, 68, 74, 186; distractions in 156–7
working time arrangements 1, 2, 4–5,
9; compressed hours 46, 51, 60, 63;
compressed working week 183; core
hours 185; fixed 8; flexible 9, 10,

31, 51, 58, 63, 93, 94, 184–5; hours
worked 5–6, 24, 117–18; ICT and
teleworking 8–9; increase in hours
24; inequalities in working time and
WLB 9–10; non-standard 5, 6–8, 23,
29–31; overtime 5, 10, 24, 50, 94,
98, 104, 171; reduced hours 31, 51,
60, 63, 74, 117; restructured hours
31; short day shift 171; short-time
working 5–6; variable schedules 1;
and work-life balance 4–9; work week
reduction 183; work schedules 6–7
Working Time Directive (WTD), 15–16,
104
work intensity and intensification 4–5,
10, 24, 180
work-life balance (WLB): case studies,
182–6; definitions xv–xvi; discourses
66, 124; and financial security
119–22; and the Recession 1; and
inequalities in working time 9–10;
management of 35–6; middle-class
112, 114, 117; and the physical
workplace 149–52; and self-
employment 131–2, 134–7, 144–5;
and technology use 34–5; and time
116–19; and trade unions 93–4; and
the triple agenda 180–81; working-

class 112, 114–16; and working-time
arrangements 4–9
work-life balance practices: changes in
provision of 50–5; employer support
for 45–8; family-friendly policies
45–6, 48–9, 52–4, 79; initiatives
for 11–17; limited availability of
59–61; understanding of needs by
management 54–6
Workplace Employment Relations
Study (WERS) 24, 46–50
workplaces: amenities in 153–4,
158–9; centralisation of 154;
change initiatives 64; consolidation
of 149; contemporary provision
152–5; evolution of 150–2; family-
friendly 150–1; important aspects of
157–60; nurseries in 49, 52, 53, 151;
simplification in 159–60; spatially
distributed 160–2; and technology
149–50; 'third places' as 160–2; and
workers' realities 155–7

Yahoo 165

Zappos 166
zero-hours contracts 4, 31, 96, 121,
189